MERTON &
INDIGENOUS
WISDOM

Edited by Peter Savastano

FONS VITAE

The Fons Vitae Thomas Merton Series
Merton & Sufism: The Untold Story, 1999
Merton & Hesychasm: The Prayer of the Heart, 2003
Merton & Judaism: Holiness in Words, 2003
Merton & Buddhism: Wisdom, Emptiness,
and Everyday Mind, 2007
Merton & The Tao: Dialogues with John C. H. Wu
and the Ancient Sages, 2013
Merton & The Protestant Tradition, 2016
Merton & Indigenous Wisdom, 2019

First published in 2019 by
Fons Vitae
49 Mockingbird Valley Drive
Louisville, KY 40207
http://www.fonsvitae.com

Copyright Fons Vitae 2019

Library of Congress Control Number: 2019948953

ISBN 978-1891785-993

This book was typeset by Neville Blakemore, Jr.

Printed in Canada

MERTON &
INDIGENOUS WISDOM

Dedicated to those venerable indigenous elders who, over countless centuries, have placed their hands on the shoulders of the next generation to instill wise ways forward through the vessels of ceremony, tradition, and custodianship of the Earth and all its inhabitants.

CONTENTS

THE FONS VITAE THOMAS MERTON SERIES   IX

THOMAS MERTON'S PRAYER   XI

INTRODUCTION   XIII
Peter Savastano

THE INDIANS OF THE AMERICAN IMAGINATION
Vine Deloria, Jr.   1

THOMAS MERTON AND NATIVE AMERICA
Lewis Mehl-Madrona and Barbara Mainguy   21

NORTH AMERICAN ABORIGINAL SPIRITUALITY AND
THOMAS MERTON'S CHRISTIANITY
Lewis Mehl-Madrona and Barbara Mainguy   43

ISHI, A PARABLE FOR OUR TIME
Robert G. Toth   83

PAYING HIS DEBTS TO NATIVE AMERICAN PEOPLES:
THOMAS MERTON ON THE "SPIRITUAL RICHNESS OF
THE INDIAN RELIGIOUS GENIUS"
Donald P. St. John   93

SEEKING TRUTH ELSEWHERE: THOMAS MERTON
AND ENTHEOGENS
William Torres   143

THE SPIRIT OF THE TLINGITS
Kathleen Witkowska Tarr   163

DANCING DEEPLY IN THE THICKET OF THE CROSS:
THOMAS MERTON'S OPENNESS TO FIRST NATION ARTS
AS ICONS OF TRADITIONAL BELIEF SYSTEMS
Allan M. McMillan   183

WITH MALINOWSKI IN THE POSTMODERN DESERT:
MERTON, ANTHROPOLOGY, AND THE ETHNOPOETICS OF
THE GEOGRAPHY OF LOGRAIRE
Małgorzata Poks   223

Contents, continued

INTRODUCTION TO THE PREFACE FOR LATIN AMERICAN READERS
IN MERTON'S *OBRAS COMPLETAS (COMPLETE WORKS)*
Marcela Raggio   251

PREFACE FOR LATIN AMERICAN READERS
IN MERTON'S *OBRAS COMPLETAS (COMPLETE WORKS)*
Thomas Merton   261

CONTRIBUTORS   267

ACKNOWLEDGMENTS   271

APPENDIX
OBRAS COMPLETAS   273

THE FONS VITAE
THOMAS MERTON SERIES

Scholars, lay readers, and spiritual seekers in a broad spectrum of religious theories and practices regard the Cistercian monk Thomas Merton (1915-1968) as one of the most important spiritual writers of the last half of the twentieth century. The late Ewert Cousins, a Professor of Religion and the General Editor of the World Spirituality Series by Paulist Press, distinguished Merton as an "axial figure" who bridged estrangements between religious and secular perspectives. Dr. Cousins opined that Merton is more important today than in his lifetime. He is an iconic figure who modeled inter-religious dialogue for those who seek a common ground of respect and understanding for the varied ways in which human beings realize the sacred as a foundation for their lives. Merton's life and writing remain a bridge for others to cross and engage one another in the pursuit of common moral values that acknowledge the dignity of all earth's inhabitants. Merton's inclusive intellect, expansive religious imagination, and his heart's zeal for unity among peoples were the fruit of his monastic inner work. In his personal journal for April 28, 1957 he highlighted these dimensions of his vocation as a monastic writer:

> If I can unite in myself, in my own spiritual life, the thought of the East and the West, of the Greek and Latin Fathers, I will create in myself a reunion of the divided Church, and from that unity in myself can come the exterior and visible unity of the church. For, if we want to bring together East and West, we cannot do it by imposing one upon the other. We must contain both in ourselves and transcend them both in Christ.

The Fons Vitae publishing project for the study of world religions through the lens of Thomas Merton's life and writing brings Merton's timeless vision of all persons united in a "hidden ground of Love" to a contemporary audience. The previous six volumes in our series – *Merton & Sufism, Merton & Hesychasm, Merton & Judaism, Merton & Buddhism, Merton & Protestantism, and Merton &*

The Tao – feature essays by international scholars that assess the value of Merton's contributions to inter-religious dialogue. In addition to these volumes, Fons Vitae celebrated Merton's centenary (1915-2015) with a special volume, *We Are Already One: Thomas Merton's Message of Hope*, in which over one hundred contributors reflected on their first encounters with Merton's writing and the continued pressure that the Christian monk's life and witness has exerted on their spiritual engagements for world peace.

This seventh volume in our series, *Merton & Indigenous Wisdom*, gathers reflections that expose Merton's appreciation for the spiritual and religious genius of American and Canadian indigenous peoples. A new translation of his "Preface for Latin American Readers," originally written and published in Spanish for an Argentine project to present his complete works, is a significant manifesto of Merton's universality and "catholic" approach to the phenomenon of seeking God and the Sacred in all the world's cultures.

The forthcoming eighth volume, *Merton & Hinduism*, will end our Thomas Merton and the World's Religions project that seeks to promote the study and practice of contemplative traditions north and south, east and west.

Jonathan Montaldo and V. Gray Henry
General Editors for the Fons Vitae Thomas Merton Series

THOMAS MERTON'S PRAYER

The following prayer was offered by Thomas Merton at the First Spiritual Summit Conference in Calcutta. It appears as part of Appendix V in *The Asian Journal of Thomas Merton*. We offer it again here as the context from which this book arose and in which it has been prepared for publication.

Oh God, we are one with You. You have made us one with You. You have taught us that if we are open to one another, You dwell in us. Help us to preserve this openness and to fight for it with all our hearts. Help us to realize that there can be no understanding where there is mutual rejection. Oh God, in accepting one another wholeheartedly, fully, completely, we accept You, and we thank You, and we adore You, and we love You with our whole being, because our being is in Your being, our spirit is rooted in Your spirit. Fill us then with love, and let us be bound together with love as we go our diverse ways, united in this one spirit which makes You present in the world, and which makes You witness to the ultimate reality that is love. Love has overcome. Love is victorious. Amen.

INTRODUCTION

Peter Savastano

In 2014, I had taught my course, "Thomas Merton, Religion and Culture" for the third time over five years. I decided to use my upcoming sabbatical to make deeper sense of my life's long attraction to the life and writing of Thomas Merton. Just before my sabbatical, I had written an essay, "Thomas Merton Saved My Life And Opened My Heart To What It Really Means To Be Truly Catholic,"[1] for *We Are Already One, Thomas Merton's Message of Hope, Reflections in Honor of His Centenary (1915-2015)*. I had recounted how at the age of twelve in a local branch of the Newark, New Jersey Public Library, I had stumbled upon Merton's *The Silent Life*. My family and I had just moved from an Italian Catholic enclave. I had little if any idea that there was a world that existed beyond the parochial one in which I had lived.

Encountering *The Silent Life* in that library only three years before his death was revolutionary. Merton's engagement with other world religions moved me. I found it hard to reconcile what I had learned in Roman Catholic elementary school with Merton's positive engagements with so many religions of the world. Here was a Roman Catholic Trappist monk who was doing more than reading about other religious traditions. He was putting some of what he read about them into practice. He was engaging, mostly through correspondence, many of the contemporary masters of those traditions. Merton was not Catholic like I was at the time. I do not for a moment think that he believed, as I did, that all other denominations of Christianity were in error except for the Roman Catholic tradition, nor that all other religious twenty-first century were "pagan," and therefore dangerous to the salvation of his soul. As a child, our Catechism taught me I should never enter a Protestant Church; to do so, without confessing this "sin," would send me, upon death, immediately to Hell.

Reading Merton provided me with a model that expanded

---

1. Peter Savastano, "Thomas Merton Saved My Life..." *We Are Already One* (Louisville: FonsVitae, 2014) 176-180.

my awareness of the treasures within other religious traditions. He taught me what it meant to be "catholic," i.e., universal and all-embracing. Having read all of Merton's journals and having read most of the volumes of the Fons Vitae "Merton &" series, I enthusiastically accepted the opportunity to edit a volume in the series that focused on Merton's engagement with the indigenous sacred traditions of the Americas, North, South, and Central.

My engagement with "integral spirituality" inspired my wanting to edit *Merton & Indigenous Wisdom*. My progress through my religious life has been a deepening involvement with the task of being a Christian "interspiritually." My intellectual approach to studying, teaching, and, more importantly, living my theology is to embody a "theology without walls." While I have not located myself outside the Christian orientation of my youth, I have enriched my inherited Roman Catholicism with other traditions of seeking and realizing God and the Sacred in my personal life. While the "Theology Without Walls" endeavor is a twenty-first-century project, nevertheless, I must count Merton among the pioneers of such an interspiritual approach to the study and practice of religion. He is a living witness of the reality of what has become, academically and in practice, a "theology without walls."

Although Merton remained a Roman Catholic Christian and a Trappist monk, later in his maturity the boundaries between one religious tradition and another became more porous and fluid. I even sensed that when Merton made his Asian journey, he might not have returned to the Abbey of Gethsemani, had his accidental death not made such a momentous decision moot. I have intuited that in 1968 Merton would have remained in Asia to become the student of a meditation master of the Nyingmapa tradition of Vajrayana Buddhism. His journals in Asia attest that he desired to immerse himself in Dzogchen meditation, the highest form of Tantric Buddhist meditation, practiced by both the Nyingmapa Buddhists and also by Bon Buddhism, the indigenous form of Buddhism that existed in Tibet before Padmasambhava brought the Indian form of Buddhism to Tibet in the Eighth Century, CE.

Whether or not Merton was moving towards becoming a Buddhist is no longer important. What is more important is that Merton was finding spiritual nourishment in the Buddhist tradition and many other traditions, in theory, practice, and his relentless pursuit of the Sacred.[2] Before his practice could aptly be named an "integral spirituality" in our twenty-first century, he already embodied a "theology without walls" in word and deed.

Merton's interest in indigenous sacred traditions emerged in the second period of his life, or during what I have termed Merton 2.0. In my course on Merton, I have divided his life, and particularly his life as a searcher for the Sacred, by naming the first part of his earnest search for God as Merton 1.0. Merton 1.0 is the period in which he experienced his dramatic conversion to Catholicism, his entry into the Abbey of Our Lady of Gethsemani as a novice through his ordination to the priesthood. Merton 1.0 is the Thomas Merton of *The Seven Storey Mountain, The Silent Life, The Sign of Jonas, The Waters of Siloe,* and *The Ascent to Truth.* Conservative Catholic websites approve Merton 1.0 as "safe."

Merton 2.0, on the other hand, is the Merton who wrote *Conjectures of A Guilty Bystander, New Seeds of Contemplation, Raids on the Unspeakable, Zen and The Birds of Appetite, Mystics and Zen Masters,* and the series of articles and book reviews for *The Catholic Worker* that eventually were published posthumously as *Ishi Means Man.* Liberal or progressive Roman Catholics tout Merton 2.0 as representing the best the Roman Catholic Church has to offer for the twenty-first century. While I, as a professor and a disciple, love all phases of his life as his progress toward integrating his adult personality, a process that Merton touted as the culmination of the development of us humans to our full potential as moral, social, political, religious, and spiritual beings,[3] my students decidedly prefer and love Merton 2.0.

In the second half of his life, his Merton 2.0 phase, Merton examined his life's trajectory and began to "decolonize his mind." He was in the process of coming to terms with the colonization of his life by western standards of thinking and living. He recognized the oppressive effects of European colonization as it happened to indigenous peoples, African-Americans, to black and brown and southern hemisphere persons the world over, and to those persons

---

2. An excellent account of Merton's exploration of Vajrayana Buddhism and of Dzogchen meditation while in India is Harold Talbott's posthumous memoir *Tendrel: A Memoir of New York and the Buddhist Himalayas* (Marion, MA: Buddhayana Foundation, 2019).

3. For a more in depth understanding of what Merton meant by "final integration of the adult personality" see his *Contemplation in a World of Action* (Notre Dame, Indiana: University of Notre Dame Press, 1998), especially Chapter XIII.

who did not conform to the approved categories of sexuality and gender of the Global North. Students in my classes enthusiastically identify with Merton as a model of their need to be "decolonized" from the narratives and fictions they have learned as the true and only way the world operates. Merton is a "living text" for this decolonization process that women, Native Americans, African Americans, all persons of color, and LGBTQIA persons must endure to recover the value of their indigenous selves if one can speak metaphorically.

From an anthropological perspective, everyone has had their particular worldview and way of life mediated by their birth cultures. All learn that their culture, religion, politics, socialization, and gender categories are superior to those of any other peoples, cultures, religions, and periods of history. Emphasis on a mono-cultural education is what I call "the sin of ethnocentrism." Sadly, Merton was not spared the sin of ethnocentrism any more than the rest of us. This ethnocentrism is unconscious. "Decolonization" is a difficult inner process since our cultural scripts and the lens with which we view the world operate implicitly, shaping our understanding of reality and truth even when we want to change our points of view. Ethnocentrism is universal, unconscious, and insidious.

Merton studied Native American cultures and traditions, North, Central, and South. He corresponded with and interacted with various anthropologists, writers, artists, spiritual healers, and visionaries who were themselves encountering indigenous sacred traditions. Merton began to understand and speak out in protest of the injustices and the near genocide that was perpetrated by Euro-Americans against Native Peoples, persons of color, and those not Catholic or Christian. In protesting in his writing these various oppressions and injustices endured by those excluded, marginalized, and disenfranchised from American culture and its historical narrative, Merton began divesting his mind from the prison of his ethnocentric, imperialistic attitudes and beliefs, all of which he inherited from the European and Euro-American perspectives that had shaped his life and his education.

Did Merton always get it right as he began to decolonize his mind and deconstruct the world in which he lived as he studied Native American cultures and sacred traditions, in all of their complexity and diversity? Of course, the answer is NO. Decolonization of the mind is a life-long project. Each time we attempt to deconstruct one layer of our habitual perspectives, another layer comes to the surface. The essays contained in *Merton & Indigenous Wisdom* are written by those who are likewise in the process of decolonizing their minds, both in terms of their understanding and engagement with Merton and with their understanding and experiences with indigenous wisdom and anthropology and, in some cases, in their direct relationship with indigenous peoples.

Unfortunately, we cannot ignore that fact that much of Merton's exposure to Native American cultures and sacred traditions was through his reading books and articles by anthropologists. Given anthropology's complicity with the imperialistic colonial enterprise of Europeans and Euro-Americans, we must factor into the mix yet another insidious level of decolonization of the mind and deconstruction of the world that we must not ignore in receiving the essays included in this volume.[4] While some of the contributors to this volume are Native American, most of them are not. Like Merton, many of us might not have gotten it right or "hit the mark" either.

Some years ago, I discovered the writings of Vine Deloria, Jr., and particularly his book *God Is Red*. To read Deloria was to have the scales removed from my eyes and to realize the limited epistemological categories through which I, as a Christian, understood the Great Mystery, as some Native Peoples refer to the Creator. In including a chapter from Vine Deloria's *God Is Red* in our volume, we have invited a powerful and moving voice of a Native American. Deloria discriminates the differences in worldview between many indigenous sacred ritual and healing traditions and the Christianity that many of us have been conditioned to accept as the pinnacle of all truth. Independent of Merton, I have always been drawn to Native American history and sacred traditions, or at least what I imagined them to be. As a small child, I had recurring dreams with Native Americans as central figures. Often in these dreams, I was present at sacred rituals, none of which seemed to depict Native Peoples negatively in the way the Westerns I had seen on television or in the movies did.

Even though I am an anthropologist, I always knew that for me it would be morally wrong to do fieldwork among Native Americans, given anthropology's complicity with the pillaging and

---

4. Toward that end see Charles King's *Gods of the Upper Air: How a Circle of Renegade Anthropologists Reinvented Race, Sex and Gender in the Twentieth Century* (New York: Doubleday, 2019).

plundering of so many Native American peoples, their cultures, and sacred artifacts. I would not have, and earnestly pray I shall not have by editing this volume, contributed to the incredible harm that has been done to Native Peoples by us non-Native Americans. I realized, too, that when it came to learning about Native American religions and the wisdom they contain, I would have to content myself with what Episcopal priest and scholar Barbara Brown Taylor names "Holy Envy."[5] Whatever knowledge I have of Native American sacred traditions has come mostly from books. Gratefully, many of these books were written by Native Americans rather than by anthropologists, so I am trusting that some of what I know is genuine. I have also read the novels, memoirs and the poetry of Native Americans such as Leslie Mamon Silko and Joy Harjo. I still listen to the music of Native Americans such as Buffy Sainte-Marie, and Patrick Sky, both of whom I was fortunate enough to discover when I was in my early teens back in the 1960s. I have educated myself in the beautiful and scathing cultural, political, and spiritual critiques of these Native American artists to the historical plight of Native Peoples in the Americas, and the beauty, depths, and sorely needed wisdom of their sacred traditions.

Despite the Native American presence in my childhood dreams (and sometimes even in my current dreams), most of my exposure to Native American history and sacred traditions comes in response to a central question to which I hoped to find an answer when I went to graduate school. That question was (and still is): "Is it true that every single religious tradition in the world condemns same-sex desire and sexuality?". The famous twentieth-century anthropologist Margaret Mead once said that the reason why anthropologists study other cultures and traditions is that we might, perchance, find a solution to a problem for which we have none at the time. In one of her many testimonies before Congress, specifically about "homosexuality," Mead said that a "civilization" that condemns entire groups of people for their sexuality is a civilization that is in decline. Here is another area in which Merton had yet to grow, for, sadly, in his journals he belittles the women anthropologists he read in the same way he did the writings of some women mystics. While certainly not uniform across the board, it was in many Native American cultures, and especially their sacred traditions, that

---

5. Barbara Brown Taylor, *Holy Envy, Finding God in the Faith of Others* (San Francisco: HarperOne, 2019).

I found the answer to my question in what is currently referred to, even by some Native Peoples themselves, as "two-spirited" persons, the closest we can come to in our non-Native culture as LGBTQI persons. It was both a breath of fresh air and enlightening to learn that in many Native traditions, people whose sexual desire or gender roles do not conform to the "norm," are not condemned but rather celebrated and often became renowned healers and leaders because of their difference. Some Christian traditions still condemn such persons as "abominations." Before the appearance of Christian missionaries and sometimes in spite of them, many Native American cultures received and valued persons with same-sex desire or gender discordance. These cultures received their two-spirited status as holy and sacred. Such persons possessed gifts of sacred power and healing which they gladly shared with those conforming to the cultural, sexual, and gender norms of a particular group of indigenous peoples.[6]

Some years ago, I had a conversation with a monk of the Abbey of Gethsemani who had lived with "Fr. Louie," Merton's monastic name. The monk, who was gay, told me that he thought Merton was a homophobe and would probably continue to be had he lived beyond 1968. I disagreed with the monk then and still do.

Given that Merton was in the process of decolonizing his mind by engaging so many religious, cultural, and social issues at the time of his sudden death, he would have continued to grow, spurred on by Native American spiritual traditions, especially in matters of gender and human sexuality. I would also suggest that Merton would have surpassed his lack of understanding of the role that entheogens (psychedelics such as Peyote, Mescaline, and Ayahuasca) play in some indigenous sacred wisdom traditions, as one essay in this collection attempts to address. Had Merton lived, I like to think he would have surely encountered the plethora of scholarship currently available both about "two-spirited persons" and the important role that they played in many Native American cultures and healing traditions, as well as the importance of entheogens in many of the sacred rituals and healing rites of such traditions. The same is true for an understanding of gender as being fluid and not concordant with biological sex.[7] It was approximately six months

6. See especially Will Roscoe, *The Zuni Man-Woman* (Albequerque: University of New Mexico Press, 1991).

7. See Ruth Benedict, *Patterns of Culture* (Boston: Houghton Mifflin

after Merton's death that the Stonewall Uprising took place in New York's Greenwich Village in 1969 thus inaugurating what would become the modern LGBTQI Liberation Movement. 1969 saw the emergence of Second Wave Feminism followed by the emergence of the American Indian Movement (AIM) shortly after that. All three of these important movements for religious, cultural, and political change have had an incredible impact on American culture, politics, and religion.

Merton was a product of his times. His desire to grow and to learn from other spiritual traditions is as germane today as it was when he explored with such interest and enthusiasm indigenous people's experiences, histories, and sacred wisdom. Thomas Merton still inspires those of us who are not Native American to receive and learn the wisdom of indigenous people with sensitivity and respect. Like Merton, we must also confess in sorrow and lamentation what has been done to Native Peoples by "civilized" Christian tradition. Attempted genocide is not to be taken lightly or dismissed as no longer relevant. Native American sacred traditions contain much wisdom which can lift us all in understanding human diversity and in enlarging our capacities to learn what it truly means to be "catholic" human beings.

Company, 1934); Will Roscoe, *The Changing Ones, Third and Fourth Genders in Native North America* (New York: St. Martin's Press, 1998); Will Roscoe, coördinating editor, *Living the Spirit, A Gay American Indian Anthology Compiled by Gay American Indians* (New York: St. Martin's Press, 1988); and Walter Williams, *The Spirit and the Flesh, Sexual Diversity in American Indian Culture* (Boston: Beacon Press, 1992).

THE INDIANS OF
THE AMERICAN IMAGINATION

Vine Deloria, Jr.*

Until the occupation of Wounded Knee, American Indians were stereotyped in literature and by the media. They were either a villainous warlike group that lurked in the darkness thirsting for the blood of innocent settlers or the calm, wise, dignified elder sitting on the mesa dispensing his wisdom in poetic aphorisms. Strangely, the malevolent image can be attributed to the movie caricature while the benign image comes from anthologies, pageants, and the fervent wish by non-Indians to establish some personal sense of Jungian authentication.

As the Civil Rights movement began to be eclipsed by antiwar protests, and Martin Luther King, Jr., linked Vietnam with American domestic problems, the public began to turn to other minorities for the reassurance that they were, in spite of themselves, good guys. American Indians were a natural choice for public attention: their protests had so far taken place in remote areas of the country, they wanted to be left alone, they would not be purchasing homes in one's neighborhood, and they were a very colorful part of America's past isolated from modern problems. With a growing interest in America's history and the heightened visibility of American Indians in 1967, the publishing industry made a deliberate effort to feature Indian books. A year later Stan Steiner's *The New Indians* described the recent exploits of younger Indians "leading the way" in the 1960s.

Many of the Indians appearing in Steiner's book were sought

* First published in 1972, Vine Deloria, Jr.'s *God Is Red* remains the seminal work on Native religious views, asking new questions about our species and our ultimate fate. Celebrating three decades in publication with a special 30th anniversary edition (Golden, CO: Fulcrum Publishing, 2003), from which this chapter is excerpted, this classic work reminds us to learn "that we are part of nature, not a transcendent species with no responsibilities to the natural world." It is time again to listen to Vine Deloria, Jr.'s powerful voice, telling us about religious life that is independent from Christianity and that reveres the interconnectedness of all living things (from the back cover of the anniversary edition).

1

out by publishers and contracts were given out freely. The publication of *Custer Died for Your Sins* helped focus the anger of young Indians on specific targets such as the anthropologists, the Bureau of Indian Affairs, and the Christian churches. A year later *Bury My Heart at Wounded Knee* by Dee Brown, a well-written accounting of the Indian wars, presented another dimension of the American Indian experience to the reading public.

These books stand out in the literature about the American Indian because the rest of the field is so easily classified and deals primarily with a fantasy image of Indians, the kind of Indians that many groups of Americans would like to believe exist. The Indians occupying Wounded Knee knew they could benefit from the publicity that the book had already achieved. Insofar as they believed that the existing literature on Indians would provide people with additional background to help explain their struggles, they were sorely disappointed. A review of the literature available on American Indians during the years when the activist movement was so predominant indicates the tremendous conceptual barrier they were facing.

With the exception of N. Scott Momaday's Pulitzer Prize-winning novel *House Made of Dawn* and Hal Borland's *When the Legends Die, Stay Away, Joe,* [sic] there have been few successful novels about modern Indian life. *Little Big Man,* Thomas Berger's very successful novel of the old West, covers Indian life and culture obliquely, and its time period could hardly be said to relate to contemporary Indian life. Many novels have not even had the success of *Little Big Man.* In attempting to present, in fictional format, Indian life as it was experienced in the last century, most novels have fallen into a "go-in-peace-my-son" style, with the credibility of the plot dependent on the lonely white trapper, gunfighter, or missionary who comes across the Indian princess. The parallel between the unexpected and fortunate event in the Horatio Alger stories that catapults the hard-working hero to fame and the fortunate "salvation" event that makes the Indian tribe accept the white hero in the Indian novel is no mistake. It is virtually impossible to change cultures or economic status without what would appear to be an almost supernatural intervention.

Where other fields of literature have so successfully enabled people to empathize with conditions and cultural variances, novels about Indians have been notably bereft of the ability to invoke sympathy. Rather they have been dependent on an escapist attitude for their popularity. As a consequence the Indian activist movement could not make contact with a group of informed, sympathetic readers for there were none. There is no emotional unconscious that Indians and non-Indians share that can be tapped on behalf of American Indians, insofar as they are people, like other people. Their sufferings are historic and communal; this is the lesson that America has learned from its literature on Indians.

The communal nature of Indian personal existence is further supported by the presence of a large body of literature on the histories of the respective tribes. For generations it has been traditional that all historical literature on Indians be a recital of tribal histories from the pre-Discovery culture through the first encounter with the whites to about the year 1890. At that point the tribe seems to fade gently into history, with its famous war chief riding down the canyon into the sunset. Individuals appear within this history only to the extent that they appear to personalize the fortunes of the tribe. A mythical Hiawatha, a saddened Chief Joseph, a scowling Sitting Bull, a sullen Geronimo; all symbolize not living people but the historic fate of a nation overwhelmed by the inevitability of history.

Some of the earliest Indian protests challenged this image of Indians and the numerous false stereotypes projected by this type of literature. Sincere but uninformed whites honestly asked Indians during the height of the activist movement if we still lived in tents, if we were allowed to leave the reservations, and other relevant questions, indicating that for a substantial number of Americans, we were still shooting at the Union Pacific on our days off. On one memorable evening as a guest of the Bill Barker show in Denver, I was asked by a radio listener how the Indians celebrated Christmas before the coming of the whites. Bill and I broke out laughing and he had to punch in a commercial so I could compose myself before trying to answer this silly question. There were constant protests directed to whites writing books on tribes to include something about modern Indians in their books. The result of this protest was that several writers of books on Indians added a final chapter in which a quick sketch of the contemporary condition of the tribe was reviewed.

As late as 1964, many publishers thought (1) Indians could not write books, and (2) any book written by an Indian would be "biased" in favor of Indians.[1] Whenever the subject of Indians writing their own books arose, even the friendliest of non-Indians stated that a great many Indians had written books and that we should be content with what they had left. The trail of books written by Indians is significant if considered as the recorded feelings of a race once extant, but insignificant if it is meant to communicate modern social and legal problems that have created and intensified poverty conditions among a segment of the American population.

It was disconcerting to realize that many people felt that the old books on Indians were sufficient to inform the modern American public about the nature of Indian life and to give sufficient information about Indians to make an intelligent choice as to how best to support Indian goals and aspirations. One historian wrote that there are already a sufficient number of books by Indians, and that books chronicling contemporary outrages should not be published because they stir up bad feelings between Indians and whites.[2] He recommended *Sun Chief* (the autobiography of a Hopi, published in 1942), *The Son of Old Man Hat* (the autobiography of a Navajo, published in 1938), and Black Hawk's autobiography (published in 1833). Could these books have correctly informed the reader on the struggle of the Navajo and Hopi against Peabody Coal Company at Black Mesa or explained the protest at the Gallup ceremonial?

This fundamental gulf between the available information about Indians and information that Indians wanted communicated about particular and pressing problems came to dominate Indian concerns. For that reason the activists made maximum use of television and greatly simplified the issues that concerned them. When the National Indian Youth Council was coming into existence and young Indians were attempting to get sympathetic non-Indians to listen to their story, a non-Indian law professor replied that he was very interested in the plight of Indians and had recently read

---

1. Stan Steiner, the writer who broke open opportunities for Indian writers with his *The New Indians* (New York: Harper & Row, 1967), told me in 1968 that he had recommended me to several publishers in 1965 and 1966, but the universal response was that I would be "biased" in favor of Indians and could not get a contract.

2. I presented these same ideas in *Natural History Magazine* in a book review of *Seven Arrows* by Hyemeyohsts Storm (New York: Random House, 1970) and received a barely rational letter informing me of the greatness of the books listed in this paragraph. I have basically summarized the feelings of the letter writer in this paragraph.

Ishi in Two Worlds (a story about the last member of a California Indian tribe, who spent his final days as a mascot of a California museum in the first decade of this century). As a result, Indians, particularly young, educated Indians in their twenties who wanted to do something about conditions, were very frustrated.

The tension being experienced by young Indians, the awareness that something was dreadfully wrong, was recorded in Steiner's *The New Indians.* In this book Steiner reviewed the developments within Indian country since World War II. He pointed out that the tremendous sums the federal government had spent for Indian education were beginning to produce results. Rather than a quiet group of civil servants, however, the younger Indians had become political theorists, activists, and cultural revivalists. Steiner warned of the impending landslide of concern, which was bound to manifest itself in continuing protests against federal policies that had never taken into account the nature of Indian society or the historic feeling of betrayal that the Indian community has held throughout the twentieth century.

However, the reading public, the literary critics, and many of the people directly concerned with the problems of modern Indians were attracted to two other books also published in 1968. Alvin Josephy published *The Indian Heritage of America* and Peter Farb published the book with the long title, *Man's Rise to Civilization as Shown by the Indians of North America from Primeval Times to the Coming of the Industrial State.* Both books were best-sellers and popular book-club selections. Josephy devoted all of 20 pages in a 365-page book to the period from 1890 to 1968, failing to cite any contemporary Indian political leader at all and mentioning the National Indian Youth Council once in passing.

Farb did a brilliant analysis of prehistoric Indian cultures, covered items that had not previously been on any anthropological agenda, and cleverly wove together almost all of the relevant information on Indian cultural traditions into a 332-page book. His work was considered by reviewers as a major step forward in understanding the American Indians. He did not, however, mention the Indian Reorganization Act of 1934, which has formed the basis for communal survival in the postwar world. He did not mention the Indian Claims Commission of 1946, which attempted to redress the injustices of land confiscation through relitigation of land claims. Farb frankly stated that he would leave such a job to another. How he came to figure that he had taken Indians up to the modern industrial state, however, is another question, since his book appears chronologically to stop shortly after the Dawes Act of 1887.[3]

The incongruity of the impact of the three books became more apparent with the addition of other facts. Josephy and Farb were among the inner circle of consultants upon whom then-Secretary of the Interior Stewart Udall relied for his knowledge regarding the formation of policy for American Indians. Steiner was regarded as a itinerant relic of the Jack Kerouac school of wanderers, a person who could not conceivably possess any information on Indians that would be relevant to the formation of policy. In 1968, the inherent schizophrenia of the Indian image split and finally divided into modern Indians and the Indians of America – those ghostly figures that America loved and cherished.

In the next four years it seemed as if every book on modern Indians was promptly buried by a book on the "real" Indians of yesteryear. The public overwhelmingly turned to *Bury My Heart at Wounded Knee* and *The Memoirs of Chief Red Fox* to avoid the accusations made by modern Indians in *The Tortured Americans* and *Custer Died for Your Sins.* The *Red Fox* book alone sold more copies than the two modern books. It was later revealed to be a re-printing of an older book that "Chief Red Fox" had simply copied.[4] Each takeover of government property only served to spur further sales of Brown's review of the wars in the 1860s. While the Indian reading public was in tune with *The New Indians, The Tortured Americans, The Unjust Society* by Harold Cardinal, a Canadian Indian, and other books written by contemporary Indians on modern problems, the reading non-Indian public began frantically searching for additional books on the Indians of the last century.

---

3. Peter Farb was a keen observer of social realities, but he was also perhaps the last writer of the 1960s to perpetuate the old "Indians are exotic and also children" attitude that had been characteristic of whites writing on Indians during the early decades of this century.

4. *The New York Times* did an investigation of Chief Red Fox and found that almost every fact he had presented did not check out. A significant number of people still believe that he was an Indian, although he was unable to name any relatives on the Sioux reservations (see *The New York Times* [March 10, 1972]: 1, 22).

In recent times there have been more frauds than real Indians writing books. In 1991, it was revealed that Forrest Carter, author of *The Education of Little Tree* (New York: Delacorte Press/E. Friede, 1976), was in fact a virulent racist who had devoted a good deal of his life to the Ku Klux Klan.

The result of this intense, non-Indian interest was the publication of a series of books that were little more than cut-and-paste jobs, the anthologies. *Touch the Earth* by T. C. McLuhan and *I Have Spoken* by Virginia Armstrong consisted of a series of excerpts of the speeches by famous chiefs with a few short quotations from living Indians to give the book a timely flavor. McLuhan inserted a number of sentimental sepia pictures of old chiefs riding along the crest of a canyon to add further maudlin emotions to an already overemotional book. The public took McLuhan to heart, and *Touch the Earth* also hit the book clubs. There were also dozens of other anthologies printed following the success of these books but they simply recycled some 150 quotations between new covers. They added nothing new about contemporary Indians and events. Unfortunately, this kind of book still continues to be produced with equally dismal results.

In addition to the sentimental anthologies, a number of books were rushed into print and hopefully to judgment; they were little more than editing jobs on reports to government agencies. Among them was *American Indians and Federal Aid* by Alan Sorkin, a study done by the Brookings Institution under a grant from the Donner Foundation. The book featured numerous tables demonstrating Indian poverty but was devoid of any mention of the forces then moving in Indian affairs that sought to combat poverty and racism. *Big Brother's Indian Programs with Reservations* by Sar Levitan and Barbara Hetrick, a study funded by the Ford Foundation, was published shortly after Sorkin's book. It was distinguishable from Sorkin's book chiefly through its use of photographs as if there really were Indians alive today, its big words, and its utter lack of knowledge about hiring Indians.

In the fall of 1972, there were no less than seventy-five books on American Indians released. Most staggered into print, received few reviews, and collapsed. It was plain that the initial phase of interest in Indians was over. Then, just before Election Day, the Trail of Broken Treaties arrived in the nation's capital, ready to do battle with the Nixon administration. In little over a week the Administration, the tribal leaders, and a great segment of the American public sat stunned as the Indian activists completed their destruction of the Bureau, collected some $66,000 in travel money from the federal government, and set off to terrorize the headquarters of some tribes and Bureau of Indian Affairs field offices. Somehow

American Indians had arrived in the twentieth century.

In order to understand why this particular event occurred, we must try to understand the reception that modern Indians received when they have tried to communicate their immediate problems to an uncomprehending society. When a comparison is made between events of the Civil Rights movement and the activities of the Indian movement one thing stands out in clear relief: Americans simply refuse to give up their longstanding conceptions of what an Indian is. It was this fact more than any other that inhibited any solution of the Indian problems and projected the impossibility of their solution anytime in the future. People simply could not connect what they believed Indians to be with what they were seeing on their television sets. Let us pretend that the black community received the same reception in the Civil Rights struggle that the American Indian community received when its movement was attracting public attention.

It is 1954, and the Supreme Court has just handed down its famous case, *Brown v. Topeka Board of Education;* the Civil Rights movement is beginning to get under way. Soon there is a crisis in Montgomery, Alabama, and Dr. Martin Luther King, Jr., begins to emerge as a credible leader of the Civil Rights forces.

At a news conference King is asked about the days on the old plantation. He attempts to speak on the bus boycott, but the news media rejects his efforts. It wants to hear about Uncle Tom, the famous black of literature. The news conference ends with the newsmen thoroughly convinced that King is merely a troublemaker, that everything is fine down on the old plantation, and that everything will be all right if the blacks simply continue to compose spirituals. Sympathetic supporters stand in the background dressed in slave costumes cheering him on.

Two books are published recounting the blessed days of slavery on the one hand and the cultural achievements of the tribes of black Africa in the 1300s on the other. They are almost immediate successes on the best-seller lists. The American public now worries about the Muslims confronting the primitive tribes of the interior of the African continent and changing their culture. Mohammed becomes a public villain. In a desperate effort to raise the issue of Civil Rights in American society, Martin Luther King, Jr., writes *Stride Toward Freedom.* Outside of a few people who seem to intuit that things are not well down South, King's ideas are ignored. Two new black writers, James Baldwin and LeRoi Jones, publish books that have a sporadic, perfunctory reception, and they are ignored.

The movement continues to grow with television coverage and feature-length descriptions of the poverty conditions of the black community, prefaced by quotations from Booker T. Washington and George Washington Carver to the effect that blacks should remain separate until earning the right to participate in American society. The Freedom Rides begin, sparking a series of anthologies of Negro spirituals about traveling to the promised land. A Negro Travel Book, showing the great migrations in Africa in the 1300s, becomes a best-seller. Boy Scout groups drop their camping activities and begin to perform minstrel shows complete with authentic black dialog.

Finally the movement grows intense as plans are made for a march on Washington. People rush here and there, preparing for the march; the activists down in the Deep South are in trouble. Some have been killed for attempting to register voters. On the literary front, however, things are different. A new book, *Bury My Heart at Jamestown,* has rocketed to the top of the best-seller list. More than 20,000 copies a week are being purchased. People reading the book vow never again to buy and sell slaves. Sympathy for the slaves is running at a fever pitch, while Martin Luther King, Jr., is downgraded because "he doesn't speak for all the Negroes."

As the march gets under way, television finds a new hero. Field Hand Boggs, an elderly black who claims to be 101 years old and a nephew of Nat Turner, is discovered almost simultaneously by *The New York Times* and the "Oprah Winfrey Show." Field Hand Boggs has copied 13,000 words from *Uncle Tom's Cabin* by Harriet Beecher Stowe and is passing it off as his "notebooks" laboriously compiled over a century of struggle. Field Hand Boggs becomes the number one folk hero of America, and he recounts for thrilled television audiences his glimpse of Abraham Lincoln and General Grant sitting on the White House lawn the day that he gained his freedom. The march is conducted in virtual isolation.

As the Civil Rights movement proceeds, the literature shifts its emphasis; old government and foundation reports complete with charts and graphs are trotted out with fancy dust jackets that make them appear to be the latest battle communiqués from Atlanta. Anthologies of spirituals become very popular, and those that are inter-spaced with faded photographs of slaves working in the cotton fields prove the most popular. Introductions to these anthologies sternly inform us that we must come to understand the great contributions made by slaves to our contemporary culture,"More than ever," one commentary reads, "the modern world needs the soothing strains of 'Sweet Chariot' to assure us that all is well."

And finally Watts. As the section of Los Angeles burns, people resolve to do better. Government officials ask for full prosecution of the rebels, all the while handing out $100 bills to the rioters and advising them to go back to Virginia and South Carolina and sin no more. A task force is created of officials of various government departments to study the federal relationship to Civil Rights problems and to report back its findings no later than six months after it authorization.

In the summer of 1967, spontaneously in all parts of the country, professional and amateur archaeologists invade black graveyards. They disinter skeletons, label them, and send them to the city museums for display. Down South people rush to isolated slave graveyards with bulldozers, hoping to find some artifacts of that time when it was possible to own a human being. The National Park System locates sites where the underground railroad once ran and sets them aside for tourists, charging a minimal fee.

Anthropologists rush to the defense of the looter explaining that it is necessary for anthropologists to have the bones of blacks because they derive immense scientific knowledge from them, but they refuse to publish any reports of this precious information.

What seems ludicrous in the black situation as recounted here is precisely what happened in the American Indian situation without anyone cracking a smile. For example, at the height of the Civil Rights struggle, would anyone have seriously entertained the idea that a 101-year-old man with a tenuous claim to black blood or heritage would truly represent the struggles of the black community? Certainly no intelligent critic would be taken in by such a hoax (fraud is rarely used when discussing minority groups).[5] Yet it not only happened to American Indians, but a substantial portion of the public yearned for it to happen.

What we dealt with for the major portion of a decade was not American Indians, but the American conception of what Indians should be. While Brown's *Bury My Heart at Wounded Knee* was selling nearly twenty thousand copies a week, the three hundred state game wardens and Tacoma city police were vandalizing the Indian fishing camp and threatening the lives of Indian women and children at Frank's Landing on the Nisqually River. It is said that people read and write history to learn from the mistakes of the past, but this could certainly not apply to histories of the American Indian, if it applies to history at all.

As Raymond Yellow Thunder was being beaten to death, Americans were busy ordering *Touch the Earth* from their book clubs as an indication of their sympathy for American Indians. As the grave robbers were breaking into Chief Joseph's grave, the literary public was reading his famous surrender speech in a dozen or more anthologies of Indian speeches and bemoaning the fact that oratory such as Joseph's is not used anymore.

The most remarkable body of literature in the years preceding the emergence of the Indian movement was the beginnings of a serious literature on Indian religions. Ruth Underhill's *Red Man's Religion* presented a quick survey of the various religious beliefs of the tribes, but it was phrased in traditional anthropological con-

---

5. The problem of individuals alleging to have Indian blood has become exceedingly serious. Imposters regularly gain access to federal jobs claiming Indian preference and being upheld in their claims. New Age gurus claim to be medicine people of an "intertribal" nature, which is traditionally impossible because individuals had to belong to one tribe or another. Even in litigation on Indian rights it is not always possible to determine if the plaintiff is an Indian. *Bowen v. Roy*, a Supreme Court case involving an individual alleging to be an Abnaki Indian, was adversely decided against Indian rights and the allegations of claims to Indian religious traditions were problematical at best in this case.

cepts and had the expert-lecturing-to-novice point of view. While it provided information, the subject could just as well have been the pottery styles of long-vanished peoples. Anthony F. C. Wallace examined the religion of Handsome Lake in *The Death and Rebirth of the Senecas*. It was a respectable effort but again plagued with the detachment of a historical point of view that gave no sense of urgency to the religious feelings then stirring in the younger generation of Indians.

Father Peter Powell completed his great two-volume work, *Sweet Medicine* explaining tribal religion in a serious vein. Powell's work, particularly his style of exposition, was based primarily on conversations with reservation people and reflected their language. An Anglican priest who operated St. Augustine's Indian Center in Chicago, Powell viewed all religious expressions as sacred and consequently treated the Cheyenne tradition with respect. His book did not take the superficial approach of listing the quaint beliefs of the Cheyennes as if the reader and the author were beyond such superstitions. Sweet Medicine impressed Indians with the validity of their own traditions.

The two most popular books dealing with Indian religion were *Black Elk Speaks* by John Neihardt and *The Sacred Pipe* by Joseph Epes Brown. Some universities had already installed American Indian studies programs by the early 1970s and almost every course included the two Black Elk books as required reading. Consequently they formed a kind of sacred national Indian religious canon by themselves. The Sioux teachings were phrased in a universal manner. Because they had close relationships in theological concepts with the beliefs of other tribes, many Indian young people who had grown up in the cities and who now formed the backbone of the activist wing of Indian affairs, believed them to be an accurate statement about Indian religions.[6]

---

6. Most of the books discussed in these paragraphs had some contact with reality and were done with some degree of scholarly concern. In the last decade there has been a deluge of nonsense as non-Indians, along with a few Indians such as Wallace Black Elk and Sun Bear, have developed a curious interpretation of Indian religion that includes crystals, medicine wheels, sweat lodges, prayer circles, and almost any other kind of adaptation of popular non-Indian group dynamics to Indian traditions. The deluge of books on tribal religions is simply an appropriation of external Indian symbols to meet the emotional demands of the age and has no relationship whatsoever to what traditional Indians did religiously even several decades ago.

As Indian country was tensing for the eventual showdown in the fall of 1972, two major books on Indian religion were published. One was *Lame Deer, Seeker of Visions* by John (Fire) Lame Deer and Richard Erdoes, an autobiography of a Sioux holy man. The book revealed a great deal about the general conditions of reservation life and had an immediate clientele among the very people who had decided to march on Washington. It also had a saucy style typical of the well-experienced Sioux elder making cynical but incisive comments on human behavior. Readers accustomed to the pious rigidity of Protestant tracts on the devotional life were shocked at Lame Deer's casual approach to such taboo subjects as death, sex, growing old, and religion. Yet from the pages of the book shone a wisdom found in few devotional materials.

The second book, *Seven Arrows* by Hyemeyohsts Storm, was even more controversial. *Seven Arrows* was unique because it tried to make a contemporary religious statement using traditional stories, mythologies, and symbols of the Cheyenne people. In a sense it modernized and simplified some of the ideas articulated by Powell in *Sweet Medicine.* People expecting to find a record of ancient Cheyenne rituals and ceremonies were stunned to see garish quasi-psychedelic shields, modernistic representations of culture heros, and the advocacy of the so-called "medicine wheel" that was supposed to enable a person to adjust their lives in order to solve pressing personal problems.

Seven Arrows had an incredible impact on young non-Indians. Accustomed to simplistic teachings from their own churches they found the key to an exotic religion that they had been led to believe was very complicated. Younger Indians living in isolated urban areas away from the reservation ceremonials also liked the book and believed that it was a true representation of their own tribal religions even though it was written for the 1960s. *Seven Arrows* provided a linkage between the emerging groups of non-Indians who were adopting non-Western religious traditions and the Indians who were asserting or relearning their own religious traditions. While it helped to create a groundswell of support for the Indian occupations of federal buildings, it also brought the subject of tribal religions into the marketplace of ideas for the increasing number of people looking for a personal religion and new kinds of religious experiences.

Several years before Storm's book a "cult" following for Indian religion had already been created by a series of books written by Carlos Castaneda, beginning with *The Teachings of Don Juan* and *A Separate Reality,* and a succession of clever titles. In this series of narratives Castaneda purported to have spent several years as an apprentice to a Yaqui medicine man Don Juan who lived in the Sonoran deserts and other obscure places in Mexico. Castaneda had learned very quickly all the secrets of the shaman's trade until the current book sales began to wane and he would pick up the narrative and reveal even further sophistications about making reality in your own mind. The Don Juan books were just what young whites needed to bolster their shattering personal identities, and the books were immensely popular.[7]

Movies did not keep pace with the Indian image during these years. The movie Indian was a thinly disguised young white who wished to have both the simplicity of nature and the modern involvement with social and political issues. The most popular movie alleged to deal with Indians was *Billy Jack,* a mixed-blood Indian and a war veteran who was an expert in the martial arts. He demonstrated his commitment to peace by breaking people's limbs in a spectacular fashion. One scene showed Billy Jack dancing in an abandoned Pueblo ruin and allowing a rattlesnake to bite him as he danced, purporting to be some kind of ceremony that enabled him to be a brother to the snakes. The scene was pure Lutheran theology since Billy Jack's faith was supposed to make him immune to snake poison. Sequels to this movie did not do as well. The phenomenon was a passing fad but an extremely important one because it informed young non-Indians that their goals and the Indian goals were identical, that through mastering Indian religious ceremonials they could become invincible and heroic.

Tell Them Willie Boy Is Here, starring Robert Redford and Katharine Ross, chronicled an earlier incident in this century in which a sheriff's posse pursued a young California Indian. The movie had a ring of authenticity regarding both the reservation and the historical period. Because it did not show the Indian using magical tricks or being particularly religious, *Willie Boy* did not attract the great crowds that attended *Billy Jack,* and few people

---

7. People appeared to be divided on whether or not Castaneda had actually met any Indians, let alone studied under Don Juan. The consensus is that the religious experiences were either made up or came out of a sugar cube somewhere on the West Coast.

connected the conditions of Indians on California reservations with the demands of the protestors in Washington.

If we compare the image of Indians projected in literature and somewhat in film with that of the Indians who marched on Washington one thing stands out clearly – underneath all of the symbols and ideologies is a religious context and religious motivation. But there was no way to communicate the complexities of this worldview to non-Indians and there was no way that Indians could articulate how this religious perspective could resolve existing problems. Two entirely different views of the world, of human beings, and of human history were about to clash and there was not a single bridge over which the exchange of ideas and sentiments could take place. Moving from the Bureau of Indian Affairs occupation through the Wounded Knee occupation, the trials and the investigations by the American Indian Policy Review Commission, one of the first pieces of legislation passed to resolve Indian problems was the American Indian Religious Freedom Resolution (1978). So there could be no doubt that religion played a critical, if unarticulated, role in the Indian movement.

Two entirely different developments characterize the period from 1972 to 1990. First, Indians in their respective tribes began a serious revival of their religious traditions. Ceremonies that had long been discarded or suppressed were once again performed. Traditional people were sought out for their knowledge of ceremonies and customs. Young Indians all over the country felt it imperative to experience a vision quest, and some groups even reinstituted a version of the Ghost Dance. The movement even intruded upon the congregations of Christian Indians as Indian priests and ministers sought to combine the teachings and practices of both religions. Some traditional ceremonies were even carried out in Protestant churches so that it became difficult to tell whether one was going to attend a hymn-singing or a healing ceremony when people gathered.

The reasoning behind this integration of two religious traditions is interesting because it goes to both the nature of religion and the nature of cultural identity for answers. Christian Indian priests and ministers felt no sense of guilt in conducting traditional ceremonies because they felt that the ceremonies were as much Indian cultural expressions as religious acts. Additionally, with the argument that there was but one deity, the difference in religions was merely one of choice and expression. Hence a universal sense of religious feeling replaced what had been rather precise formulations of religious beliefs. Some Indians expressed the thought that every culture was in effect an "old testament" with the "new testament" topping them off and making sense of all earlier cultural reaching toward God.

The churches eagerly embraced this new movement for the most part. Their congregations had been declining drastically for years as reservation residents gained more mobility and small settlements on the reservations could no longer support churches and chapels that had been founded during the 1880s and 1890s, a period of impressive conversions. Much nonsense occurred during this period. Episcopal bishops, already looking silly in ecclesiastical costumes standing on the South Dakota prairies looked absurd when this dress was topped off with awkward fitting war bonnets. Indian Christians and traditionals alike were offended when masses were held coincident with the sun dance in spite of the arguments given for merging the two traditions.

Christianity among Indians has fared rather badly during recent years. When placed next to traditional religions, it has very little to say about responsibilities to family and community; most Christians deal simply with the church as if it were the deity. Indian symbolism is not symbolic in the same way that Christian symbolism is; therefore, mixing liturgical objects has become anathema to many Indians. Indian cultural traditions provided an easy explanation for certain kinds of religious acts whereas Christian religious acts depended primarily upon the acceptance of Western culture. It was this cultural and historical perspective that Indians rejected. The result we see today is the rapid movement away from secularism and Christianity toward a more serious traditional religious life.

The second development that emerged following the cresting of the Indian movement was the intense interest in tribal religions by non-Indians and the seemingly wholesale adoption of some of their beliefs and practices by significant segments of white society. The medicine wheel was the symbol most easily adopted by whites through workshops, conferences, and gatherings. The seven directions to which the Plains Indians pray with the pipe became a means of orienting people to the natural world so that the pipe and some semblance of Indian ceremonies were also taken over. Whites then began making and using drums and feather fans for their own use in ceremonies they were holding. The first wave of appropriation, therefore, was simply the symbolic costumes that non-Indians believed would place them closer to nature.

As the demand for authenticity increased so did the fees paid to real Indians to hold ceremonies. Sun Bear, a Chippewa from Minnesota, created his own tribe, the Bear tribe, and found a way to bring non-Indians into his own version of Indian ceremonial life. Eventually he expanded and had an advertisement in *Shaman's Drum,* a magazine devoted to educating the thousands of young whites who wished to be Indians – and shamans. The ad featured a nice picture of Sun Bear with the caption, "Sun Bear needs spiritual warriors." This ad exemplified the motivation of non-Indians – they wanted some kind of power so they could deal with their own culture and be successful.

A variety of Indian medicine men and purported medicine men moved into white society where there were easy pickings. Whites would pay hundreds of dollars for the privilege of sitting on the ground, having corn flour thrown in their faces, and being told that the earth was round and all things lived in circles. The next step was performing sweat lodges for non-Indians. Another step was to cut out the best-looking blonde for a "special ceremony" in which she would play Mother Earth while the medicine man, or whoever had conned the blonde, would be Father Sky. They would couple to preserve the life on the planet. In short, the arena between cultures became a scene of intense exploitation.

Added to this confusion was the elevation of whites once again to be the primary exponents of Indian religion and culture. This phenomenon was triggered unexpectedly by Ruth Beebe Hill in a badly written novel entitled *Hanta Yo.* Hill purported to "know" the Dakota language before missionaries had written it down and therefore ruined it. She claimed to have written a 1,500-page book in this language, translated it from an early English dictionary in order to get authentic English sentence structure, and published it. Her informant was a strange Santee Indian named Chucksa Yuha. Otherwise known as Lorenzo Blackmith, his personal history and claim to ancient knowledge was refuted by investigators at every turn. Hill's major thesis was that she alone knew the truth about the original Dakota/Lakota Indians, that their descendants were pale imitations, and that the original resembled nothing less than Ayn Rand's *Fountainhead,* rugged individuals who bowed to nothing including the deity.

Hanta Yo, according to its editor, was thrown over the transom (in other words, came in unsolicited), read avidly, and seen immediately as a classic – the first time anyone had rendered an accurate version of traditional Sioux life. Without delay it was announced that the book was an Indian "Roots" and that David Wolper, who had produced the original "Roots," had somehow acquired the television rights to the work. Indians protested vigorously and slowed down production of the television movie. A group at Pine Ridge, however, could not resist the money being offered by Wolper and endorsed the film. It was finally shown under the title *Mystic Warrior* and thankfully disappeared.

Ruth Beebe Hill had proved a very important point. As interested as whites were in Indian culture and religion, they preferred to learn from non-Indians who posed as experts in the field. Thus, the books on Indian religion written by Thomas Mails, complete with very good drawings of Indians and sacred objects, and the books by Richard Erdoes, confidant to a group of traditional people on the Rosebud Sioux Reservation in South Dakota, did a brisk sale and continued to be popular. These books were within the scope of respectable offerings because so much of their material was taken directly from existing literature and was sullied only by their own occasional personal interpretations of events and activities.

Beginning in the late 1970s and continuing through present time, the literature on American Indians includes not only books on Indian religion written by non-Indians but also anthologies and treatises on ecology allegedly using Indian principles. One example of this fantasy literature are books by Lynn Andrews, a talented show business performer. Andrews has demonstrated that it is possible to say almost anything and have it believed providing it is packaged correctly; at that job she is without peer.

Andrews' first offering was *Medicine Woman* in which she purported to have been an apprentice to a Canadian medicine woman named Agnes Whistling Elk. The narrative is thrilling because almost without pain or discomfort Andrews is given all the secrets that every white person has sought for centuries. We learn in the last chapters of the book that her mission is not to live among the Canadian Indians performing simple healing and condolence ceremonies like other medicine practitioners. Instead she is commissioned to go throughout the world revealing religious secrets of the Indians. Following *Medicine Woman* are an incredible number of books in which Andrews visits the outstanding medicine women in the world and is accepted immediately into secret societies that have been preserving the ancient knowledge for thousands of years.

The concept of proselytizing on an apostolic commission inspired some Indians to claim similar missions. Today an alleged shaman can explain his or her absence from the reservation or absence of Indian blood with the excuse that after being trained by elders, the individual has then been authorized and commanded to go among all peoples and preach the Indian gospel. It seems that this surplus of shamans could severely tax the credibility of these practitioners. How can there be so many medicine people who have been commissioned to hold ceremonies for non-Indians while their own people suffer without religious ministrations?

In what has been called the "New Age" circuit, Indians have devised a clever answer to this question. They insist that they are "pipe carriers," an office that has rather hazy historical and cultural antecedents. No definition is ever given of the exact duties of the pipe carrier except that he or she can perform all the ceremonies that a shaman can perform without being called to account when nothing happens. This status was just what non-Indians need to avoid the accusation that they are practicing traditional ceremonies without any real knowledge or understanding of Indian ways. Now everyone from movie stars to gas station attendants has claimed to be an authorized pipe carrier. The belief is that one need only recite these magic words to turn aside all criticisms and skeptical expressions of the listeners.

In the 1990s, Indian religions are a hot item. It is the outward symbolic form that is most popular. Many people, Indian and non-Indian, have taken a few principles to heart, mostly those beliefs that require little in the way of changing one's lifestyle. Tribal religions have been trivialized beyond redemption by people sincerely wishing to learn about them. In isolated places on the reservations, however, a gathering of people is taking place and much of the substance of the old way of life is starting to emerge. Some keen observers predict that within a decade people serving on tribal councils will have to have a full traditional ceremonial life to get elected.

THOMAS MERTON
AND NATIVE AMERICA

Lewis Mehl-Madrona and Barbara Mainguy

In the 1950s, Merton began to address the relationship between the Government and the Churches to Native nations in the United States. He left only a small number of works in which he directly engaged his interest in and questions about Native Americans. His research and writing about Indians were his way of entering into a humanistic discussion of the moral and spiritual failures of those in the United States' dominant culture in their dealings with indigenous peoples.

Several authors have located Merton's interest in indigenous cultures as his pursuit of social justice for all peoples, especially for those who have suffered most from rapid industrialization. In *Thomas Merton and the Monastic Vision*, Cunningham[1] suggests that Merton personally identified with those whom the dominant culture misidentifies and marginalizes. He personalized the past unjust treatment of indigenous peoples to influence new perspectives that valued the culture and rights of Native Americans. In her essay, "Thomas Merton's Re-Visioning the New World at Intercultural Borders," Małgorzata Poks[2] suggests that Merton was questioning his own American identity to project the idea of an America that can resolve tensions across intercultural borders. He confronted the paradoxes of the *Civitas Christiana* that had manifested itself below a lofty rhetoric as an "exploitative, genocidal, corrupt, destructive, mad, totalitarian police state." Merton was intent on tearing away any shreds of a romantic fabric that covered the state of the Union with regards to civil rights and humanism and insisted on taking a rigorous look at American policy.

---

1. Lawrence Cunningham, *Thomas Merton and the Monastic Vision* (Cambridge: Cambridge University Press, 1999).

2. Małgorzata Poks, "Thomas Merton's Re-Visioning the New World at Intercultural Borders," *Cross Currents* 58, no. 4 (Dec 2008) 570-591.

REFLECTING ON MERTON'S WRITING ABOUT
NATIVE AMERICAN CULTURES

Two primary texts permit insight into Merton's engagement with Native American cultures and the narrative of the social and political catastrophe of the interactions between these cultures and the American government. This narrative of catastrophe had been analyzed in the writings of Ohiyesu (Charles Eastman) that were penetrating even mainstream culture around the time of his writing (1890-1920). One of these Merton texts is a long poem, "The Geography of Lograire," in which the poem's "West" section features the Ghost Dance ceremony.[3] The second and more important text *Ishi Means Man* is a collection of essays on Native Americans many of which Merton had written for *The Catholic Worker* in the year preceding his death in 1968.[4] The title of this volume refers both to the literal meaning of *Ishi*, which means "man" in the Yana language and to a book about a man who was a Yahi tribal member (or possibly mixed Yahi-Namiatu [one of the Wintun tribes of Northern California]). After genocidal gold rush participants had enacted a series of murderous raids on them dated between 1865-70, the Yahi people went into hiding, successfully evading contact with settlers, but decreasing in population until only a tiny group remained. After further attacks on this group, only four tribal members escaped. When his mother and sister died, the man who would come to be called Ishi walked half-starved from the forest near Orovo, California, in 1911, and after a news media furor, he encountered the University of California anthropologists, Alfred Kroeber and Thomas Talbot Waterman. He was called *Ishi,* the word for "man" in his language because Yahi tribal custom forbade him speaking his name. Kroeber and Waterman arranged for his release from jail, took care of him, and welcomed him to the University as a teaching assistant. He spent his last days living in his apartment at the University of California, Berkeley, Museum of Anthropology (so called at the time), teaching about his people. Ishi never disclosed the fates of the other three members of his group.

We can't predict how Merton's appreciation of Native American cultures would have changed beyond these two texts if he had

3. Thomas Merton, *The Collected Poems of Thomas Merton* (New York: New Directions, 1977) 455-609.

4. Thomas Merton, *Ishi Means Man: Essays on Native Americans* (Greensboro, NC: Unicorn Press, 1976).

received the opportunity to interact personally with a Native community. We have in these texts at best a glimpse into his process of attempting honest engagement with the sprawling whole of the political, emotional, personal, and spiritual struggle of Native Nations. We can see at the outset that Merton wished to stretch his understanding beyond any anthropological or political science review. But there are too few essays here to judge if he did this. Our reading suggests that he might have stopped short of truly embracing the otherness he sought, but he certainly presented a rigorous framework for our understanding.

In the first essay of *Ishi Means Man*, "The Shoshoneans," he explores the social and political life of Native Americans. He addresses the exclusion and oppression of the members of the tribal culture, who are rendered symbolic, turned into fixed points, by the treatment he describes. In 1965, writer Edward Dorn and photographer Leroy Lucas traveled through the west to meet the Shoshone people and to encounter them not as exotic Indians but as people with full inter-subjective status. Merton first gives voice to his awakened sense of the awful injustices perpetrated against the Native Nations and the continuing attempts at the time to cover up and defend the genocidal practices. He then ventures into a sarcastic exposition of the type of mind that could have created the government documents and histories which described the atrocities committed against Native Americans as the necessary containment of a fundamentally depraved people. Merton is scathing in his reading of these government-described "Indians," stereotyped on popular television shows as shiftless and primitive, so lacking in intelligence as to need protection as wards of the state, perpetually minors due to their incapacity to care for themselves. Indeed, they are mysteriously drawn to live in impoverished areas and run down places. They lacked any capacity for effective stewardship of the lands upon which they dwelled. Their stories of their relationship to the land, involving ancestors, hunting, and other "romantic nonsense" served as evidence of their "minor" (minority) standing and need for supervision.

Merton judges this rhetoric as so much propaganda. It was a deliberately constructed fake story intended to render Indians as "other," as diminished in status because of their diminished capacities. Their minds are simply not sophisticated enough to comprehend a bigger picture. They lack the correct approach to land stewardship, sales, development, and money making. Their interference in these objectives shows a stubborn adherence to wrong-mindedness and a simple-minded neglect of the responsibility of "citizenship." Thus, the settlers had to take responsibility for this neglected land. They needed to wipe out or contain these disreputable people. These were ample reasons to justify their imprisonment whenever Indians mounted a defense or offense when they attempted to re-acquire land (and to survive).

Merton uses the writings of Dorn and Lucas to counterpoint this understanding. He approved of their approach. He called their book a pilgrimage, a journey to the source, a looking for a renewal of life; in this case, a renewal of the life of the tribal people in which they appear *as themselves*. He speculated that Lucas' African-American status enabled him to slip past the picturesque façade of Indians as foreign objects in the glory of the western landscape. Merton's project in this essay is to disturb our assumptions about the political project of colonialism – that *others* must be taught to be like us. He troubles any self-congratulatory dialogue about human rights that might be occurring in the complacent field of U.S. politics. Merton speaks urgently and passionately about the need to see people as they are. Otherwise, we forever trap them in the circular inscription of their otherness, forever rendering them as people who fail to be versions of ourselves; almost like us, but not quite, and not successfully. In a way that Merton finds horrifying, we offer them a definition of themselves that is "arbitrary and unlivable." We consign them to a symbolic existence that is tragic and profoundly affects the lives and identities of our fellow beings. As Dorn and Lucas have done, Merton writes that we must see these indigenous peoples with a clear vision of their personhood and autonomy. We must approach them with a sense of understanding and repentance for our actions against our common humanity. Indeed, at this point in history, after imposing through our ignorance several generations of suffering, we must offer a now a lifeline to the peoples we have oppressed and subjugated. This enraged opening launches Merton's writing into appreciating the context of Native American experience. He launches himself into a nascent dialogue with Native American peoples and invites his audience to join him in grappling with these issues of injustice. Our past and current approaches to Native American experience are very wrong.

Merton found evidence for our cultural resistance to Native

American personhood in the casual disregard for Native American voices. He invites engagement with the question, "What do they think of themselves?" He attempts an answer by describing a series of current inter-cultural struggles. He comments about how a local Kentucky radio station casually thanks the Shoshoni Bannocks Sun Dance for Peace in Vietnam, knowing nothing about the dance, reading it only as a nice gesture for peace. A non-Indian argues for practicing the peyote church ceremony, while "highly articulate" Native Americans counter his arguments as detached from Native American authenticity. Merton notes a speech by a young Ponean man named Clyde Warrior as an articulate commentary in which the young man argues for Indian autonomy in managing resources, and comments that the disenfranchised are controlled by the very institutions that exclude them, and do not permit them a voice at the table. Organizers of this conference to end poverty would not place Warrior's speech on their agenda.[5] The group was just not ready to hear what he had to say.

Having opened to his scrutiny the seam of deceptive, illegal, genocidal practices in the colonial struggle with the Indians of the United States, Merton changes his emphasis in his essay, "War and Vision." He explores the nature of a profound spiritual experience, an idea inherent in Native American culture and central to its spirituality: "the vision quest." He investigates this Native American lifeway as inherently mystical. He uses the term "mysticism" to make the scope of understanding this ritual as broad as possible, avoiding the "vision quest's" becoming entangled in religious identifiers from Catholicism. He states that "such visions were taken for granted as a normal part of life in an archaic culture." He locates "fasting" for a vision as an important rite of passage into adult life. He explores its meaning and purpose in the contexts of a "hunting and warring culture." "Visions," he points out, are potent and could be damaging, so their significance required examination by tribal elders who assisted in deriving the meaning of the vision after much collaborative consideration.

Merton proposes that the "vision quest" belongs to a disappearing past. When we read this, we feel uncomfortable. Perhaps Merton did not realize that cultures are dynamic. The notion of an "archaic" culture seems to reference a system that is a discrete segment as if there were a dividing line between archaic and modern

---

5. Merton, *Ishi Means Man*, 14.

as if cultures don't live and change with time and pressure. Perhaps the "vision quest" provoked dissonance with Merton's concept of "visions," and he feared their vulnerability to manipulations. He complains that "vision quests" are susceptible to a blindness inherent in the aims of a system. He seems to prefer a vision that is received randomly and from outside. A culture that relies on visions for life's direction is unattractive to him. He apparently overlooks that apparitions or visions play a strong role in Catholicism. He seems to imply that an encounter with the Great Mystery through a vision was shaky ground on which to base life decisions. Is he being hypocritical here or expressing his view out of an implicit sense of Catholic superiority?

Merton appears to be guarded about "visions" after studying the "vision quest" in the autobiographical account of Two Leggings, a Crow warrior who co-wrote his biography (with Peter Nabokov). Two Leggings wrote of forcing himself to have a vision. He pretended a vision to have access to a deeper knowledge of leadership and medicine in his community. The Elders sensed his partial confabulation and did not affirm or support his vision, to his perpetual bitterness. Merton accounts for Two Leggings' choice when he remarks, ". . . we must not be too romantic about all this. There would be no point in merely idealizing primitive men and archaic culture." Merton remarks that Two Leggings failed because he tried to skirt existing protocols for gaining spiritual knowledge. He tried to seize "mystical knowledge" as useful information before it naturally came to him through experience. Merton considered these spiritual protocols to be obsolete soon after the elimination of bison hunting and war parties. The shift in focus for Indians was to create, in Merton's reckoning, a Pan-Indian non-warring group to work for survival, never mind obtaining status in the pre-contact ways. He remarks that "stone age" warriors were no longer relevant and he seemed in accord with Two Leggings' final commentary that without those lifeways, without the hunt and warrior life, "There is nothing more to tell." Merton suggests that a role for the "vision quest" has ended. "Vision quests," and the self-humbling that comes in seeking a vision, have no place in a warless society. Leadership need not have this spiritual dimension; working for survival has nothing to gain from a fast.

We know, however, that there is considerably more to tell. Native American spirituality was not relegated to a "back then," a movement or philosophy that died out due to a lack of utility. We know from Lakota elders such as Albert White Hat, Sr., and John Around Him that the spiritual practices continued, stopping only when forced to be discontinued because of being made illegal for the "protection" of the people. We know that in the 1950s and 1960s, word began to spread in the Native American community that the ceremonies still existed. Albert White Hat, Sr., in a lecture at Sinte Gleska University, detailed his coming into awareness that there were those who had preserved the ancient ceremonies and had taught them to him before they once again became legal.[6] The information was underground, out of view of scholars, and certainly of missionaries. In *Coyote Medicine,*[7] LMM wrote about attending his first *inipikaga* (revitalization ceremony) in 1973 when it was still illegal in the United States. A Roman Catholic priest was there with his collar at the ready in case the police came, prepared to declare the ritual a proper Catholic ceremony. LMM heard stories about other members of the Catholic clergy similarly supporting Native American ceremonies before legalization in 1978. The water-kettle drums of the Native American Church's vision quest ceremonies were fabricated to appear like to cookware if discovered. The entire ceremony resembled people sitting around a fire cooking if discovered by police.

Merton's selection of Two Leggings' story seems tendentious. As his study of Native American lifeways and what remained of his natural life was to be cut short, he seems to have made no obvious attempt to interview Indians who had embraced a contemporary identity, and he thus relegates the relevance of Indian lifeways to the "Stone Age." He uses language to suggest that Indian spiritualities were coming to an end with the demise of the buffalo. He offers a view of nothing alive. The atonement that he vigorously announces in his first essay begins to seem like an obituary, a conversation of apology that is only a dialogue with the dead. We can listen, he says, to how the Indians are, but, in truth, they are nowhere, floundering in the spiritual vacuum left by the disappearance of the buffalo and, therefore, of the meaning and purpose of the whole people.

In some principled way, this seems unfair. Sociologically

---

6. Albert White Hat and John Cunningham, *Life's Journey – Zuya: Oral Teachings from Rosebud* (Salt Lake City: University of Utah Press, 2012).

7. Lewis Mehl-Madrona, *Coyote Medicine* (New York: Simon & Schuster, 1997).

speaking it may be true of the pragmatic structure of old, but can we truly claim that there was no capacity to adapt? If buffalo were the metaphor for the sustenance of life, could there be no new metaphor?[8] Could there be no continuity of existence beyond the functional, no possibility for the DNA of this mystical trait to be preserved in the inevitable morphing that would take place? Could no life in a thousand of years of continuous culture survive this decimation? In a culture that is rich in values and a lifeway that some have compared with that of Jesus,[9] how is it that Merton apparently could not see this possibility? To be fair, perhaps his views on visions expressed in *Ishi Means Man* resulted from his perceived need for scholarly discipline so that he judged the Indian responses to their mistreatment with the same rigor as he examined actions taken by the U.S. Government against them.

In the essay "Ishi: A Meditation," Merton tends to muddle the Indian identity and he critically limits Native American cultures as emerging from a past 'age.' Merton seems to walk further into his view of the anachronistic Indian. The warrior identity was shifting but not, as Merton thought, disappearing. He certainly could have found provocative reading to challenge his views of a disappearing people. In the 1950s, he could have readily found Indians who were grappling with the realities of the imposition of the dominant culture on their own. While sparse, the cultural landscape was not as barren as he proposed.

Merton was familiar with the people and ideas that would influence the American Indian Movement. Merton's fellow monk, Ernesto Cardenal,[10] assures us that Merton had read Black Elk. He certainly could have obtained his account of the Wounded Knee massacre from that reading and would have heard in rich detail about Black Elk's vision. Perhaps this is why he allows for visions to have a universal quality but he limits their effectiveness as a means of social and spiritual direction.

Merton is likely to have read the work of Ohiyesu published in many forms and detailing a rich and painful conversation between Native American social and spiritual values and the "new" Christian culture. After fifteen years of living with his Dakota tribe, Ohiyesu,

8. Across Native North America, people today say, "Education is the new buffalo."

9. Charles Alexander (Ohiyesa) Eastman, 1858-1939. *The Soul of the Indian: An Interpretation* (Boston and New York: Houghton Mifflin Company, 1911).

10. Polks, ibid.

Charles Eastman, attended Indian Boarding School, then Dartmouth College, the Boston University School of Medicine, and walked in both worlds. This included time spent as an Indian lobbyist, trying to get the legislators and governors of the day to honor the treaties. The transitional moment for Ohiyesu was the massacre of the Ghost Dancers. He was the doctor on the Pine Ridge Reservation where and when it happened, and afterward wrote fourteen books. In his most political autobiography, *From the Deep Woods to Civilization*,[11] he speaks highly of Jesus, but meticulously tears apart the Christian conceit of being better than Indian culture and values. Merton does not mention this account, though the books were bestsellers. Instead, he appears to have based his thinking on Native American identity on the very appearances of poverty and listlessness that he advises us to question.

What motivated Merton in this way? Did he want to clear the space for a genuine relationship between his Church and the Native Americans that provided something necessary – in this case, a new liturgy?

When it came to Ishi's plight, Merton felt the poignancy of a man's living in a museum as the last living survivor of his tribe, brought to extinction by European conquest and colonial policies. Merton was sad and enraged at the destruction of indigenous cultures by what he considered to be an aggressive culture of exploitation. Merton appreciated the concepts of cultural and spiritual genocide achieved through residential schools, which forbade the practice of aboriginal language and culture, as well as through the entire reservation system. He believed that these practices created a false identity for Native Americans, a mask imposed by others, which was illusory and destructive. He recognized how this constituted psychological destruction. Merton had similar feelings about nuclear proliferation – that exploitive and aggressive cultures of violence behaved amorally against others without regard to consequences and effects.

Even so, he uses the "Ishi: A Meditation" essay to close his thinking. He reflects on the cruelty of the Indians and the compassion toward Ishi and seems to suggest that those things have an equalizing effect – could Merton absolve his culture of blaming

---

11. Charles (Ohiyesa) Eastman, *From the Deep Woods to Civilization: Chapters in the Autobiography of An Indian* (Boston: Little, Brown, and Company, 1916).

the victim because Indians in the heat of battle could use tactics invited by the white men? Could he be saying that one example of compassion to an Indian by an anthropologist is enough to provide redress to the criminal activity again and again of the United States government? Here are Merton's words, and we must read much from the tone compared to the stridency found elsewhere as he discusses Ishi:

> Ishi spent the rest of his life in San Francisco, patiently teaching his hitherto completely unknown (and quite sophisticated) language to experts like Sapir. Curiously enough, Ishi lived in an anthropological museum where he earned his living as a kind of caretaker and also functioned, on occasion, as a live exhibit. He was well treated, and, in fact, the affection and charm of his relations with his white friends are not the least moving part of his story. He adapted to life in the city without too much trouble.[12]

Merton also attempts to mitigate the genocide, attributing it to lawless ones who disobeyed the government because they were crazed by gold (an idea directly echoing Ohiyesu). He neglects the truth that from the President Andrew Jackson forward the tacit assumption was that treaties made with Indians could be broken and that the genocide was sanctioned.

Merton's reception of the Ghost Dance Movement does not seem to have caused a re-evaluation of his negative view of "visions" in Indian culture. Merton devoted a section of his process poem, *The Geography of Lograire*, to a critical moment in Native American history. According to Charles Eastman (Ohiyesu), the original Ghost Dance was a ceremony envisioned by a Paiute named Wodziwob, in Nevada, who in a dream envisioned a ritual dance that would inspire a cultural resurgence of the Paiute people and affect the demise of the whites. Wodziwob's prophecies included the eradication of Europeans, either following a giant earthquake or an ascension, neither of which came true, so the movement died out. Twenty years later, after twenty more years of abuse, broken treaties, starvation, and deprivation by the U.S. Government, Wovoka, a Northern Paiute, offered his reinterpretation of the message. In Wovoka's dream, the dance again resulted in the disappearance of white people and the return of tribal lands. This dream troubled

---

12. Merton, *Ishi Means Man*, 31.

the Indian Agency leaders, who were already facing increasing resistance as their abusive practices and failure to comply with treaty obligations was becoming less easy to hide.[13]

As widespread discontent was being swept up into the religious initiative of the Ghost Dance, the U.S. Government began to consider a military response. Two *Miniconjou* (*Plants By the Water,* a Sioux sub-tribe), Kicking Bear, a man of spirit who famously sun danced for Crazy Horse, and Short Bull, brought the dance to their people in central South Dakota. Fearing the movement would captivate followers of Sitting Bull, who supported the Ghost Dance, the agents at Standing Rock in North Dakota became concerned and conspired to arrest Sitting Bull. This arrest famously resulted in his murder, long held as the desired intended result. Some of his relatives fled toward Pine Ridge to the Southwest. Passing through the Cheyenne River Reservation, Chief Big Foot joined them. The Government preventatively arrested Kicking Bear and Short Bull. According to Eastman, the press fomented the idea of an Indian Rebellion and encouraged panic. Eastman in his telling this history comments upon the considerable profits resulting from "Indian Uprisings." Chased by soldiers, Ghost Dance practicing Indians moved towards Wounded Knee. Meanwhile, the Indian Agency "called in" all those who were not part of this new religion on the pretext of protecting them. When Indians began gathering to dance under the inspiration of Wovoka's vision, the soldiers insisted they disarm. Though the majority did, there was some opposition, and one dancer (who was known to be deaf) fired a gun into the air, giving the U.S. soldiers the excuse they needed to open fire. In a short time, they slaughtered over 300 hundred unarmed men, women, and children dancers in the area of Wounded Knee, including Chief Big Foot.

Merton does not negotiate the slaughter in the Ghost Dance portion of *Lograire* (Part III). Reflecting on the Ghost Dance as a ceremony as he understood it, Merton presents the Ghost Dance as a desperate attempt by a critically abused culture to find meaning in their suffering. He judges elements of the ceremony as tragic spiritual exercises. He notes the superhuman qualities attributed to those who practiced the ritual. Wearing shirts that deflected bullets

---

13. For a poignant description of those abuses, see Thomas King, *The Inconvenient Indian: A Curious Account of Native People in North America* (Minneapolis: University of Minnesota Press, 2013).

and protective boundaries that soldiers could not cross were fantasies of true freedom based on magic. In his poem's brief *Prologue,* he imagines a meeting of the leaders in attendance on November 27, 1890: American Horse (who Ohiyesu considered to be a great voice of reason), Fast Thunder, Spotted Horse, Pretty Back, and Good Lance. They enumerate their grievances against the U.S. Government who negotiated with them in bad faith and was acting contrary to its current laws in an almost surreal denial of accountability. In the second section, *The Ghost Dance*, Merton offers a historical account of the dance movement, his narrator being on the ground to observe it, giving the poem the air of a debriefing. We learn in this account that this is not a ceremony that reaches for transcendence, nor even, as in a vision quest, for connection to spirit. By creating the poem, Merton transcends analysis. He offers, instead, a blunt account of the features of the dance without added commentary as if he were practicing a disciplined spiritual empiricism. Under Merton's passively observant scrutiny, he allows the Ghost Dance to manifest itself.

George Kilcourse has described *The Geography of Lograire* as a chronicle of the historical, widespread degradation of indigenous peoples that manifests the "resilient hopes of the weak, the abused, and the damaged of the earth, who are now known as Third World Peoples."[14] Cunningham saw the poem as presaging the yet unborn critiques of liberation theology. Merton's essays on Native Americans argue that every human being has an irreducible human dignity always threatened by the incursion of large forces deriving from modern culture.[15] The Ghost Dance was a response to a deep sense of impending self-destruction experienced by Aboriginal people in the face of a holocaust that was beyond their historical comprehension. Merton believed that this arose through the triumph of what Jacques Ellul had called *techne,* which overwhelms the humanizing instincts of people in contemporary society. In a 1967 letter to Rosemary Reuther, Merton described his reading of anthropology as an attempt to make sense of the trauma that happened to traditional cultures when being overrun by European-derived cultures. He believed the Ghost Dance religion had eschatological manifestations.[16]

---

14. George Kilcourse quoted in Cunningham, *Thomas Merton*, 161.
15. Cunningham, *Thomas Merton*, 64.
16. Cunningham, *Thomas Merton*, 64.

Relating Merton's Spiritual Views
to Those of Native Americans

Merton believed that God is closer to us than we are to ourselves. To understand this is to realize that God unifies everyone through the divine presence within us. The difficulty in comparing Native American spirituality to that of Merton's comes in understanding definitions. Since Native American tribes differ, we will concentrate our reflections on the Lakota tribe, about which we know the most, as our prototype for this discussion. To further complicate this comparison, contemporary spiritual practice on reservations today often blurs Christian concepts with those of Native America. The Lakota speak of the *nagili* translated as "that which arises through interaction with the divine." Finding a parallel for the Christian God can be difficult within Lakota. The Creator, *dakuskanskan,* is genderless, lives at the end of the "milky road," and is more removed from humanity than the Christian God. *Dakuskanskan* is translated as "that which moves everything that moves." Within Lakota spirituality is an understanding that we are first and foremost spirits linked to a material form.

Merton's Concept of Self

Merton's concept of self differs from that of the Lakota. Merton believed in the idea of a "true" or "authentic" self, which emerges through contemplation and prayer. This self became progressively more spiritual through living the monastic life (and to some degree, non-monastic spiritual counterparts). Merton's concept of the self was, however, largely European, similar to that imagined by Jung or Freud. Lakota lacks such a concept, having instead the concept of the *nagi*, which is the swarm of stories (and a part of all the beings who told those stories) that surrounds our bodies and shapes our minds into who we are. We are *swarminess* in the sense of a swarm of bees that moves as one body. This concept of the self most closely resembles Bakhtin's polyphonic self or Hermans' concept of the dialogical self. However, within dialogical self-theory, just as in the worlds in which Merton interacted, there are interesting cultural differences.[17] Non-European societies can be more contextualized in

---

17. J. Valsiher and G. Han, "Where Is Culture within The Dialogical Perspectives on The Self?" *International Journal for Dialogical Science*, 3, no. 1 (2008) 1-8.

social relationship hierarchies,[18,19] which call for functional fluidity to adapt to changes in the relationships and limit the degree to which a differentiated self can arise in relation to the Other.

The indigenous self may be/is an extended or connected self.[20] An extended self contrasts with Merton's more European-derived concept of the self, which places stress on values such as self-efficacy and individuality,[21] competitiveness and its management, and assertiveness and self-assuredness.[22] These attributes manifest in what Merton called the authentic self. This authentic self is an independent and self-contained entity, separate from the context in which it is embedded and struggles to reconnect with the Spirit or the Divine or God. This concept of an authentic self is rooted in European philosophical traditions and especially to the influence of Cartesianism.[23] In an experimental study, when Americans were asked to comment on their personalities, they rarely made reference to the context in which they existed.[24] Implicit in Merton's ethos of self-actualization and the discovery of authenticity is this concept of the autonomous self in the West.[25]

Within the concept of *nagi*, the self is decentralized. Aspects of the self can exist quite separately in space and time from the present and the observed physical body. For example, my grandmother

18. N. Chaudhary, "Persistent patterns in Cultural Negotiations of the Self: Using Dialogical Self Theory to Understand Self-Other Dynamics within Culture," *International Journal of Dialogical Science*, 3, no. 1 (2008).

19. T. Van Mejil, "Culture and Identity in Anthropology: Reflections on 'Unity' and 'Uncertainty' in the Dialogical Self," *International Journal of Dialogical Science*, 3, no. 1 (2008).

20. T. B. Benning, "Western and Indigenous Conceptualizations of Self, Depression, and its Healing," *The International Journal of Psychosocial Rehabilitation*, 17, no. 2 (2013) 129-137.

21. L. J. Kirmayer, "Psychotherapy and the Cultural Concept of the Person," *Transcultural Psychiatry*, 44, no. 2 (2007) 232-257.

22. L. J. Kirmayer, G. M. Brass, and C. L. Tait, "The Mental Health of Aboriginal Peoples: Transformations of Identity and Community," *Canadian Journal of Psychiatry*, 45, no. 7 (2000) 607-616.

23. S. Kitayama and H. R. Markus, *Emotion and Culture: Studies of Mutual Influence* (Washington, D.C.: American Psychological Association, 1994).

24. R. A. Schweder and E. J. Bourne, "Does the Concept of the Person Vary Cross-Culturally?" *Culture Theory: Essays on Mind, Self and Emotion,* eds. R. A. Schweder and R. A. LeVine (Cambridge: Cambridge University Press) 158-199.

25. F. Johnson,"The Western Concept of Self," *Culture and Self: Asian and Western Perspectives,* eds. A. J. Marsella, G. M. Devos, F. L. Hsand, and K. Hsu (London: Tavistock, 1985) 91-138.

together with all the stories she ever told figures prominently in my *nagi,* but she is not present in ordinary space-time. Similarly, I often identify with my self-criticizer, my stepfather, who died years ago. Within *nagi,* we are many stories, all of which shape us into what we are. To know what we are entails knowing all the stories that have made us what we are.

Bakhtin's polyphonic self[26] is the European version of the *nagi.* Bakhtin referred to the self as composed of a multiplicity of independent, autonomous voices or characters, each with its point of view, some shouting out the others, some forming coalitions, breaking coalitions, while others cower in the corner in the face of this cacophony. He pointed to Dostoevsky's novels as his best example of what this would resemble. In the midst of this, we construct an identity narrative to keep these characters in some semblance of order that allows us to operate in the world. Some narratives are better than others. Some generate more friction in the self's interface with the world than others. These voices or characters have distinct functions in our lives and are available when we need them. If one of our internal characters resembles the Red Queen in *Alice and Wonderland,* as was the case for one of our clients, she should probably not be allowed to drive the car in rush hour. For Lakota and Bakhtin, all the characters living within our *nagi* are authentic. The question becomes one of negotiating the right character for the job presented to us. A different character goes to war from the one who contemplates spirituality. Both are authentic within the context in which they operate. Merton was more concerned with finding a context-free authentic self. Lakota and Bakhtin are more concerned with matching the leading character to the context in which he or she functions more productively.

Merton believed it was possible to enter into a dialogue with God at an experiential level despite the obstacles of modernity. Here Merton's concepts are directly in line with Lakota thought, especially as presented by Charles Easton (Ohiyesa) in his writings such as *The Soul of the Indian.*

CULTURE AND SPIRITUALITY

Culture is not an essence within the minds of people from the given

---

26. M. Bakhtin,"Problems of Dostoevsky's Poetics," *Theory and History of Literature,* vol. 8, ed. Carl Emerson (Minneapolis: University of Minnesota Press, 1984).

society, but an organizing principle of every human mind, in any society.[27] Culture is thus everywhere – always in action, but usually rarely noticed. Merton was drawn to the spirituality of diverse cultures presumably because participating in those other cultures allows us to see ourselves from perspectives different from our own. The perspective of another culture provides us a certain ironic distance from which to view ourselves. When we see ourselves as persons of another culture would see us, we become more aware of ourselves. Merton appeared to become more aware of his spirituality through considering himself from the standpoint of Native Americans, but also from perspectives of Buddhists, Hindus, and other representatives of other cultures. The Lakota worldview as we understand it would relate culture to a collection of stories and practices derived from those stories, shared by an inter-related group of people. If one person has a swarm of stories surrounding him or her that creates who he is, then a group of people shares an intersecting swarm of stories that define individual and group identity and membership. Typically these stories are performed through the medium of language so that those who share these stories speak a common language in which to tell these stories.

CONTEMPORARY EXTENSIONS OF MERTON'S WORK

The story of Merton's interactions with religious perspectives other than his own has impacted members of his Roman Catholic Church who are today in active relationships with the world's traditional religions. Merton's story is surely part of the "swarm" attached to the person of Father Achiel Peelman, Oblate of Mary Immaculate, who was born in the Flemish part of Belgium in 1942 and has been teaching at the St. Paul University in Ottawa since 1971. He was part of a symposium on "traditional religions and their contribution to peace," held at the Vatican, January 12-15, 2005. The initiative for this meeting came from Pope John Paul II who wanted more attention paid to the traditional religions.

Peelman writes that almost everywhere, the traditional religions have a rather similar concept of peace as much more than the absence of war and conflicts; peace is more the full realization of life. "In the traditional religions, there are certain elements that form

---

27. J. Valsiher and G. Han, "Where Is Culture within The Dialogical Perspectives on The Self?" *International Journal for Dialogical Science*, 3, no. 1 (2008) 1-8.

part of a universal patrimony. But in the context of globalization, it is becoming difficult also for them to maintain their values. That is why we are concerned to help them to safeguard these values and to transmit them."[28] The Church's dialogue with the traditional religions began officially for the first time at a meeting in Assisi called by John Paul II in 1986. Before this meeting, inter-religious dialogue involved representatives only from Hinduism, Buddhism, and Islam.

Peelman's inspiration to promote inter-religious dialogue had its foundation in a dream:

> [My] decision to remain in Canada came after a dream. It was already very Amerindian, because dreams for them are like moments of "revelation." This dream was telling me that I should study the situation and the future of the Oblate Missions throughout Canada. So, I made a plan that led me to visit the Oblates from one ocean to the other. As soon as I got under way, the Amerindians made me understand that my approach was too much from within the Church and that I should concentrate more on their culture. Their spiritual leaders invited me to visit them and thus I was able to become initiated into their spirituality, in particular that of the Cree in Alberta. It is a step that I accepted without hesitation, because to understand this spirituality, there was only one way: to experience and live it from within.[29]

Peelman experienced the "Vision Quest" through which he wrote, "You subject yourself to a complete fast from food and drink for four days, in a sacred place, under the supervision of a traditional . . . spiritual leader. I was also invited to practice many other rituals and to have many contacts with the Wise ones. That enabled me to have a privileged view of them while deepening my own Christian spirituality." Peelman's views resemble Merton's but, unlike Merton, he had no sense of Native American cultures as vanishing. (Merton might have changed his perspective, had he lived longer.)

Stories like Merton's and Peelman's are changing a Church that prohibited traditional practices in the past into one that now encour-

---

28. Jean-Pierre Caloz, "Achiel Peelman, OMI, An Untraditional Involvement: Interview with Achiel Peelman, OMI." (Rome, Italy: Missionnary Oblates of Mary Immaculate, 2004). https://www.omniworld.org/interview/achiel-peelman-omi/. Last accessed 11 January 2018.
29. Jean-Pierre Caloz, "Achiel Peelman, OMI."

ages them. Peelman documents this change in his own experiences:

> I take myself as an example: this course of initiation helped
> me to reflect on the inculturation and the development
> of an Amerindian church. In Canada many Amerindians
> became Christians, but they always wonder: can one be
> at the same time Amerindian and Christian or must one
> choose? And this question comes from people who really
> want to achieve a synthesis between the Christian faith and
> their own culture. It is true that in the past the Church had a
> negative view of these practices, but the Church has looked
> more in depth at the bonds between cultures and the faith,
> and can now encourage human groups to develop them-
> selves, with the assistance of their local pastors, a synthesis
> between their cultural knowledge and the Christian faith.
> As Oblates, we are invited to take part with the people in
> this synthesis and this harmony.[30]

In 1995, Peelman published a book entitled *Le Christ est amérindien
(Christ is an Amerindian)* in which he developed the Amerindian
vision of Christ, traditional spirituality and some orientations for
the development of an Amerindian Church.[31] In 2004, he published
another work: *L'Esprit est amérindien (The Spirit is Amerindian)*[32]
where he wrote of his initiation into Amerindian spirituality and of
the relation between this spirituality and Christianity.[33]

INTER-SPIRITUALITY

Before Merton, the Roman Catholic Church resisted inter-religiosity
as a degradation of true religion. Merton, and later Peelman, believed that inter-faith dialogue with its potential to transform and
change all participants is both desirable and necessary. Merton
was open to the possibility that dialogue and contemplation could
transform historical practice and that practice should support spirituality rather than be rote and unchangeable. Religious syncretism

---

30. Jean-Pierre Caloz, "Achiel Peelman, OMI."
31. Achiel Peelman, *Le Christ est amérindien: une réflexion théologique sur
l'culturation du Christ parmi les Améridiens du Canada* (Ottawa: Novalis, 1992).
32. Achiel Peelman, *L'Esprit est amérindien: quand la religion amérindienne
recontre le christianisme* (Montréal: Médiaspaul, 2004).
33. Jean-Pierre Caloz, "Achiel Peelman, OMI." Retrieved 9 November, 2014,
from http://www.omiworld.org/ content.asp?catID=4&artID=753&N=.

is a kind of border practice performed by those who situate themselves within multiple intersecting spiritual practices and/or in the margins between them.[34] Peelman talked about syncretism as the fusion of two belief systems to form a third. Peelman's interest was in "border dwellers," those who are invested in more than one belief system and set of practices.

S. H. Hughes has written of Louise Erdrich and Joy Harjo as two syncretic theologians. These bicultural writers demonstrate both a Native American perspective and a Christian reciprocation of those views. They create a third space for religious experience that offers the possibility for integration and transformation of the two views. In doing so, Hughes says that they unsettle forces in both camps, turning their insights into what Native theologian George Tinker calls "reciprocal dualisms."[35] Each poet reveals the conflicts within the Christian system that they engage, and in a syncretic process transform that dichotomy into a productive and reciprocal relationship. In doing so, they highlight the feminine aspects of God.

Hughes calls this a blurring of boundaries, but that is only so from the European point of view. Native American philosophy does not draw sharp boundaries between inside and outside, sacred and secular, human and nature, and self and other. Within the Native American view, there is no secular; all is sacred. Humans are embedded in nature and are not considered apart or above nature. "Other" is contained in self, as we mentioned before in describing Bakhtin's polyphonic self.

Erdrich's poems, *Baptism of Desire,* highlights the tensions between natural needs and spiritual needs, between the earth-bound body and the transcendent ascent of the soul. She integrates these tensions, moving into the same realm opened by Merton in his journals, where he questions the value and meaning of a contemplative life, especially in a world demanding action to remedy injustice and oppression. Merton came first and paved the road on which these poets travel. Hughes argues that Erdrich holds together essential denial and sheer celebration, ultimate need and utter fulfillment, opening the door to a more traditionally tribal view of spiritual

34. S. H. Hughes, "Falls of Desire/Leaps of Faith: Religious Syncretism in Louise Erdrich's and Joy Harjo's 'Mixed-Blood' Poetry," *Native American Writers*, ed. Harold Bloom (New York: Infobase Publishing Co., 1998).

35. George Tinker, *Missionary Conquest: The Gospel and Native American Cultural Genocide* (Minneapolis: Augsberg Fortess, 1993) 131.

reality and "the mutually regenerative power of the earth and the body."[36] Her poems emphasize the essential changeability and multiplicity of both physical and spiritual reality. "They suggest that flexibility and adaptability determine the viability of any religious form."[37] Spiritual power is realized in the inter-connections of co-inhabitants of the material world.

Hughes described Harjo as engaged in a more Protestant dialogue, that between Word and Spirit. By relying on a more tribal and oral understanding of the relationship between these two terms, she brought nature and the body into play, asserting that the same feminine spirit inspires all religious expression. Harjo says, "Transformation is really about understanding the shape and condition of another with compassion, not about overtaking . . . God . . . who is a relative . . . [who] lives at the roots of molecular structure in all life (quoted in Ruwe, 60)."[38]

On the more practical side of daily life, Native Americans today are creating syncretisms.[39] On the Dine Reservation in Northern Arizona (USA), three major spiritual traditions are being used today: traditional healing practices used for generations having a continued dynamic existence relevant to everyday life; Christian healing traditions, ranging from Charismatic Catholicism to Protestant Pentecostal; and those of the Native American Church (NAC). The coexistence ranges from outright opposition to complex synthesis. Many people have been able to integrate two or, in some cases, all three of the major spiritual healing traditions into their spiritual way of life, in addition to making use of allopathic medicine. Begay and Maryboy examined the complexity of this spiritual synthesis through their presentation of the story of a Navajo/Choctaw Catholic nun, whom they called Sister Grace, known as Asdzaan Jobaa'ii, or "Woman of Compassion," by her traditional Dine acquaintances.

Although a devout Catholic nun, her unique spirituality also drew on the beliefs and practices of the Native American Church as well as Traditional Dine beliefs and ceremonies. Sister Grace

36. Hughes, "Falls of Desire," 43.

37. Hughes, "Falls of Desire," 43.

38. J. Harjo and D. Ruwe, "Weaving Stories for Food: An Interview with Joy Harjo," *Religion and Literature* 26, no. 1 (1994) 60.

39. D. H. Begay and N. C. Maryboy, "The Whole Universe Is My Cathedral: A Contemporary Navajo Spiritual Synthesis," *Medical Anthropology Quarterly* 14, no. 4 (2000) 498-520.

was born into all three spiritual traditions. She was a living example of multiple religious allegiances. There was no major or abrupt conversion process from one to another. Faced with serious medical problems, this devout Catholic turned to Dine Traditional Spirituality and to the Native American Church for spiritual diagnosis and treatment. She provides a practical example of Merton's inter-faith dialogue alive and functioning within one person. Her treatment exposed evidence of ancestral disharmony of a genetic and hereditary nature. Ceremonial procedures were initiated, leading to a process of healing.

The Dine worldview is naturally dynamic and holistic. Everything evolves from a cultural and spiritual way of life, which is rooted in recursive cosmic processes directly connected to the natural cosmic order. In the Dine view, cosmic processes are intrinsically interconnected through systemic movement and relationship.[40] A vital awareness and understanding of the concept of wholeness are fundamental to the consciousness of most indigenous peoples. For the Dine, this holistic consciousness manifests through language and ceremonies. This unique and comprehensive consciousness has provided the cultural nexus and dynamic order for countless generations.

DIALOGICAL THEORY AND SPIRITUALITY

Important relationships exist among Merton's theory of spiritual development, indigenous thought about self and other, and dialogical self-theory, which holds that human beings are fundamentally social, their sociality being the very condition of their individuality.[41] The social and the individual then are not in contradiction or opposition to each other; rather, they are dynamically related, generating each other. Lakota thought would see us in a similar relationship with the invisible, spiritual world. Others shape us even as we influence them. Merton speaks of a similar dialogue with God, who would appear to be an amalgam of multiple individual spirits to a person from an indigenous background. The dialogue with God changes us, though it is hard to say if Merton would

---

40. D. H. Begay and N. C. Maryboy, *Nanit'a Sa'ah Naaghai Nanit'a Bik'eh H6zh66n: Living the Order: Dynamic Cosmic Process of Dine Cosmology* (San Francisco: California Institute of Integral Studies, 1988).

41. C. M. Bertau, "Introduction: The self within the space-time of language performance." *Theory & Psychology*, 24 no. 4 (2014) 433-441.

agree that we change God, as well. Catholics have been moving toward this perspective through the process theology of Teilhard de Chardin, as have Protestants through Alfred North Whitehead.

Dialogical research rejects an individualistic methodology,[42] asserting that what matters is the relatedness of human beings to their consociates, to themselves, and to their specific historical and socio-cultural environment.[43] Otherness plays a central role in forming us. The basic move to constructing an alternative to individualistic methodology is the shift from the self-contained "I" to the related self, where the other is seen as the self's pre-condition – to acquire, develop, and perform language, thinking, consciousness as well as its self.[44] Similarly, aboriginal philosophy sees us emerging from the interaction with all of our relations, shaped and influenced by every story told and all the beings telling those stories. Merton understood the way in which the spiritual context and the dialogue with God shapes and creates the spiritual self, what he called the "authentic self" that emerged in dialogue with God.

Spiritual communication is a positioning, evaluating, and mediational process in the Lakota world. Merton would describe the monastic life as providing the positioning, the evaluating, and mediation between the person and God. Eastman described this as happening through nature, the original church for the Native American. Ultimately, all argue for an enlivening inter-faith dialogue in which the world's traditional religions have validity and the opportunity to influence (and to be influenced by) the world's dominant religions. However, many scholars would argue that these traditional religions have already been over-influenced by the dominant religions and need protection to return to their origins in non-patriarchal, non-gendered, and less hierarchical spiritualities. Merton certainly moved the Roman Catholic Church in this direction and only time will tell us the consequences of his efforts.

---

42. S. Gallagher, "A Philosophical Epilogue on the Question of Autonomy," *Handbook of Dialogical Self Theory,* eds. H. J. M. Hermans and T. Gieser (Cambridge: Cambridge University Press, 2012) 488-496.

43. J. Shotter, *Conversational Realities: Constructing Life through Language* (London: Sage, 1993).

44. C. M. Bertau, "Introduction: The Self within the Space-Time of Language Performance," *Theory & Psychology* 24, no. 4 (2014) 433-441.

NORTH AMERICAN ABORIGINAL¹ SPIRITUALITY AND THOMAS MERTON'S CHRISTIANITY

Lewis Mehl-Madrona and Barbara Mainguy

INTRODUCTION

The spiritual practices of the aboriginal peoples of North America vary widely as Indian nations have differing histories and beliefs. Our aim in this chapter is to provide an introduction to North American indigenous spirituality with an emphasis on Dakota/Lakota culture. We know this culture best, and it would have been widely discussed during Merton's lifetime thanks to the existence of the American Indian Movement in the social activist circles in which Thomas Merton circulated. Dakota/Lakota philosophy has general relevance across North American Indian cultures but is not compatible in all instances. We suggest the interested reader explore the indigenous spirituality of his or her interest to learn how it might be similar or different from what we are writing here.

Thomas Merton became familiar with Native American spirituality through his political activism, which brought him into contact with the precursors of the American Indian Movement (AIM). AIM was strongly influenced by Dakota/Lakota spirituality. Based in Minneapolis, an area close to Dakota groups, two of AIM's main founders were Ojibway from Minnesota (sometimes called Chippewa). They quickly aligned with Lakota people through the man who would become influential in their development, Russell Means.²

---

1. We shall use interchangeably the Canadian, Australian, English, and New Zealand convention of referring to the original people of a place as aboriginal along with the common U.S. term "Native American," and the term "American Indian," or "Indian." We will use indigenous synonymously with aboriginal.

2. Patrick Straub, *It Happened in South Dakota: Remarkable Events that Shaped History*, vol. 2 (Lanham, MD: Rowman & Littlefield, 2016) 112-119.

AIM's leadership made a conscious decision to align their movement with Dakota/Lakota spirituality. It would have been impossible to be a social activist in Merton's time and not come into contact with AIM and its precursors. In *Ishi Means Man* Merton demonstrated his understanding of the complete destruction of aboriginal people by European Americans, his grasp of the issues, and a sophisticated analysis of how people can do these things to other people. As an example of his writing in this volume, consider Merton's ironic perspective on aboriginal people and land ownership:

> They did once in a manner of speaking qualify as "property owners," but of course in a very mystical, primitive, irresponsible way, a way utterly laughable. They seemed to be owners of the whole continent until we arrived and informed them of the true situation. They were squatters on land which God had assigned us. They were only *aboriginal* owners. Really no owner at all. The Indian had all this real estate but never even knew it was real estate. So he never really had any legal title. He never even claimed a legal title. What a betrayal of responsibility! What a shameful disrespect for the basic value of life: property ownership! The aboriginal owner was content to put forward some fantastic story about ancestors, about living here, about having the right to hunt in order to stay alive, and other romantic nonsense. From the first, it was quite evident that the manifest destiny of the Indian was to live 'principally' on reservations as wards of the true owners of the land, the ones for whom legal title had been prepared in some mysterious fashion from the beginning of time, or drawn up perhaps in Noah's ark.
>
> He [the Indian] can never sell himself to us as fully human on our impossible terms. In practice, he is at best a second-class human who tries to dress and act like ourselves but never quite manages to make the grade. Placing them on reservations was an act to protect white settlers from psychological depredations, from any loss of self-esteem by an admission that the Indians might be humanly their equals. To protect white America from the realization that the Indian was not an inferior being. To guarantee that the Indian conformed to the white man's idea of him, the Indian

was more and more deprived of his original holdings, *since the white man's identity is coextensive with the capacity to own property, to have holdings, and to make a lot of money.*

[T]he ultimate violence which the American white man has exerted in all unconscious "good faith" upon the colored races of the earth has been to impose on them *invented identities*, to place them in positions of subservience and helplessness in which they came to believe in the identities which had thus been conferred upon them.[3]

MERTON AND NATIVE AMERICANS

As early as 1958, Merton was concerned about the indigenous people of the Americas. He believed that listening to the poorest and humblest people was essential. In a letter to Ernesto Cardenal, who had once been a novice monk under Merton at the Abbey of Gethsemani, Merton spoke of moving to South America:

[O]ne of my mad ideas is to break off and start a new kind of small monastery in Ecuador, a sort of ashram for local intellectuals and men of good will and Indians, part of the time devoted to discussions and spiritual works of mercy (and some corporal, like a clinic).[4]

When he was Merton's novice, Cardenal, who had participated in armed resistance against oppression in Nicaragua, was reading with his novice master[5] Black Elk's *The Sacred Pipe*,[6] a book that describes the essence of Dakota/Lakota spirituality. In April 1958, Merton was also reading John Collier's revisionist book, *The Indians of the Americas*,[7] which features the Dakota/Lakota among others. While he was interested but not as familiar with the history of the indigenous people of Latin America cultures, Merton appeared to have glossed the many distinct cultures of the Americas into a pan-Indian vision that drove his quest for justice and exoneration of the Christian faith

3. Thomas Merton, *Ishi Means Man: Essays on Native Americans* (Mahway, NJ: Paulist Press, 2015) 4.

4. Thomas Merton, *The Hidden Ground of Love* (New York: Farrar, Straus and Giroux, 2011) 17.

5. Małgorzata Poks, "Thomas Merton's Re-visioning the New World at Intercultural Borders," *Cross Currents* 58, no. 4 (2009) 200-220.

6. Joseph Epes Brown, *The Sacred Pipe: Black Elk's Account of the Seven Rites of the Oglala Sioux* (Norman, OK: The University of Oklahoma Press, 1989).

7. John Collier, *Indians of the Americas* (New York: Signet, 1948).

from its brutality toward indigenous people.

An example of Merton's perspicacity in appreciating the plight of aboriginal people came in *Ishi Means Man,* when he describes the 1965 visit of Edward Dorn, a poet, and Leroy Lucas, a photographer, to the Paiute Reservation in Nevada and two Shoshone Reservations in Idaho. Merton writes about their photographs:

> These are not the photographs which somehow manage to ignore Indians and treat them as if they weren't there – making them disappear in a raw, postcard colored landscape and an incomprehensible costume. The aboriginal owner has a face marked with suffering, irony, courage, sometimes desperation: always with a human beauty which sometimes defeats obvious degradation.[8]

Merton tells us that Leroy Lucas participated in the Sun Dance, fasting and dancing for three days straight. The dancers were praying for peace in Vietnam. Radio KSSN, Pocatello, Idaho, praised it as a War Dance for War.[9] Merton notes the many levels of irony in this distortion. He might not have been aware, however, that the Sun Dance (*Wiwanyang wachipi*)[10] was still illegal (it would remain so until 1978). The U.S. Government tolerated its occurrence before 1978 due to the mainstream American belief that the dance was to support aboriginal soldiers who were fighting in the Pacific Theater in World War II, and later, in Korea, and later still, in Vietnam.

> When Radio Station KSSN congratulates the Indians for their war dance, it is congratulating them for accepting an identity imagined for them by somebody else and performing a meaningless, perhaps slightly nostalgic act which defines them as non-persons. The war dance is permitted as an admission of failure. One admits failure by admitting that one is an Indian. A situation worthy of Kafka. To be an Indian is a lifelong desultory exercise in acting like somebody else's invention . . . After all, the war dance does remain ambivalent: an assertion that to be an Indian formerly meant something: a capacity for self-defense.[11]

---

8. Merton, *Ishi Means Man*, 5-6.

9. Merton, *Ishi Means Man*, 7.

10. We will continue to refer to the Sun Dance by its Lakota name to avoid any confusion with the film festival in Sundance, Wyoming.

11. Merton, *Ishi Means Man*, 10.

What Merton may not have realized is that the *Wiwanyang wachipi* was never a war dance, but was always a dance of gratitude offered by someone in thanks for his life having been saved when their death seemed imminent. It was and still is more a dance for returning warriors than it was for those going to war. Merton also may not have realized that the Shoshones were taking advantage of the mainstream culture's erroneous assumptions to perform a most sacred ceremony which they had been arrested for performing since the 1890s. The Shoshones did not care what the mainstream culture thought was happening, as long as they performed the Sun Dance without interference. The revival of the *Wiwanyang wachipi* was a part of an Indian cultural renaissance that was building in Merton's time (though he may not have noticed it) and this renaissance continues to grow to this day.

Merton also briefly discusses the Native American Church, calling it the Peyote Religion, and quotes a Shoshone man who argued that drugs were not the historical way to achieve spirituality. Merton points out that drugs had come to the Shoshone for only the past 50 years and that they had never been part of the culture before that time. This is equally true in Dakota/Lakota culture.

Merton was also aware of another aspect of Dakota/Lakota culture, the vision quest or *hanblechiya*. In one of his letters, he wrote:

> This afternoon I am going to take off into the woods. I have a rather fascinating book about a Crow Indian who made fasting retreats on mountaintops in order to get suitable visions and "medicine" in order to triumph in battle. It is quite fascinating – a study of a mystical military life![12]

We shall now more particularly describe general aspects of Dakota/Lakota religious culture and make comparisons with Merton's Christianity.

DAKOTA/LAKOTA SPIRITUALITY AND THOMAS MERTON

ORIGINS

The people now called Dakota/Lakota/Nakota are believed to have originated in the Mississippi River area and to have moved into the Ohio River Valley, making their way eventually to what is now called Wisconsin, Minnesota, Iowa, and the Eastern Da-

12. Merton, *Hidden Ground of Love*, 29.

kotas. Conflicts with the Anishnaabe and the Cree pushed the Lakota westward in the mid-to late-seventeenth century.[13] Early Lakota history was recorded on their winter counts (*waniyetu wowapi*), painted on hides since 900 C.E.[14] This is when the first mention of the White Buffalo Calf Woman giving the people the sacred pipe occurs.[15] Around 1730, the Cheyenne gave the Lakota horses (called *sunkhan wakhan*, or "mysterious/sacred dog"). The horse led to a shift in the Lakota way of life to buffalo hunting on horseback. As they were pushed west by European expansion, they brought along religious beliefs developed in the Great Lakes region to adapt to their new locale. By 1750, they had reached the east bank of the Missouri River. The powerful Arikara, Hidatsu, and Mandan prevented them from moving further west until the great smallpox epidemic of 1772-1780, which killed three-quarters of the people of these tribes. In 1765, a Lakota raiding party led by Standing Bear had discovered the Black Hills (*Paha Sapa*), which lay in Cheyenne territory. In 1776, they defeated the Cheyenne and occupied the Black Hills, which they considered sacred.[16] The U.S. government first made contact with the Dakota/Lakota during the Lewis and Clark expedition of 1804-1806, which resulted in a standoff. The Lakota refused to allow the expedition to continue upstream, leading them to prepare for a battle which never came.

COSMOLOGY

North American indigenous theology may be monotheistic, polytheistic, henotheistic, animistic, or some combination thereof. In

13. B. Pritzker, *A Native American Encyclopedia: History, Culture, and Peoples* (New York: Oxford University Press, 2000) 329.

14. One type of record common among Native People of the Plains is the pictographic *waniyetu wowapi*, or winter count, painted on animal hide and later on unbleached muslin. The tribal historian with the counsel of the old men of his tribe, decided on some event that distinguished each year and then drew an appropriate symbol for that year. Every adult could describe the events portrayed and used the calendar-like device as a visual aid when educating the tribe's children or retelling the tribe's history at gatherings. The Dakota and Lakota refer to these documents as *waiyetu wowapi* or "winter counts" because the people counted their years by winters, and so the Dakota year covered portions of two calendar years. http://www.ndstudies.org/resources/IndianStudies/standingrock/timeline_highdog.html.

15. Smithsonian Institute, Lakota Winter Counts: http://wintercounts.si.edu/html_version/html/thewintercounts.html (2012).

16. M. Liberty, Cheyenne Primacy: The Tribes' Perspective as Opposed to That of the United States Army: A Possible Alternative to the Great Sioux War of 1876: http://www.friendslittlebighorn.com/cheyenneprimacy.htm (2006).

many Native American traditions, spirituality is taught through stories and relies on direct contact with elders (knowledge carriers) in one's family and community. Dakota/Lakota theology is also learned through hearing the stories and participating in the ceremonies and the culture.

In Lakota cosmology, the Creator's loneliness sparks creation. Creator is translated as "that which moves all that moves" and has no gender. Various sources place Creator at the end of the Milky Road, which interestingly has just been found to be the site of the only black hole in this galaxy where creation is still underway.

Creator made rock (*inyan*), which is male, and earth (*makha*), which is female. A slew of sacred beings began to appear, the most important of which was the Sun (*Wi*), who is the Chief of the Sky Spirits (*wakantankan*), and exercises no small degree of power and influence over the beings of the earth. Important here is the more direct correspondence of Lakota cosmology with our contemporary understanding of the solar system (and unlike the early Christian cosmology, which put the earth at the center of the universe). The other sky spirits included the moon, the stars, the light, the darkness, the clouds, and the Thunder Spirits (lightning, thunder). *Makha* was uncomfortable with her plainness and negotiated with Creator to be covered in green clothing with blue jewelry (lakes, rivers, and seas). The adventures of the Sacred Beings are every bit as dramatic and intriguing as those of the Greek and Roman gods and goddesses.

Eventually, Creator had to prepare the earth for people and dispatched the Wind and his four sons to do so. *Wazi*, a wise male who will eventually oversee human males, aided Creator while *Iktomi* opposed Creator. His name is usually translated as a "man who looks like a spider." His questionable parentage and oppositional nature cause him to create obstacles to any process that leads to the good. *Iktomi* is as close as Dakota/Lakota comes to the Christian devil and is different in that he is accepted as a necessary aspect of the world and is invited to take part in some ceremonies to help us know where he is. Dakota/Lakota cosmology minimizes an epic struggle between good and evil. Despite *Iktomi*'s opposition, with the help of the designees of the Plant People (the Sage Plant) and the designees of the Animal People (the Eagle), with the aid of the Thunder Spirits, and with an intervention by the Bird Nations, the four sons of the Wind become the Four Directions. The Four Directions are sometimes also called the Four Winds who even today are considered guardians and helpers. The establishment of each of the Four Directions is a story of how they each acquire attributes, activities, and colors that are unique to each direction. In the South direction sits the South Wind, who comes to be married to the White Buffalo Calf Woman, an important messenger to and from Creator.

Coming closer to our ordinary lives and to contemporary times, we find the characters who populate today's ceremonies and spiritual rituals. There are the Four Sons of the Wind, or Four Directions, whom songs acknowledge by asking them to look this way at us and see what we are about to do. There are the Sky and the Earth. The Sky protects us (also a scientific story) and the earth nurtures, feeds, and heals us. We connect to each other from our "center" which a common contemporary greeting translates as, "I shake your hand in greeting with a warm heart." As in some Asian and African religions, ancestors remain available to help as spirit beings and are honored and acknowledged in song and ceremony.

EQUALITY OF ALL BEINGS

Central to the Lakota spirituality is the idea that all beings are equal. Lakota lacks the "specism" commonly encountered today. Animals are not held superior to people, nor are plants held superior to animals. All have spirit and are equal. Physical places have spirit – mountains, lakes, and rivers. One can enter into dialogue with trees, dogs, eagles, and even mosquitoes. One can see how Merton might have been sympathetic to the results of such beliefs. In his poem, "O Sweet Irrational Worship," he writes:

Wind and a bobwhite
And the afternoon sun.

By ceasing to question the sun,
I have become light,

Bird and wind.

My leaves sing.

I am earth, earth

All these lighted things
Grow from my heart.

A tall, spare pine
Stands like the initial of my first
Name when I had one.

When I had a spirit,
When I was on fire
When this valley was
Made out of fresh air
You spoke my name
In naming your silence:
O sweet, irrational worship

I am earth, earth

My heart's love
Bursts with hay and flowers.
I am a lake of blue air
In which my own appointed place
Field and valley
Stand reflected.

I am earth, earth

Out of my grass heart
Rises the bobwhite.

Out of my nameless weeds
His foolish worship.[17]

I read Merton as supporting these ideas of the power of nature and what happens when nature is primary. Being nature is automatic worship. He saw our destruction of the world of nature, and the use of animals in factory farming in particular, as a sign of the increasingly destructive and irrational behavior of technological man.[18] Merton's sense of letting creation be itself appears to extend to animals and the rest of non-human nature. We're particularly drawn to his poem, "The Ox Mountain Parable," which appears to link the destructiveness of man to nature to the destructiveness of man to his mind:

17. Thomas Merton, *The Collected Poems of Thomas Merton* (New York: New Directions, 1977) 345.

18. Andrew Lizey, *Christianity and the Rights of Animals* (Eugene, OR: Wipf and Stock Publishers, 2016) 20.

Master Meng said: There was once a fine forest on the Ox
    Mountain.
Near the capital of a populous country.
The men came out with axes and cut down the trees.
    Was it still a fine forest?
Yet, resting in the alteration of days and nights,
    moistened by dew,
The stumps sprouted, the trees began to grow again.
Then out came goats and cattle to browse on the young shoots.
The Ox Mountain was stripped utterly bare.
Our mind too stripped bare like the mountain
Still cannot be without some basic tendency to love.
But just as men with axes, cutting down the trees every morning
Destroy the beauty of the forest,
So we, by our daily actions, destroy our right mind.

Where then do our likes and dislikes differ from those of
    animals?
In nothing much.
Men see us and say we never had anything in us but evil.
Is this man's nature?[19]

NON-VIOLENCE

Inter-Indian wars existed, but Kirkpatrick Sale[20] writes from having reviewed multiple sources of European descriptions of Native
American peoples, that war was less organized and intense than
in Europe. Skirmishes occurred between neighboring tribes who
encroached on each other's hunting territory. One European wrote
that a war between two tribes could last seven years with only
seven people being killed. North American aboriginal people did
not duplicate the level of warfare that Europeans created. Nothing like the Crusades or the Hundred Years War occurred. In that
respect, less emphasis on destructive violence existed, which would
have pleased.

INTER-CONNECTEDNESS OF BEINGS

Every aspect of the environment is a being in a system perme-

19. Paul M. Pearson, "'Wisdom Cries the Dawn Deacon': Thomas Merton
and 'The Ox Mountain Parable,'" *CEA Critic* 75, no. 3 (2013) 278-284.
    20. Kirkpatrick Sale, *The Conquest of Paradise* (New York: Anchor Books,
1992).

NORTH AMERICAN ABORIGINAL SPIRITUALITY • 53

ated with beings, which may be physical or non-physical. Lakota spirituality does not make a distinction in the way of European thought between what is called the natural and the supernatural. What Europeans called the supernatural is folded back into the natural, but also the natural world is both infused by and contained within the spiritual.

LIFE WAYS VS. BELIEF SYSTEMS

Cornille[21] writes about Native American spiritualities as being all-embracing life ways and not as belief systems. She emphasizes the Native person's intimate experience of the Great Mystery and his or her connection with the universe as a spiritual or animated environment. Peelman writes that Native American religions are both profoundly sacramental and mystical, that they present themselves as being on an ongoing spiritual journey or religious process, which is experienced first on the level of tribe, clan, extended family or nation.[22] Native authors like Sam Gill point to the performative or practical/ritual dimension of any Native American religious experience.[23] Though these writings involve a certain element of glossing over the many differences among tribes and traditions, nevertheless great similarities exist across North America. We don't know Merton's level of awareness of differences among peoples, or if he was aware that Dakota/Lakota spirituality dominated among many of the political activists of his time. There is a tendency to romanticize or destroy the other. Native American genocide resulted from the latter. Today we see more of a romanticizing, which, from a historical perspective, is, of course, more positive.

Merton's spiritual path was quite sacramental and mystical for him and was an ongoing spiritual journey experienced within a community. Gill points to the practical dimension of spirituality as the specific procedures one follows during ceremony – the construction of the altar, the preparation, the specific songs to be sung, the activities proscribed by the ceremony. Merton would have had similar concerns in following ceremonial ritual actions.

---

21. Catherine Cornille, ed., *The Wiley-Blackwell Companion to Inter-Religious Dialogue* (Hoboken, NJ: Wiley-Blackwell, 2013) 347.

22. Achiel Peelman, *Christ Is A Native American* (Eugene, OR: Wipf and Stock, 2006) 39-60.

23. Sam Gill, *Native American Religions: An Introduction (Religious Life in History)* 2nd ed. (Belmont, CA: Wadsworth Publishing, 2004) 81-101.

Dakota/Lakota and other aboriginal spiritualities are more performative and practical in their ceremonials. Christian, Judaic, and Islamic ceremonies are more observational. Dakota/Lakota ceremonies happen in circles where everyone sees each other, while Christian ceremonies happen with an audience watching a leader performing a ceremony in which all face the leader and not each other. Participation is intense in Native American ceremonies, quite different from some Christian services where most of the action happens in the front of a seated congregation with minimal audience involvement. I suspect Merton would have preferred circles to lines of chairs facing the front. He did perform many liturgies with participants standing in a circle as he celebrated the Mass at the altar in the small chapel of his hermitage at Gethsemani.

SPIRITUALITY AND EVERYDAY LIFE

Lakota spirituality is not separable from everyday life. Some stories tell about times when animals and humans were out of harmony. Emissaries from either camp would seek the other to offer gifts and promises of cooperation for the common good to restore harmony and balance (*wicozani*). For example, a girl had bad manners and was left alone in the forest by her friends. She became lost and was found by bear people. Eventually, she married a bear man and had a bear child. She had not realized that if her people were to see her, they would have seen a bear. One day her brothers trapped and killed her husband in the forest. She came to them as a human-bear and negotiated a kind of peace among humans and bears in which bears would offer medicine to heal the people, and people would follow specific conventions and rules about how to relate to bears. In another story, long ago buffalo had behaved aggressively toward humans. They sent an emissary, the White Buffalo Cow Woman, to give a gift of the Calf Pipe and its rituals. Following the White Buffalo Cow Woman's instructions established a relationship of respect and honor between buffalo and humans. As part of this relationship, buffalo would provide food and other necessities to the people. Humans would continually renew this relationship through prayer which both invokes the interrelatedness of all things and asks spirit beings to provide the kindness and generosity one would expect of a good relative.

Dakota/Lakota philosophy does not separate good and evil, sickness and health, or right and wrong as distinct entities; nor does the Christian concept of evil exist. The closest parallel is *Iktomi*, or spider-man, an amalgamated creature, whose purpose is to oppose whatever Creator (*Takuskanskan*) wants. *Iktomi* can change shapes, which explains some of his capacity for trickery. However, *Iktomi* is invited to most major ceremonies and often plays a role. Apparently, Dakota/Lakota thought followed the aphorism, "Keep your friends close, but keep your enemies closer." *Iktomi*, who opposes whatever Creator wants, is still accepted as a necessary part of Creation.

OVERLAP OF SPIRIT AND ORDINARY WORLD

Lakota spirituality does distinguish between human and non-human, between ordinary and extraordinary or incomprehensible realms. Humans coexist with multiple types of non-humans, physical and non-physical, but also intersect with the extraordinary or incomprehensible as a part of ordinary life. The concept of *wo'onshila* speaks to a sense of being thrown into a world of incomprehensible and invisible forces manipulated by beings who barely notice us and who can crush us without noticing. Within this sense of existential "thrown-ness," our task is to work with all beings who will establish contact with us, to create meaning and purpose in an otherwise (to us) seemingly meaningless world. Merton was very mindful of this existential aspect of our existence.[24]

> My own monastic vocation is constantly being called into question . . ., and if I hold on to it, which I certainly do, it is no longer on the grounds that it is "best" but on more existential grounds: 'It may be absurd, I may not understand it, it may look like madness in the eyes of all these cats, but it happens to be what I am called to, and this is what I am going to do.' Ultimately, I think it is on this level that all our decisions have to be made today. What does God ask of Me?[25]

Through prayer and ceremony, we ask the spirits to intervene on our behalf if they're able and it's not too much trouble, and it just happens to be for our highest good. We do not assume that we know what the highest good is. Since there are so many unseen beings

---

24. Thomas Merton, *Zen and the Birds of Appetite* (New York: New Directions, 2010).

25. Merton, *Hidden Ground of Love*, 302.

with so many different types of power and influence, it makes sense to live in peace and harmony with all beings to the extent possible. This concept is at the root of Lakota spiritual humility.

The non-material and transpersonal reality is considered the source of health and power.[26] Healers (not what they call themselves) work by cultivating relationships with powerful beings in the spirit world, who will help them when needed. Healers speak of becoming hollow bones so that the spirits can work through them. This stance is the opposite of the view of "shamans" that exists in European-derived cultures in which the shaman possesses the power and magic. The European view emphasizes the individual, while the Dakota/Lakota healer relegates the individual to the background and minimizes the person of the healer. These spirit helpers give the healer permission to work with people and to conduct ceremonies. Of course, in Indian country, it's always problematic what to call those who heal with the help of the spirits. They would object strenuously to the term shaman[27] as belonging to another language, another culture, and a derisive term based upon "New Age" practitioners who take a weekend course and become "shamans." However, many of those who heal object to being called healers, as well, saying they don't heal anyone, that they're just ordinary persons. In one gathering of such elders, the group consensus was to call them "fix-it men," for they helped fix things up if that were possible, using aid from the spirit world. However, others not at this gathering also objected to that term. Typically, within communities, these healing elders are entitled quite vaguely with terms such as "that man." Such a vague title relates to the Dakota/Lakota concept of humility. It's hard to accept a title if the credit for the work goes to the spirits. However, one elder told me that it's entirely acceptable to receive the cash donation that often comes to those who heal for the spirits aren't in any position to use the money. He was, as is typical, both joking and serious. He joked in the sense that he would have helped someone for as little a donation as one cigarette. And he was serious in the sense that he had to pay his rent and he needed help doing that. All this, of course, reads very monk-like in Merton's sense of the term. One

26. R. W. Voss et al., "Tribal and Shamanic-based Social Work Practice: A Lakota Perspective," *Social Work* 44, no. 3 (1999) 228-241.
27. Lewis Mehl-Madrona, *Modern Day Shamanism in Future Health* (Newtown, PA: Future Health, Inc., 2010).

of Merton's poems makes this even more clear:

> Dawn. The Hour of Lauds. There is in all visible things an invisible fecundity, a dimmed light, a meek namelessness, a hidden wholeness. This mysterious Unity and Integrity is Wisdom, the Mother of all, Natura Naturans. There is in all things an inexhaustible sweetness and purity, a silence that is a fount of action and joy. It rises up in wordless gentleness and flows out to me from the unseen roots of all created being, welcoming me tenderly, saluting me with indescribable humility. This is at once my own being, my own nature, and the Gift of my Creator's Thought and Art within me, speaking as Hagia Sophia, speaking as my Sister, Wisdom. I am awakened, I am born again at the voice of this my Sister, sent to me from the depths of divine fecundity.[28]

In *The Wisdom of the Desert* Merton writes that "St. Anthony remarked that 'the prayer of the monk is not perfect until he no longer realizes himself or the fact that he is praying.'"[29] Later on, he writes:

> In many respects, therefore, these Desert Fathers had much in common with Indian Yogis and with Zen Buddhist monks of China and Japan. If we were to seek their like in twentieth-century America, we would have to look in a strange, out of the way place. [W]e might perhaps find someone like this among the Pueblo Indians or the Navahos. You would have simplicity, primitive wisdom: but rooted in a primitive society.[30]

He also writes that "Abbott Pastor said: 'There are two things which a monk ought to hate above all, for by hating them he can become free in this world. And a brother asked: 'What are these things?' The elder replied: 'An easy life and vain glory.'"[31]

The relationship with spirits is direct and personal, similar to Catholic practice, where people are free to commune with saints and maintain personal relationships with them; personal relationships

---

28. Thomas Merton, "Hagia Sophia" in *The Collected Poems of Thomas Merton* (New York: New Directions, 1977) 363.

29. Thomas Merton, *The Wisdom of the Desert* (New York: New Directions, 1970) 8-9.

30. Merton, *Wisdom*, 9.

31. Merton, *Wisdom*, 9.

but perhaps, unlike Catholicism, the spirits are not predetermined but are found locally and incidentally and encountered as spirits through personal contact. Christianity is not uniform when it comes to spirit-human relationships. The Catholics of Brittany appear to have one or more specific saints for healing any given part of the body. Some Protestant sects do not acknowledge saints but only God the Father, Christ the Son, and the Holy Spirit. Catholicism permits a panoply of Saints who can intervene and to whom one prays, not to mention angels and other beings. Thus even as orderly a religion as Catholicism can be confusing to one looking at it from the outside. However, the saints in Catholicism appear to have been most often historical people, while the spirits in Native American spirituality can be anyone or anything – former people; elements of nature such as rocks, mountains, trees, rivers; animals; cosmological beings like Coyote or *Iktomi*; or unfathomable entities.

In general, however, the Native American relationship with spirits is more personal and more direct. One talks to the spirits frequently and typically the same ones often appear. One does not have to be a "holy man" or a "saint" or a "priest" to talk to the spirits and to be answered. However, if one's resources prove insufficient, then one might visit someone who is reputed to have powerful spirit relations and be able to implore them to intervene for a good outcome in human affairs. These spirits can give specific instructions that may not even make sense to the healer. In an interview with one of us (LMM), a healer delivered a message that the person should eat watermelon every day for thirty days. I asked why but the healer replied that he did not know. He said perhaps watermelons have some nutrient she needed or perhaps it was just a way to determine if she was serious or not. I also heard a healer tell a woman with poor luck in love that she should talk to 101 men before deciding on one to date. She didn't listen to him and stopped at 17, and ended in yet another miserable relationship. He didn't criticize her, of course, because elders are in general not to do that, but he did say that the spirits probably knew best. And who knew what was waiting at the end of 101 meetings? An elder told me once to alternate black and white prayer "ties" (pieces of cloth filled with tobacco and tied onto a string) and to hang them from a tree in a place where nobody goes. I knew better than to ask why, and just did it.

The helping process begins and ends with spiritual powers and influences, for all healing and helping is ultimately spiritual, returning to the idea that we are spirit beings living in borrowed bodies.

HUMILITY

Related to this valuation of humility (a concept familiar to Merton and compatible with his monastic practices and life) is the concept of tribalism which emphasizes the importance of kinship and community relationships over the needs and wishes of the individual. Merton includes an example of monastic humility in *The Wisdom of the Desert*:

> A brother in Scete happened to commit a fault, and the elders assembled and sent for Abbot Moses to join them. He, however, did not want to come. The priest sent him a message, saying: Come, the community of the brethren is waiting for you. So he arose and started off. And taking with him a very old basket full of holes, he filled it with sand and carried it behind him. The elders came out to meet him, and said: What is this, Father? The elder replied: My sins are running out behind me, and I do not see them, and today I come to judge the sins of another! They, hearing this, said nothing to the brother but pardoned him.[32]

Recognition of kinship ties and demonstration of generosity are important among Native American peoples. One's kinship network and ancestors are part of one's identity, which can span across time and space for several generations backward and forward and for long physical distances. Naming ceremonies can bestow a name (which comes with the qualities of that person) of an ancestor upon a person, which then links this recipient with that ancestor henceforth.

SPIRITUALITY AND COMMUNITY

Dakota/Lakota culture integrates spirituality into the life of the community. Within the Lakota worldview, everything is spiritual due to our having come from the spirit realm and being a spirit taking a ride in an earthly body. Direct contact with spirits is fostered and encouraged, and a lively dialogue exists among the tribe and our ancestors. Beings from the spirit realm guide our contact with each other and show us how to live together in peace and harmony with all beings. Merton appreciated the

---

32. Merton, *Wisdom*, 40.

integration of spirituality and everyday life:

> It is my belief that all those in the world who have kept
> some vestige of sanity and spirituality should unite in firm
> resistance to the movements of power politicians and the
> monster nations, resist the whole movement of war and
> aggression, resist the diplomatic overtures of power and
> develop a strong and coherent "third world" that can stand
> on its own feet and affirm the spiritual and human values
> which are cynically denied by the great powers.[33]

BIG SELF/LITTLE SELF

Merton followed a long line of Christian mystics such as Meister
Eckhart in the idea of seeking to unite with a larger Self. Lakota
spirituality provides something similar in the idea of the *nagi*, a
concept that is difficult for conventional European thinkers to grasp,
though one that has its parallel in the writing of Mikhail Bhaktin[34]
and Hubert Hermans.[35] The *nagi* is the swarm (as in a swarm of
bees or a school of fish) of stories that surround one's physical body
and form the being who occupies the physical body. Each of these
stories in this swarm of stories (for a story is alive and has a soul; it
is a being) also contains a bit of the being who told that story. One
can imagine it as a spark that flew off his or her soul. The stories
and the beings who told those stories coalesce to make us who we
are. We are the swarm formed by these stories that have been told
about us, around us, by us. Mathematicians and engineers now talk
about "swarminess," the behavior of swarms that are completely
unpredictable from an understanding of any of the individual members of the swarm. These properties only emerge when a swarm
forms and there are critical thresholds attained for the formation of
a swarm. Personal growth in Dakota/Lakota spirituality consists of
becoming more aware of the nature of one's swarm and enlarging
the size of one's swarm through hearing more stories and connecting with more beings who tell one stories.

Native American spirituality and Merton's diverge in the concept of the self. Merton's concept developed within the European

33. Merton, *Hidden Ground*, 50-51.
34. M. M. Bakhtin, *Art and Answerability: Early Philosophical Essays*
(Austin, TX: University of Texas Press, 1990).
35. H. J. M. Hermans, "The Dialogical Self: Toward a Theory of Personal
and Cultural Positioning," *Culture Psychology* 7, no. 1 (2001) 243-281.

tradition located the self in an "I" that is fixed in time and place. He believed in a "true self":

> The Desert Father could not afford to be an illuminist. He could not dare risk attachment to his own ego or the dangerous ecstasy of self-will. He could not retain the slightest identification with his superficial, transient, self-constructed self. He had to lose himself in the inner, hidden reality of a self that was transcendent, mysterious, half-known and lost in Christ. He had to die to the values of transient existence as Christ had died to them on the Cross and rise from the dead with Him in the light of an entirely new wisdom.[36]

Dakota/Lakota philosophy does not share the idea of a separate, independent, individual ego.[37] It places less emphasis on the search to unite with a "larger self." The self is already embedded experientially in larger contexts. The Dakota/Lakota "me" resembles more the dialogical self of Hermans, which weaves together the concepts of "me" and of "me-in-dialogue" so that "me" becomes "this body" + "all those other beings with whom it is in dialogue."[38] This "dialogical self" brings the external into the internal and, in reverse, introduces the internal into the external, thereby transcending the dichotomy between self and society that has plagued European psychology. Native American, and specifically Dakota/Lakota psychological theory did not suffer this same divisiveness. Kemper[39] also approaches the Dakota/Lakota world view when he proposes that the concept of the self may be an extraneous item. Since the internal self is created by the social milieu, it might make sense to work with that milieu directly rather than with its product. The Dakota/Lakota view would be that my relation to the "other" creates my awareness. I become my awareness as I become the recipient of another's attention. I see others looking at my body and construe that what they are viewing must be "me." Having discovered "me," I am compelled to construct a

---

36. Merton, *Wisdom,* 84-89.

37. R. W. Voss et al., "Tribal and Shamanic-based Social Work Practice: A Lakota Perspective," *Social Work* 44, no. 3 (1999) 228-241.

38. H. Hermans, "Dialogical Self," *Encyclopedia of Critical Psychology,* ed. Thomas Teo (Berlin: Springer Reference, 2014) 428-432.

39. T. D. Kemper, "After the Dialogical Self, What?" *Roczniki Psychologiczne* 17, no. 1 (2014) 155-169.

story to explain "me," which becomes my identity narrative, the story told in response to the question, "Who are you?" In answer to this question, the Dakota/Lakota person responds by listing his or her relatives, his/her mother and her people, his/her father and his people, the land from which they arise, his/her river, mountain, and lake. Dakota/Lakota identity includes a continual awareness of those to whom we are connected; hence, the common Dakota/Lakota greeting, *Hau mitakuye oyasin,* which means, "Recognition that we are all related." The Dakota/Lakota is never separated from his/her social milieu.

What is similar to Merton's and Meister Eckhart's quest would be the Lakota quest to connect with more powerful spiritual beings. Paradoxically this is done for the benefit of others and to become more of a "hollow bone" for the spirits to work through. Though we have heard and read others talking about powerful Lakota shamans and "medicine men," we have not encountered that idea in our travels through Dakota/Lakota country. Mostly we hear people talking about creating a safe space for the medicine (aka power) to work. We hear about people getting out of the way of the medicine. We hear people working to become less for the spirits to become more. We do hear about some people seeking personal power, but this is usually described critically and often linked to the person seeking power to do ill, usually something selfish. Dakota/Lakota spirituality usually gives more credit to the spirits and less to the person interceding, communicating, or entreating the spirits. Recently, we spoke with a friend about an elder who was known to be a drunk and taking advantage of women. He was, nevertheless, associated with some powerful and amazing healing. We talked about how this behavior conflicted with the Christian idea that spiritual healers had to be holy people and do things morally and ethically correctly. Our friend, also a lifelong student of Dakota/Lakota spirituality, reflected that the convenient moral rules of European religions don't seem always to work. He did remark that people in the community of this elder believed his medicine would have been more powerful if he had lived a more moral life.

SPIRITUAL AMORPHOUSNESS

Unlike Christianity, Dakota/Lakota spirituality has no orthodoxy, no creed, and no dogma. It differs from region to region, family to family, practitioner to practitioner. It is a personal family affair, not regulated by an authoritarian body. Therefore, whatever we say about Dakota/Lakota spirituality as a whole is the result of listening to all the stories and tellers of those stories that we have encountered and observing the practices and ceremonies where we have been. We hope we have had a sufficiently broad experience to create a synthesis of what is common, though some room for inaccuracy exists. Raymond Bucko[40] had a similar experience when he went looking for the Dakota/Lakota sweat lodge (now called an *inipikaga*, which is properly translated as revitalization ceremony and not sweat lodge, which was the Jesuit description of the ceremony that stuck). Bucko found that there was no one correct way to perform an *inipikaga*. Every family had slightly different practices. However, he discovered some commonalities, which emerged in his book. We have made the same approach to describing Dakota/Lakota spirituality by addressing what seems to be common among all the families and practices we have encountered.

We have heard varying stories about what happens after death, but none resemble the Christian story of resurrection. The majority of the stories we have heard hold that we are reunited with our relatives and enter into the work of the spirit world, which is somewhat of a mystery. Reincarnation is a common belief across North America (see *Amerindian Reincarnation*[41]) and familiar to Dakota/Lakota spirituality, though to the extent people have been influenced by Christianity, belief in reincarnation is less. However, we hear people talking about how we are spirits who have come to earth to occupy a body for a specific reason. We receive a heart which we must protect and nurture. We cannot give it away because we would die. Sometimes we take on tasks that seem reasonable in the spirit world but turn out to be insurmountable in the ordinary world. Unlike Asian religions, no cycle of karma exists. We can return to earth, or not. We do not have to keep returning until we resolve our karma. Lakota spirituality is aware that most of what happens in the spirit world is a great mystery to us and will remain so until we get there. I have also heard elders saying that they have met spirits who tell them that there are levels of the spirit world and that these levels take beings further away from the

40. R. A. Bucko, *The Lakota Ritual of the Sweat Lodge: History and Contemporary Practice* (Lincohn, NE: University of Nebraska Press, 1998).

41. A. Mills and R. Slobodin, eds., *Amerindian Rebirth: Reincarnation Belief Among North American Indians and Inuit* (Toronto: University of Toronto Press, Scholarly Publishing Division, 2009).

realm of human beings and an understanding of the suffering of humanity, but toward a more abstract understanding of the purpose and meaning of Creation. These beings need the more local spirits who are closer to humans to help them to communicate with and understand humans. Dakota/Lakota spirituality, however, doesn't seem to spend a lot of time contemplating these issues. Mostly we see good-natured shrugs and sayings, like, "we'll find out when the time comes."

CHARLES EASTMAN

The Dakota physician Charles Eastman described Dakota/Lakota spirituality in a book originally published in the late nineteenth century.[42] Though Eastman died at age 80 in 1939, Merton would have resonated with Eastman's aims. Eastman believed that Native American spirituality, while different on the surface from Christianity, was essentially the same. He advocated for the rights of Native American people to practice their religions without persecution from the agents of Christianity. Eastman had reluctantly assimilated to white culture until the Wounded Knee Massacre in 1890 on the Pine Ridge Reservation. This event radicalized him and led him to advocate separate and equal status for Native Americans with the rights to practice their spirituality and speak their tribal languages. In a Merton-like passage, he wrote:

> "[W]e also have a religion which was given to our forefathers, and has been handed down to us their children. It teaches us to be thankful, to be united, and to love one another! We never quarrel about religion." Thus spoke the great Seneca orator, Red Jacket, in his superb reply to Missionary Cram more than a century ago, and I have often heard the same thought expressed by my countrymen. I have attempted to paint the religious life of the typical American Indian as it was before he knew the white man. I have long wished to do this because I cannot find that it has ever been seriously, adequately, and sincerely done. The religion of the Indian is the last thing about him that the man of another race will ever understand. First, the Indian does not speak of these deep matters so long as he

believes in them, and when he has ceased to believe he speaks inaccurately and slightingly. Second, even if he can be induced to speak, the racial and religious prejudice of the other stands in the way of his sympathetic comprehension. Third, practically all existing studies on this subject have been made during the transition period, when the original beliefs and philosophy of the native American were already undergoing rapid disintegration.

Merton was very familiar with this destruction of aboriginal spirituality, a practice he opposed. He considered this practice to be spiritual genocide and aimed his activism toward protecting the spiritualities of aboriginal peoples.

Eastman was born near Redwood Falls, Minnesota in the winter of 1858.[43] His birth name was *Hakadah*, meaning "the pitiful last," because he was the last of three brothers and one sister, and his mother died shortly after his birth. She was the granddaughter of the Dakota chief Cloud Man and the daughter of Stands Sacred and a well-known U.S. Army officer, Seth Eastman. In his early youth, Eastman received the name Ohiyesa, meaning "the Winner." Hakadah's father was named Many Lightnings – *Tawakanhdeot*a. He lived with his family until the "Sioux Uprising of 1862," when he became separated from his father, elder brothers, and sister. He traveled with his grandmother to Manitoba where the survivors took exile, believing that his other relatives had been killed.

For the next 11 years, Ohiyesa lived a traditional life with his uncle and grandmother. His uncle trained him in hunting, warfare, and spirituality. Then, Ohiyesa's father unexpectedly reappeared when he was age 15 and preparing to go on a raid to seek revenge for his father's death. Calling himself Jacob Eastman, his father had come to get Ohiyesa and take him back to a homestead in Flandreau, Dakota Territory, a place for Indians who had adopted the religion and customs of the whites.

Ohiyesa attended a mission day school. He wanted to run away and return to the traditional lifestyle that he knew, but his father convinced him to remain and to cut his hair.

Ohiyesa did well in school and at age 17 walked 250 km to attend a better school at Santee, Nebraska. He was soon accepted

43. Charles A. Eastman; Ohiyesa (The Winner). Akta Lakota Museum and Cultural Center. Available from: http://aktalakota.stjo.org/site/News2?page=NewsArticle&id=8884.

to Beloit College in Wisconsin, where he spent two years before eventually graduating from Dartmouth College in 1887. He then studied medicine at Boston University, graduating in 1890. His first job was to be the physician at the Pine Ridge Reservation in South Dakota. Before this, Eastman believed that assimilation was the best policy for Indians. The Massacre at Wounded Knee radicalized him and he no longer advocated for assimilation. He became very involved in exposing the fraud and corruption in the management of provisions and funds on the Reservation, which caused his reassignment to the Crow Creek Agency in South Dakota. He eventually moved east again and spent the rest of his life advocating for Indian rights. He and his wife, Elaine Goodale Eastman, disagreed over the future of Indians. She advocated total assimilation into white society, while Charles promoted cultural pluralism in which Indians would retain their identity, beliefs, and customs, even while interacting with white society. The two separated in August 1921, probably related to their conflict over these issues and Eastman's belief that the teachings and spirit of his adopted religion of Christianity and traditional Indian spiritual beliefs were essentially the same, a belief that was controversial to many Christians.

MYSTICAL STATES

The turn of the century Harvard psychologist, William James,[44] believed that the inner aspects of spirituality could not be expressed or understood totally through behavioral, affective, or cognitive concepts. He wrote, "The ordinary waking consciousness is but one form of consciousness. All around us lie infinite worlds, separated only by the thinnest veils." Referring to noetic or mystical states of consciousness, James said they might be similar to but different from feelings or emotions. He continued, "Mystical states seem to those who experience them to be also states of knowledge." James referred to mystical states of consciousness as ineffable and paradoxical. He wrote that the mystical experience eludes words and logic. Kelly and fellow psychologists[45] describe the mystical experience as a unitary experience during which one feels an inter-

---

44. William James, *The Varieties of Religious Experience: A Study in Human Nature* (New York: Philosophy Library/Open Road, 1902) 300.

45. E. F. Kelly et alia, "Irreducible mind: Toward a Psychology of the 21st Century." *Journal Of Transpersonal Psychology* 39, no. 2 (2009) 227.

connection with an ultimate all-encompassing reality. Richards[46] wrote, "Consciousness includes infinitely more than our individual egos. Mystical consciousness includes a conviction that, within this unitive world, all of us are interconnected and inter-related." All of this seems compatible with both Merton's spirituality and Dakota/Lakota spirituality.

Robbins and Hong[47] conducted a qualitative study of a traditional North American aboriginal healer, White Bear (pseudonym) from Oklahoma, who they related "never offered, and even resisted a definition of the self; he did suggest meanings about the self. For instance, after a purification ceremony, I asked him if he would be White Bear after he died. This following is the essence of what he said and in a harsh tone I might add. 'No! Hey nobody knows what happens after we die. You really want to be a reference point? You want to be your memories? Really? Listen. The center, which you are always in, whether you know it or not, is everything and one. It is that simple.'"

White Bear exemplified many aspects of Dakota/Lakota spirituality, and his reflections offered in the Robbins and Hong study are similar to Merton's:

> We found White Bear's recurrent remarks about his limitations and his dismissive, self-effacing comment that often ended the interviews refreshing: "Take this information or leave it. I just say what I am told. If it is helpful good, but it is really none of my business."[48]

> Although he has limited formal education, he discussed his spiritual experiences in a highly sophisticated fashion. For the most part, he spoke out of his personal experiences, though, often relating them to the hundreds of Native American events in which he has participated over the years. He said he simply reported what the "spirits" taught, whether they were "Native American or other religions." The interviewer told him that some of his teachings sounded

---

46. W. A. Richards, "The Rebirth of Research with Entheogens: Lessons from the Past and Hypotheses for the Future," *Journal of Transpersonal Psychology* 41, no. 2 (2009) 141.

47. Rockey Robbins and Ji Y. Hong, "Building Bridges Between Spirituality and Psychology: An Indigenous Healer's Teachings About Befriending the Self," *Journal of Transpersonal Psychology* 45, no. 2 (2013) 175-195.

48. Robbins and Hong, "Building Bridges," 179.

similar to Eastern religious ideas. He responded that he "did not know about that." But that he did not have time to read about it if that was what I was suggesting, because he already had too much to think about just dealing with what the spirits taught him.[49]

I continued, "I have heard Christians talk to you about the importance of dying to the self or sacrificing the self. I have listened, wondering how that may or may not fit into Native American views about realizing our interconnection to everything. Would you comment on this?"

White Bear responded, "That is not an Indian perspective. I can tell you what the spirits are telling me. They say, 'Don't kill it. You can't kill it.' The self tries to keep us safe from suffering right now. The self is important because it protects us and it keeps us on top of problems. It is helpful. I might have been hit and buried by the dirt when we were digging that ditch the other day if not for self. But it likes to look good all the time and the false one the Christians are talking about is a 'control freak' [he seems to mean what the Christians refer to as the false self; possibly White Bear was reacting to phrases such as Bonhoeffer's 'death of the self' described in the literature review]. It is supposed to be viewing all this . . . this creation that is always going on right now, but when it is in control, you just see only its protective vision that is not totally true and keeps you from seeing the beauty right in front of you."[50]

The entire interview with White Bear is interesting, for it shows the lack of definition of "self" for White Bear and the attempt to construct something about which he and the researchers could have a meaningful conversation.

Merton[51] wrote about the idea of "submitting oneself to God" being paramount for spiritual healing. He argued that a false self tends toward self-glorification, but that God facilitates our awareness of our true self. God helps us transcend the depravity of reason to experience ourselves as part of his mystery. We suspect that

---

49. Robbins and Hong, 180.
50. Robbins and Hong, 183.
51. Thomas Merton, *The Ascent to Truth* (New York: Harcourt, Brace & Co., 1957).

"submitting oneself to God" would map onto the Dakota/Lakota idea of "becoming a hollow bone" through which the spirits can work. Dakota/Lakota spirituality would not use the term "false self," but would describe a person as being overrun with "bad" stories. In this context, "bad" could mean selfish, ungenerous, unkind, uncompassionate; in short, not in alignment with the Lakota fundamental values. The idea of "experiencing ourselves as part of God's mystery" seems to resonate with the idea perpetuated and accentuated through the ceremony of entering completely into the present moment without looking forward or backward. Dakota/Lakota verbs do not conjugate into the past or present forms. All verbs are in the perpetual "now." A future time frame is made clear by including the word *kta* in the sentence or by the context. Likewise, there are specific verbs that only refer to the past. Communion with spirits as achieved in fasting, praying, dancing, drumming, and singing is part of that experience of inter-connectedness with that which is greater than our physical body and our swarm, the craving for communion which is common to both Dakota/Lakota spirituality and Merton.

Corneille[52] writes about how the high priority that Native American spirituality gives to experiential learning does not mean it is less "theological" or "philosophical" than the dominant world religions. Hartley Burr Alexander[53] demonstrated how the aboriginal people of North America developed an extraordinary awareness of the sacred and how many rituals like the Sun Dance represent complex symbolic forms of thinking. The opportunity for inter-religious symbolism and cross-fertilization is rich, and Merton recognized that.

THE CHANNUPA

Central to Dakota/Lakota spirituality is the pipe or *channupa*. The bowl symbolizes the earth and the stem, the sky. When earth and sky are joined, communication with the Creator and to the spirit world can happen. The White Buffalo Woman provided the procedures to follow in making this communication. An important song says, "Friend, do it in the way you were taught (*Kola le c'un*

---

52. C. Cornille, ed., *Many mansions? Multiple Religious Belonging and Christian Identity* (Eugene, OR: Wipf and Stock Publishers, 2010).

53. H. B. Alexander, *The World's Rim: Great Mysteries of the North American Indians* (North Chelmsford, MA: Courier Corporation, 1998).

le c'un wo)." The song goes on to say, "If you do it in that way, your prayers will be answered." Christian writers have likened the smoking of the pipe to communion. The smoking mixture (*kinincki-nick*) absorbs the prayers and becomes spirit as it is smoked. The White Buffalo Woman (or a related spirit) is attracted to the smoke and carries the prayers to the Creator, changing them if necessary to preserve balance and harmony. In the version of this story, told along the East Coast of North America, White Buffalo Woman is displaced by First Mother, who saw that her many children were dying of hunger. She announced to her family that she would die. When she did, they were to drag her body across a field. When all the flesh had been removed, they were to bury her bones in the middle of the field. Six months later, they should return, and a gift would be bestowed. She sang her death song and they reluctantly carried out her wishes. Six months later, tobacco had sprung forth from her bones. Corn, bean, and squash had come from her flesh. In this version of the story, First Mother sits in the smoke when tobacco was smoked. She would translate the prayers into the form spirits could understand and arrange for them to be answered. These activities of White Buffalo Woman and First Mother are perhaps not dissimilar to the Virgin Mary intervening with God on behalf of those who pray to her.

Tobacco is the most sacred herb in North America and was used in ceremonies in concentrations varying with the distance from where it was most easy to grow. In the American southeast, tobacco sticks (now called cigars) were used. In Dakota/Lakota country, small bits of tobacco were placed in a mixture of willow bark, chokecherry bark, osha root, and other herbs. Tobacco was not inhaled and did not become a drug of abuse until Europeans co-opted it.

IMPORTANT CEREMONIES

We will conclude our discussion of Dakota/Lakota and other Native American spiritualities with a description of some of the important ceremonies.

THE *INIPIKAGA*

The *inipikaga* ceremony was originally translated into English as the "sweat lodge," but this translation minimized the spiritual purpose of the ceremony, so newer translators prefer "purification ceremony" or "breath of life" ceremony. The word *inipi* means "they breathe in a way of revitalizing themselves," which is a much better translation. In the *inipi* ceremony (*inipikaga*) there are many variations, but in general, people sing and pray in the dark. Heat comes from hot stones placed into a central pit. Water is placed onto these stones to produce the steam that becomes the breath of life.

J. R. Walker has described the *inipi:*

> [The people] enter a sweat lodge to *ini*, or vitalize. *Inipi*, or vitalizing, is a . . . ceremony to stimulate the *ni*, or vitality, so that it may increase strength and purify the body. Vitalizing may be merely a means of refreshment, a remedial measure for disease, or to purify the body for some important undertaking. It ought always to be done as a preliminary to ceremonies. In its simplest form, it is done by releasing the spirit-like[54] of water in a confined space so that it may enter the body. This spirit-like stimulates the vitality so that it overcomes harmful things that may be in the body and the spirit-like of the water washes them out of the body, and they appear upon the skin like sweat and can be washed or wiped away. Thus, the vitality is strengthened and the body purified. If the vitalizing is a remedy for disease, medicines may be added to the water so that their potency, or spirit-like, may be released and enter the body, and there cause the desired effect.
>
> . . . A lodge is made by thrusting slender saplings into the ground in a circle, the diameter of which is a little longer than the height of a tall man. The tops of these saplings are bent and bound together to form a dome-like support for a covering. This support is covered with robes to confine the vapor from boiling water, this vapor being the spirit-like of the water released. At any place on the border of the covering, except toward the north, an opening that may be tightly closed, should be made large enough so that a man can crawl through it. Assistants, usually women, heat the stones in a fire near the lodge and, when the occupants are within, should bring the stones and pass them through

---

54. Walker uses the term "spirit-like," whereas in modern usage we would say that the spirit of the water enters the body as well as acknowledging that the vapor itself has physical healing properties.

the opening, then pass the water into the lodge and tightly close the opening. Those inside should place the hot stones at the center of the lodge and at intervals pour small quantities of water on them. This releases the spirit-like of the water, and as it cannot escape upward, it enters the bodies of those exposed to it. It is propitiated with smoke from the pipe and will stimulate the vitality. When it appears again upon the surface of the body, like sweat, it will have in it the harmful things that were in the body, and it should be wiped away, or better, it should be washed away, which is best done by plunging into water.[55]

Walker captures the sense of the *inipi* better than any contemporary writing we have read. It captures the sense of the spirit-essence of the water revitalizing the body. The word *inipi* means to revitalize or to resuscitate. The sense is that the spirit of the water dispels toxins and evil humors in the person and brings them out of the body onto the skin to be wiped or washed away.

Walker made it clear that in the nineteenth century, an *inipi* could last for the duration of time required to smoke two pipes of tobacco to more than twenty-four hours. It could consist of one person or many. At least one song must be sung while pouring water onto the hot stones, or as many as time permits. For more elaborate ceremonies, sage and sweetgrass are burned in the lodge. Sage expels the evil powers from the lodge. Sweetgrass propitiates the powers for good.

THE *HANBLECHIYA*

Charles Eastman made the "vision quest" part of popular culture when he helped include it as an activity into the Boy Scouts of America. In 1910, he became their Indian advisor and incorporated many elements of his culture into their activities, including the Order of the Arrow and Webelos.[56,57] The *hanblechiya* is a one to four-day ceremony of fasting and praying in a sacred spot in nature that begins and concludes with an *inipi* ceremony. There

55. J. R. Walker, *The Sun Dance and Other Ceremonies of the Oglala Division of The Teton Dakota* (London: Forgotten Books, 2008).

56. Charles A. Eastman, *The Essential Charles Eastman (Ohiyesa): Light on the Indian World (Sacred Worlds)* (Bloomington, IN: World Wisdom, Inc., 2007).

57. Ojibwa. American Indians in 1915. Native American Netroots 2015. Available from http://nativeamerican-netroots.net/diary/1834.

are as many subtle variations on how a *hanblechiya* is performed as there are families doing them.

Walker wrote about the *hanblechiya*:

> If an Oglala[58] contemplates an important undertaking, he ought to seek a vision, and if he has the vision, he should be governed according to the interpretation of it. To seek a vision, one should strip and wear only a robe, a breechclout,[59] and moccasins.[60] Clothed thus, he should take a pipe, smoking materials, and a knife, and go to the top of a high place where others are not likely to intrude. There he should remove every living or growing thing from a space on the ground sufficiently large for him to sit or lie upon. Then he should go, to this space and remain on it until he has a vision, or until he is convinced that he will have none. When he enters the cleared space, he should invoke the Four Winds in order that they may not bring inclement weather upon him. Then he should await a vision, meditating continuously upon his quest. He may invoke the gods, verbally or mentally, either in song or prayer. He may stand, sit, or lie awake or asleep, but he must not go away from the space he has prepared. He may smoke as often as he wishes, but he must neither drink nor eat while making the quest. The vision may come to him, either when he is awake, or when he is asleep. It may appear in the form of anything that breathes or as some inanimate thing. If it communicates with him, it may speak intelligibly to him, or it may use words that he does not understand, or speak in the language of birds or beasts. By something that it says or does it will make known to him that it is the vision he seeks. He should wait for such a vision until he receives it, or until he is so exhausted that he can wait no longer without danger of losing his life: If he should receive a vision, he should return to his tipi singing a song of victory. If one seeks a vision and it is not granted to him, he should

---

58. Oglala is a branch of Lakota.

59. Today it would be written "breech-cloth."

60. Buffalo robes were also permitted, which are amazingly warmer than I could imagine before I wrapped myself in one. We perform a *hanblechiya* once yearly before the Sun Dance.

meekly come from the quest as privately as possibly.[61]

Merton was aware of the *hanblechiya*:

> The practice of "fasting for vision" was once almost uni-
> versal among North American Indians for whom it might
> almost be said that a certain level of "mysticism" was an
> essential part of growing up. The Indian based his life on
> a spiritual illumination beyond the ordinary conscious
> level of psychic experience. [S]uch visions were taken for
> granted as a normal part of life in an archaic culture. They
> were an essential component in the concept of the mature
> human personality and hence they were to some extent
> institutionalized. For although the practice of fasting for
> vision was an entirely individual project, there was a pre-
> scribed ritual, and the value of the vision was not decided
> on the individual's own judgment. [V]ision, for good or
> evil, could be quite momentous for the rest of the tribe.
> Hence the chiefs and elders passed judgment on the vision
> and its interpretation.[62]

Merton goes on to say that ecstatic dancing, self-torture, and drugs
were also used to obtain visions. Here he was mistaken. We are
unaware of anything that could be called ecstatic dancing in North
America, though it may exist south of the Rio Grande. We are
also unaware of any self-torture. Merton may be describing the
piercings of the *Wiwanyang wachipi*. Both of us have experienced
multiple piercings in that dance: it is not self-torture. Nor were
drugs used except perhaps as by those living in proximity to what
is now Mexico. Hallucinogenic drugs were not used except that
the Cherokees did have tobacco healers, who drank tobacco tea
in sufficient concentrations as to have visions. This was a tricky
business, however, for the lethal dose was not that far removed
from the hallucinatory dose, and great experience was required to
make and take tobacco tea.

Merton over dramatizes the role of visions in the ordinary life
of a tribe. Visions were a personal matter, and, while all personal
matters were subjects of communal discussion, the lack of a vision

61. J. R. Walker, *The Sun Dance and Other Ceremonies of the Oglala Division of The Teton Dakota* (Seattle: Amazon Digital Services, 2012) Kindle Locations 236-256.

62. Merton, *Ishi Means Man*, 16.

did not doom someone to be a poor hunter or prevent him from going to war. Not all visions were important for the life of the tribe. Merton misses a subtle point of distinction in discussing visions. As someone from an individualistic culture, he did not understand that people did not make individual decisions. All decisions were made communally, through dialogue with all stakeholders involved in the issue.

ALTARS AND THE SUN DANCE

Altars are important in all Native American ceremonies. Walker tells how they were constructed:

> An Oglala Shaman makes an altar by removing everything that breathes or grows from the space where the altar is to be. This should be done because the altar is a sacred thing which should have nothing in or upon it except that which may be an offering acceptable to the Gods.[63] Any other thing that may touch this space while it is an altar should either be destroyed or purified in an incense of sage and then in one of sweetgrass. This space must be square, for the altar must have four sides of equal length because each side pertains to one of the Four Winds and each of these must receive equal consideration in every respect. The sides of the altar should be toward the west, the north, the east, and the south so that one side will be toward the tipi of each of the Four Winds. The sides should measure not less than four handbreadths, nor more than the height of a man. They may vary anywhere between these extremes. The smallest altars should be made in tipis and the largest in the Sun Dance Lodge. At each angle of this square, a pointed space should project halfway between two of the directions. These are the horns of the altar that guard it against all malevolent beings. The square space and horns should be dug to the depth of a finger length and the loosened soil removed and freed from everything. Then it should be pulverized, replaced, level. The one who replaces and levels the soil should utter an appropriate invocation, or sing an appropriate song, or both, for in this manner the

---

63. Walker uses the term "Gods" whereas we would use "spirits" today.

altar is consecrated to the purposes for which it is made.[64]

THE SUN DANCE

One of the main sources of information about the traditional Sun Dance ceremony was James Walker, a physician to the Oglala Lakota and an amateur ethnologist. He interviewed many of the elders during the late nineteenth century and carefully recorded their answers about this sacred ceremony:

> The Sun Dance of the Oglala is a sacred ceremony which may be undertaken by any one of mankind, provided he or she: 1. Undertakes it for a proper purpose. 2. Complies with the essentials for the ceremony. 3. Conforms to the customs of the Oglala. 4. Accepts the mythology of the Lakota.
>
> The proper purposes for undertaking the Sun Dance are: 1. To fulfill a vow. 2. To secure supernatural aid for another. 3. To secure supernatural aid for self. 4. To secure supernatural powers for self.
>
> The stages are: 1. Announcement of the candidacy. 2. Instruction of the Candidate. 3. Occupation of the ceremonial camp. 4. Dancing the Sun Dance.
>
> The time is: 1. When the buffalo are fat. 2. When new sprouts of sage are a span long. 3. When chokecherries are ripening. 4. When the Moon is rising as the Sun is going down.

In the nineteenth century, before beginning to dance the Sun Dance during the ceremony, the Dancer must have made an acceptable offering to the Sun and have had a wound that will cause his blood to flow. If he dances the Sun Dance to its completion, he may expect a vision in which he may receive a communication from the Sun.

The simplest form of dancing was called "Gazing at the Sun." It was done for any of the first three purposes mentioned by Walker but did not require strict compliance with the essentials of the ceremony, although the dancer was supposed to comply to the best of his ability. It began with the first song of the Sun Dance and continued for a minimum of four songs, through the entire dance if the dancer wished. Today, it is more common to require even "gazing at the Sun" dancers to comply with all the requirements and to dance the entire dance. The offering to the Sun was expected to be of as much value as the Dancer could afford. The wound could

---

64. Walker, *The Sun Dance*, Kindle Locations 259-276.

be as small or as large as the Dancer wished. Women and children could dance "gazing at the sun."

The "gazing at the Sun Buffalo" dancing involved piercings in the back and pulling a train of buffalo skulls around the dance arbor. The "gazing at the Sun" stake involved piercings in the chest and being tied by a rope from the piercing pegs to the tree. The "gazing at the sun suspended" involved hanging from either front or back piercings from the tree:

> If the dancer is dancing for the purpose of securing the supernatural powers . . ., he must dance actually suspended. Sun dancers demonstrate their possession of the four great virtues, which are 1. Bravery. 2. Generosity. 3. Fortitude. 4. Integrity. This caused the people to honor the Dancer, and the scars made by the wounds were considered highly honorable insignia.[65]

This description of the Sun Dance did not change through the twentieth century and is as accurate today as it was in the 1890s when being recorded by Walker.

A sacred tree is raised in the center of the dance grounds (though elder Harry Charger says that trees were never cut in the nineteenth century; only living trees were used). Prayer flags and prayer ties (*chanli pata*) are placed on the tree along with symbolic objects (usually a bison deity and an eagle's nest). The Sun Dance lasts 3 or 4 days during which the dancers do not drink water or eat food. However, they are given whatever medicines are needed to keep them dancing. The dance honors the sun and the gifts it provides for the people. Some male dancers pierce with buffalo bone pegs to be connected through a rope to the tree. At the appointed moment, they break through to symbolize the action required for the answering of prayers. Others pull buffalo skulls around the dance grounds. Both men and women dance. Four days of purification precede the days of dancing.

THE MEDICINE BUNDLE

Merton was familiar with the medicine bundle as his description in *Ishi Means Man* indicates:

> Communion with the vision person was ritually formalized

---

65. Walker, *The Sun Dance*, Kindle Locations 131-132.

through the use of a "medicine bundle," a little package of magic objects which had been assembled under the explicit direction of the vision person. The ingredients of the medicine bundle were usually fragments of animal skin, bone, rock, or herbs: but all these objects were associated in some way or other with the vision person. They were things which he had used to demonstrate his friendly power and were normally revealed in a vision or dream. One prepared for battle for the hunt with a ceremonious veneration of the vision person, by ritual prayers to the medicine bundle and perhaps also a little impromptu magic suitable to the occasion. As may easily be guessed, the formalization of relations with the spirits through cult objects easily took the place of vision. Once a culture had passed its peak-vitality, one might expect the medicine bundle to become, in practice, more important than direct communion with the vision person. Then the medicine man became a kind of pharmacist of good luck charms rather than a discerner of spirits.[66]

It might be instructive to Merton scholars to realize how much Merton's interpretations of what he was reading were incorrect. Merton missed the idea of the medicine bundle. The objects in a bundle were not thought to be "magic" in any way but were thought to be a kind of homing beacon to draw the spirits to the bundle who related to that object. For example, if one has a bear claw in a medicine bundle, its presence is to draw the Spirit of the Bear (mythological) or any bear (ordinary) to that bundle. Objects in the medicine bundle invoked the spirits who related to those objects. Merton also over-emphasized the status of the mentor, who was just that, and not a "vision person." As he does in other instances in *Ishi Means Man*, Merton assumed that North American indigenous culture was dying, when in fact, it was at the time and is now revitalizing. The medicine bundle, never a collection of good luck charms, remains as powerful as ever. Direct communication with spirits remains more important than the mentor whose role is to assist in understanding that communication.

Merton had positive things to say about Native American cultures:

---

66. Merton, *Ishi Means Man*, 19.

We realize that there was really a deep psychological validity to this way of life. It was by no means a mere concoction
of superstitious fantasies and mythic explanations of realities that only science could eventually clarify. However one
may choose to explain the fact, these stone-age people had
inherited an archaic wisdom which did somehow protect
them against the dangers of a merely superficial, willful,
and cerebral existence. It did somehow integrate their
personality in such a way that the conscious mind was responsive to deep unconscious sources of awareness. Those
who were most in contact with a powerful vision person
tended to have an almost phenomenal luck and dexterity
in war or the hunt.[67]

It's sad to me (LMM) to be called a stone-age person. Our fiber
technologies were far superior to those of Europeans as were our
environmental engineering practices and agriculture. Our wisdom
is not archaic, but quite contemporary; at least as contemporary as
Asian Buddhists, whom Merton respected more.

In another place in *Ishi Means Man* Merton writes:

We must not be too romantic about all this. There would
be no point in merely idealizing primitive men and archaic
culture. There is no such thing as a charismatic culture.
Though the life of an Indian was much more individualistic than we have imagined, it was integrated in the culture
of his tribe and its complex rituals. "Vision" was perhaps
more often a deepening of the common imagination than
a real breakthrough of personal insight.[68]

When Merton calls us primitive and archaic, he falls into the same
boat as the mainstream Americans that he criticizes. His writings do
not show that he understands at all the differences inherent in living
communally from living in the contemporary individualistic society.
I believe that we (our elders) do know the difference between a
deepening of the common imagination and spirit communication.
What Merton writes leads us to believe that he does not accept the
contemporary validity of direct spirit communication.

Finally, on another critical note, Merton writes about Two

67. Merton, *Ishi Means Man*, 19-20.
68. Merton, *Ishi Means Man*, 20.

Leggings, using him as an example of a North American indigenous person, which most people agree Two Leggings was not. Merton should have questioned his view of Two Leggings, especially when he noted: "When other Indians of his time heard that his story was being taken down to be put in a book, they said 'Why him?'"[69]

Merton is more sympathetic to Central American Indians. He writes approvingly, for example about Pablo Antonio Cuadra:

> [He] absolutely refuses to regard the Indian heritage of Central America as a matter of archaeology or lavish color pictures in *Life* magazine. It is to him something living, something that boils and fights for expression in his soul, and in the soul of his people. He cannot do otherwise than attempt, as so many others have attempted, to clarify contemporary aspirations in the language of ancient myth. It is a singularly fruitful and necessary combination, and there is no longer any question of its validity.[70]

Merton is much kinder to Central American Indians than to those of North America.

CONCLUSION

Merton would have agreed with North American aboriginal activists like Charles Eastman (Ohiyesa) and Gertrude Bonney (Zitkala-sa), that the demands on Indians to convert to Christianity were excessive and constituted spiritual genocide. Merton believed that all faiths led to the same place and that all roads led to the same God. He argued for a spiritual pluralism that was rare in his time and before. Had he lived longer, he might have revised many of his assessments of Native American culture sprinkled throughout *Ishi Means Man*:

> Forest upon forest, mile upon empty mile
> The undiscovered continent lies, rock upon rock:
> The lakes awake or move in their mute sleep.
> Huge rivers wander where the plains
> Are cloudy or dark with seas of buffalo.

---

69. Merton, *Ishi Means Man*, 22.

70. Thomas Merton, introduction to Pablo Antonio Cuadra, *The Jaguar & the Moon*, trans. Thomas Merton (Seattle: Kindle Digital Media, 2015) Kindle Locations 76-79.

Frail waterbirds sing in the weeds of Florida.
Northward, gray seas stir
In sight of the unconscious hills.
There are no prints in the thin snows of Maine.[71]

Here Merton's perceptions manifest his Eurocentrism as he poetically describes a North America that was empty and undiscovered rather than teaming with sentient beings with their spiritualities that expressed their hopes and dreams. There were many footprints in the snows of Maine long before Columbus came.

---

71. Thomas Merton, "Christopher Columbus," *The Collected Poems of Thomas Merton* (New York: New Direction, 1977) 207.

ISHI, A PARABLE FOR OUR TIME

Robert G. Toth

This is a story of how Thomas Merton was profoundly affected toward the end of his life by his encounter with an indigenous mode of consciousness, through the story of Ishi. This encounter challenged the very mode of consciousness Merton had deployed most of his life as a participant in modern society, and which he had come to regard as destructive. We will refer to Ishi's mode of consciousness as holomorphic consciousness – an apprehension of the world that sees being in terms of the way the whole of life interrelates, balances, and transforms itself. It is a mode of thinking we all innately possess, but which is suppressed in anthropocentric (human-centered) societies and cultures and the anthropocentric-dominated thought patterns that developed since the Neolithic period.

The anthropocentric mode of thinking is also innate in us. It is not "wrong," but it is limited, and that is its power. The anthropocentric perspective is rooted in separation and oppositional dualities; it thinks in terms of quantities and hierarchies; its thinking is rooted in a presupposition, that the self is separate from other selves and other "things" in the world. It is a world of enemies and allies, predators and prey. It is, in short, object-based thinking.

From the perspective of anthropocentric consciousness, the whole (wholeness) is a concept not an experience; it's an idea, slightly unreal, even a contradiction in terms; something to be achieved as a spiritual culmination.

In contrast, indigenous peoples have remained grounded in an everyday experience of the whole: an everyday recognition of one's inherent interrelatedness with all beings, from insects to buffalo to medicinal plants to the pebble under foot. They, of course, possess, as we all do, an anthropocentric awareness, an awareness of themselves as separate in a world of objects, but it doesn't dominate their consciousness, as it does ours.

That is what I believe Thomas Merton discovered.

We have a record of Merton's holomorphic consciousness as a child in *Tom's Book*, the remarkable journal kept by his mother, Ruth. For example:

September 1915 [8 months] He also stood up in his p'ram, especially to see the river when we went on the bridge. He waved 'Bonjour' and pointed out the light, the flowers . . .

November 1, 1916 [21 months] when we go out he seems conscious of everything. Sometimes he puts up his arms and cries out 'Oh Sun! Oh joli!' Often it is to the birds or trees that he makes these pagan hymns of joy. Sometimes he throws himself on the ground to see the 'cunnin' little ants'

He already knew the wind and rain [when we came here,] and always holds out his hand to feel them. Lately he has taken to saying 'Monsieur Wind' and I heard him at the window saying – 'What's he say, 'Monsieur Wind,' then answering his own question by a long drawn 'Oo-oo-oo!'[1]

Soon the society and culture of the time opened its arms to embrace the young and vulnerable Merton in its anthropocentric grasp, and he learned to love this subject-object way of thinking so familiar to us – though he would later also come to abhor it. In the opening paragraph of *The Seven Storey Mountain*, Merton identifies what became a subliminal life-long struggle to retrieve the holomorphic experience of his early childhood: ". . . I came into the world. Free by nature, in the image of God, I was nevertheless the prisoner of my own violence and my own selfishness, in the image of the world into which I was born."[2]

Merton's life story could be written as a series of attempts to escape the physical and spiritual imprisonments of the world as it is structured by anthropocentric thought. Merton's journey was to find freedom for himself and assist others who are trying to escape with him. His writings record many self-reinterpretations and epiphanies that were moving him closer to recovering the original, natural freedom he sought.

In the months leading up to and including January and February 1967, Merton was engaged in yet another round of "self-interpretation," [as it is called]. He was reading and writing across a wide range of social issues: the war in Vietnam and the Peace movement; the civil rights movement; poverty; the impact of technology; the

1. Ruth Jenkins, *Tom's Book,* ed. Shelia Milton (Monterey, KY: Larkspur Press, 2005).

2. Thomas Merton, *The Seven Storey Mountain* (New York: Harcourt Brace Jovanovich, 1976) 3.

growing crisis in the environment; the past and present Native American situation; and the future of the Church and monasticism. He was also dealing with a number of personal issues: another in his ongoing disputes with his Abbot, Dom James Fox; questioning the value of his writing in light of recent critiques; struggling with how to end a close relationship he developed with a young nurse he met while hospitalized in Louisville; concerned about the implica-tions of dramatic changes in the Catholic Church as a result of The Second Vatican Council; questioning and defending his monastic vocation; and dealing with his recurring health problems. In some sense, each of these can be seen as a form of imprisonment.

During this period he read dozens of books on theology, scrip-ture, religion, philosophy, anthropology, nature, spirituality, the mystics, Zen Buddhism, social justice, the history of indigenous people, and also some fiction, especially Faulkner. And he was writing – a paper for Harvard magazine; a long essay on Faulkner; an essay on "A New Christian Consciousness"; the manuscript of *Faith and Violence*; a long essay on reading the Bible; 25 pages in his Journal; 56 letters to 35 different people; 20 pages of notes in his Reading notebooks; and also preparing his talks for the novices.

Then he received a gift, a book, *Ishi in Two Worlds,* a book by Theodora Kroeber that raises deep ontological questions, a book that turned Merton's attention to recovering something from the past that was lost by humanity and himself. While he was reading *Ishi in Two Worlds* he made an entry in his Reading Notebook on January 31, 1967 that he entitled "Food for solitary reflections on my 52nd birthday." He wrote:

> In fact, I am very resentful of a society which precisely is forcing upon me a future I do not especially want – and which I suspect even "they" do not really want. Once God & his Providence are got rid of, we find ourselves under the unconscious determinism of human myth and caprice & it occurs to me now that really I have to look for the roots of this in man's biology (importance of a book like K Lorenz *On Aggression*). But what is of immediate importance is mans' interpretation of himself & the consequences of that interpretation. In reading Ishi, I see the connection between 19th century America's self-interpretation & the Vietnam war today. Eiseley examines the trend toward "conformi-

ty." But both the conformism & non-conformism of people in this country especially seem erratic & disquieting. But there is no use in being merely "alarmed" by it – my own tendency to be alarmed & to complain really gets nowhere either – it is only a confession of helplessness. I myself need a new and deeper attitude. It is surely not enough to go on echoing the various Thoreaus that I find congenial.

This is to me a simple & helpful sentence. It helps to understand my problem with critics who have made it an article of faith to reject nature – in a kind of Barthian technologism maybe? – all now finds meaning in mans' decision (they don't seem to see that in man's "decision" there can be a revenge of nature that has been too arbitrarily handled for irrational purposes). I would myself be content to go along with the old promises – & in fact that is what I intend to do anyway. But the future is cancelling them out. What I don't want to do is make the irrational act of sub-mission & solidarity with the fantasies of people I cannot respect because to me they are doctrinaire, self-complacent and grievously limited in the "humanity" they claim to be proud of. And they are destructive.[3]

(You can hear the echos from *Conjectures of a Guilty Bystander* throughout.)

Merton connects the consequences of the nation's and human-ity's interpretations to his personal self-interpretation, expressing antipathy for the anthropocentric worldview dominating the society and culture, where "all finds meaning in man's decision" and in the "unconscious determinism of human myth and caprice" where "God's Providence is got rid of" and where man's irrational rejec-tion of nature results in a revenge of nature. While Merton is railing against a self-destructive society and culture he recognizes that he cannot escape it, and that he is every bit as capable of participating in it as those perpetrating the most heinous crimes against humanity. In summarizing his own position, he is describing the uncomfortable situation of everyone imprisoned in the dominant Western culture, seeing man's rejection of nature as a rejection of God's providence. "I would myself be content to go along with the old promises – & in fact that is what I intend to do anyway. But the future is cancelling

---

3. Thomas Merton, *Reading Notebook, 1966-1967.* Unpublished.

them out." The "old promises." Anthropocentric promises. The imagined and often illusory promises of democracy, the American Dream, the church, the monastic life, and all the guiding institutions of society that were failing to resolve the critical issues affecting the human condition, and even contributing to making it worse. These were the walls of the prison the anthropocentric world had built.

Searching to understand how the future will cancel out the old promises, he concludes that he must look for the roots of this condition in man's biology. He had been reading the works of Loren Eiseley, Conrad Lorenz and other anthropologists, including Theodora Kroeber, author of *Ishi in Two Worlds*. Theodora was an anthropologist, wife of Alfred Kroeber, who was a Professor of Anthropology at the University of California, Berkeley and the Director of the University of the California Museum of Anthropology.

Kroeber's *Ishi in Two Worlds* is divided into two sections. The first part is the history of the Yana people, their life before and during the genocide. The second part is the story of Ishi's concealment, and his adoption and adaption to Euro-American culture.

During the westward expansion and colonization of the nineteenth century, a small group of indigenous people, the Yahi, members of the Yana nation, who lived around the foothills of Mount Lassen near Oroville and Vina California, suffered the same fate as most other Native Peoples: genocide. Eventually the Yahi were reduced to five people who were able to conceal themselves in a remote, and nearly inaccessible, area of the mountains. Finally, when some surveyors happened upon their settlement, they scattered. The two eldest members died, two others disappeared and were never found. In August 1911 the one survivor was discovered, starving and delirious, draped over a fence near a slaughterhouse in Oroville, California. He had been living alone in concealment for three years, occasionally making forays into the nearby ranches to find food. He was taken to the local jail and provided food and shelter.

The second section of *Ishi in Two Worlds* presents thought provoking contrasts in two worldviews as this "stone-age" man confronts Euro-American culture. Alfred Kroeber and a fellow anthropology professor, Thomas Waterman, who had studied the Yana, took Ishi to San Francisco where he was provided lodging and employment at the recently opened Museum of Anthropology. There a small group of people from the university and the

museum cared for him and studied his history and culture. Unable
to determine his actual name Kroeber named him Ishi, which in
Yana simply means "man." Ishi returned once to his old territory
for several months where anthropologists observed him under his
natural conditions. After four and a half years living among white
men, Ishi died of tuberculosis in 1916.

"Ishi: A Meditation" – Merton in Two Worlds

Moved by Ishi's story, Merton wrote a review of *Ishi in Two
Worlds* that he entitled "Ishi: A Meditation." While he saw Ishi's
experience as "the connection between 19th century America's
self-interpretation & the Vietnam war," he also found himself
personally connected to this man who like himself came into the
world "Free by nature, in the image of God," and who unwillingly
became a prisoner of violence in the world into which he was born,
the wider anthropocentric world which exterminated his people and
sentenced him to solitary confinement. But Merton recognized that
in spite of all that happened to Ishi, he was not a captive but still
free in his holomorphic spirituality.

In the meditation Merton connects a number of reciprocal
dimensions – the past and the present, the individual and the collective, the physical and the spiritual. The initial, one word, sentence
of his meditation, "Genocide," establishes the historical context,
specifically the genocide of Native Americans and the genocide
in Vietnam. Collectively, "Men are always separating murder
into two parts: one which is unholy and unclean: for 'the enemy.'
Another which is a sacred duty: 'for our side.' . . . We were the
people of God, always in the right, following a manifest destiny."
Merton was conscious of the Catholic Church's role in establishing
the doctrine of discovery and its evolution into the United States'
concept of manifest destiny, anthropocentric forces of society and
religion that combined to allow the colonization, assimilation, and
physical, cultural, and spiritual genocide of indigenous people. He
found the lethal effects of the Doctrine of Discovery and Manifest
Destiny irreconcilable with the principles, values, and spirituality
expressed by the founders of both the Church and the country.

The spiritual dimension was more personal to Merton. It was
about the way this indigenous man, Ishi, and his culture, challenge
Merton to see another way of being human, a way to interpret

himself from a holomorphic perspective. Anthropocentric consciousness typically constructs the idea of a holistic state of mind as something to be achieved through long practice, through mystical revelation, through a negation of the anthropocentric consciousness itself, or through evolving or attaining a unitary consciousness. In contrast, Ishi experienced the whole, as the everyday recognition of one's inherent physical and spiritual interrelatedness with all beings.

As an intellectual exercise in self interpretation, understanding Ishi's worldview required setting aside the customary categories and distinctions of Western thought, and connecting with a different way of being in relationship with the source of all being and its implications for how to live.

In the months before reading *Ishi in Two Worlds,* Merton had been reading about the role of the wilderness and the desert in the spirituality of the Bible and the early Christian Church. They were places for retreat apart from the "world," places for spiritual development, solitude, and revelation where mystery was encountered and contemplated, and God was to be discovered. Special places of physical-spiritual connection.

For the colonizer the wilderness meant an uncivilized frontier to be explored, settled, and exploited, a savage and dangerous place where civil laws and behavior did not apply, but where laws also granted rights to some to take what did not belong to them. Wilderness was a place where people like Ishi live.

For Ishi and Native Americans there was no concept of wilderness, no word for it, no boundaries separating humans from any other being. Their lives were grounded in a holomorphic consciousness. Theirs was not a special place for only the most serious spiritual seekers. They lived in a sacred place where everyone can experience a balanced, physical-spiritual relationship with nature. A place of natural laws, and of responsibility for nature. Their physical and spiritual existence was rooted in close communication with the mystery of being. The place gave them meaning rather than they giving meaning to the place. The Native American sense of place is the foundation of their cultural mooring and values: it is not simply "the environment" that they "accidentally occupy" – they are the children of that place. There is no artificial distinction between themselves and some alien "other" that is termed "nature,"[4]

---

4. Viola Cordova, *How It Is* (Tucson: The University of Arizona Press, 2007) 197-98.

whether it be a mountain or a seed, a star or a tree, water or a rock. Everything shares mutual responsibility for everything else, and nothing, including humans, has special rights.

Merton feels the contrast between Ishi's contemplative life and his own. Both are in relationship with the mysterious source of all being. Ishi knows that source, and receives its instructions on how to live, from the physical world around him, not as things, but as being itself. His space and time is here and now. Nature is sufficient revelation of God's providence.

Merton sees Ishi as a man who is integrated and balanced, psychologically, physically, and spiritually. He contrasts the fact that Ishi was "not guilt ridden," "with the spectacle of our own country with its . . . psychic turmoil, its moral confusion and its profound heritage of guilt." He sees Ishi as someone who "lived by a deeply religious wisdom which can be called in a broad sense mystical . . .. As a man sustained by a deep and unassailable spiritual strength."

Those of us who knew Ron Seitz may remember his constant reminder to look beyond Merton's hand to where his finger is pointing, and this is precisely what Merton himself is telling us to do in "Ishi: A Meditation." He is very specific about the direction he wants us to take. He states:

> For the reflective reader who is – as everyone must be today – deeply concerned about man and his fate, this is a moving and significant book, one of those unusually suggestive works that must be read, and perhaps more than once. It is a book to think deeply about and to take notes on, not only because of its extraordinary factual interest but because of its special quality as a kind of parable.[5]

"Unusually suggestive," "a kind of parable." Merton does not fully explicate what he found unusually suggestive or its meaning as a kind of parable. There is a parable here, a vitally important one, a very deep one, one that is about history and the future, about all of humanity and us as individuals. Something so personally important for our self-interpretation we must discover it for ourselves. Throughout the meditation, he instructs us to consider various implications of Ishi's story and what it means to be human from an indigenous perspective, one that is grounded in biology, in the physical, in a spirituality of nature. He tells us:

5. Thomas Merton, *Ishi Means Man* (Greensboro, NC: Unicorn Press, 1976) 31.

To read this story thoughtfully, to open one's heart to it, is to receive a most significant message: one that not only moves, but disturbs. You begin to feel the inner stirrings of that pity and dread which Aristotle said were the purifying effect of tragedy.

The impact of the story is all the greater because the events are so deeply charged with a natural symbolism: the structure of these happenings is such that it leaves a haunting imprint on the mind. Out of that imprint come disturbing and potent reflections.

It has implications that are simply beyond speech. There is nothing one can say in the presence of such a happening and of its connotations for what our spiritual books so glibly call "the hidden life."

The reader should reflect a little on the relation of the Indian to the land on which he lived. In this sense, most modern men never know what it means to have a "home ground."[6]

If we are to see the story of Ishi as a parable, so, too, we might see a parable in the story of Merton's self-interpretation in the context of an indigenous worldview.

"Ishi: A Meditation" became the centerpiece of a collection of five essays Merton wrote on books about Native Americans that was published as *Ishi Means Man*, with a Foreword by Dorothy Day. In the Forward she expresses her "guilt at knowing so little about the Indians of the Americas," and being brought out of her "abysmal ignorance" by a book by John Collier, *Indians of the Americas, The Long Hope* written in 1947. She wrote, "That book had far-reaching influence, as I hope this book of essays will have." Retrospectively, it seems Day's hope was not realized. A search for reviews, articles, essays, and conference presentations on *Ishi Means Man* reveals it has received very little attention.

John Collier was the U.S. Commissioner of Indian Affairs from 1933 to 1945. When first appointed to that post, he believed that indigenous cultures would die out as a result of "civilization" and "progress." Over time, Collier realized that their traditional values have something critically important to offer to the world – a pro-

6. Thomas Merton, *Ishi Means Man* (Greensboro, NC: Unicorn Press, 1976) 26-29.

found sense of living and a new hope, spiritual possessions which kept Indian societies alive that centuries of cultural genocide had dimmed, but not destroyed. He opened his book with the following:

> They had what the world has lost. They have it now. What the world has lost, the world must have again, lest it die. Not many years are left to have or have not, to recapture the lost ingredient.
>
> They had and have this power for living, which our modern world has lost – as world-view and self-view, as tradition and institution, as practical philosophy dominating their society and as an art supreme among all the arts.
>
> If our modern world should be able to recapture this power, the earth's natural resources and web of life would not be irrevocably wasted within the twentieth century, which is the prospect now.
>
> The deep cause of our world agony is that we have lost the passion and reverence for human personality, and for the web of life, and the earth which the American Indians have tended as central, sacred fire since before the Stone Age. Our long hope is to renew that sacred fire in us all.[7]

Morgan Atkinson's film, *Soul Searching, the Journey of Thomas Merton* concludes with these words spoken by Michael Mott, "Merton is dead. The fire is gone to quote his own poem. These are the ashes. It's over, the fire is gone somewhere else. Where has the fire gone?"

"Ishi: A Meditation" is calling us to look where Collier, Merton, Day, and Mott are pointing us. What are we to find? The lost ingredient? Something we once had that is now critical for survival? The limits of an anthropocentric interpretation of life? A connection with the divine source of all being that predates institutional religion? . . . or simply, a way to embrace mystery.

---

7. John Collier, *Indians of the Americas: The Long Hope* (New York: The New American Library, 1947) 7-8.

PAYING HIS DEBTS TO NATIVE AMERICAN PEOPLES: THOMAS MERTON ON THE "SPIRITUAL RICHNESS OF THE INDIAN RELIGIOUS GENIUS"

Donald P. St. John

PART ONE

THIS LAND IS OUR LAND?
A PROPHETIC VOICE FOR LAND AND PEOPLE

The sickness is in history. The sickness is in this country itself, in the injustices committed against the Negro, the Indian, against the wildlife of the country, the beautiful nature God made.

Thomas Merton, *Witness to Freedom*

INTRODUCTION BY WAY OF A STRANGE COINCIDENCE

I preface Part One of this essay by reviewing a powerful piece that appeared in the Opinion Pages of *The New York Times* on May 29, 1915 by Lydia Millet, titled "Selling Off Apache Holy Land."[1] Millet's article provides an illustrative introduction as I focus on the prophetic-moral voice of Thomas Merton in his writings and conferences on Native Peoples of North America and their land. I request that my readers keep Millet's discussion in mind as they review this essay's Part Two that features Merton's discussions on the more poetic-contemplative and spiritually transformative practices of Native Peoples. The continuing assaults on Native American culture and aspects of Native American spirituality are indivisible considerations. Merton in his writing was prone to uniting heretofore hidden connections between disparate facts and

---

1. Lydia Millett, "Selling Off Apache Holy Land," *The New York Times* (May 29, 2015).

to pulling varied aspects of a topic together holistically. Millet's article, at first glance disconnected from the focus of this essay, demonstrates the continued relevance of Merton's insights into Native American spirituality.

"About an hour east of Phoenix, near a mining town called Superior, men, women, and children of the San Carlos Apache tribe have been camped out at a place called Oak Flat for more than three months, protesting the latest assault on their culture (NYT 5/29/15)." Millet notes that they had "marched" 44 miles from their tribal headquarters to begin their occupation of this "ancient Apache holy place." The Apaches had dedicated this site with beautiful "coming-of-age ceremonies" for many generations of young women. (We will briefly discuss this rite in Part Two in the context of a 1967 talk to contemplative nuns by Merton where he mentions "callings" and vocations among Native American women.) Despite all of the prior protections granted such Apache sites by a host of diverse Washington officials and departments, the U.S. Congress in 2014 had "promised to hand the title for Oak Flat over to a private, Australian-British mining concern." (Merton will issue harsh judgments on such broken promises and how they reflect an underlying lack of respect for indigenous peoples and their traditions.)

According to Millet, once Resolution Mining Company (a subsidiary of Rio Tinto Mining) had its way, what will remain of the Apache Oak Flat site will be a "two-mile-wide, 1,000-foot-deep pit," that Resolution Mining compared to a "nearby meteor crater." The duplicitous deal would trade 5,300 acres of private land to the Forest Service for 2,400 acres of land given to Resolution to mine with no oversight. Arizona politicians had tried to get such a deal approved by Congress numerous times in the past but without success. This time "the giveaway language was slipped into" a defense bill at the eleventh hour by Arizona Senators Flake and McCain and thus escaped "public scrutiny." Both Senators have long standing connections to mining interests and their contributions. (Merton will, in his review of Nash's *Wilderness and the American Mind* and elsewhere expose this link between the traditional Euro-American contempt both for Indians and for their "wilderness," large parts of which are considered as "sacred land.")

In an interview with Millet, a former chairman of the San Carlos Apache asked: "Why is this land so holy? No different to

Mt. Sinai. How the holy spirit came to be." Millet, in turn, asks, "If Oak Flat was a Christian holy site, or for that matter Jewish or Muslim, no senator who wished to remain in office would dare sneak a backdoor deal for its destruction into a spending bill – no matter what mining-company profits or jobs might result. But this is Indian religion. Clearly, the Arizona congressional delegation isn't afraid of a couple of million conquered natives."

Millet in a prophetic indictment not only charges that this political ruse allows "precious public land to be destroyed," but it once again makes Indians invisible and turns the American Native Peoples into "ghosts." For Millet this "deal is an impressive new low in congressional corruption, unworthy of our country's ideals no matter what side of the aisle you're on." This kind of back-door betrayal and "cynical maneuvering" reaffirms the sad lesson that makes the electorate "disrespect politicians," and overall to harbor "disdain for government that ends up hurting 'everyone.'" Merton also states strongly that our history and experience have demonstrated that as we oppress and demean Indians "we are in fact defining our own inhumanity, our own insensitivity, our own blindness to human values."[2] And this makes the international vaunting of our ideals ring hollow. "So it goes," says Merton, for if we demonstrate "no concern for rights and freedoms in the concrete, how can we expect the world to respond to the perfunctory mouthing of ideals?"[3]

Millet concludes with this charge: "If ever there was a time for Congress to prove its moral mettle to the public, this is that time." Merton not only questioned the moral mettle of politicians but the moral and spiritual mettle of the Church in its dealings with "Indians." He found it a betrayal of Christianity's core values and beliefs, insisting that because of the Incarnation, every human being must "be seen and treated as Christ . . .."[4] He asserted that the cosmic dimension of the Incarnation working through the Catholic sacramental imagination and "natural contemplation" can assist greatly in the development of a spiritual sensitivity to Native Peoples' deep

2. Thomas Merton, *Ishi Means Man*. Unicorn Keepsakes Series 8. Forward by Dorothy Day (Greensboro, NC: Unicorn Press, 1976) 10; hereinafter, *IMM*.

3. Thomas Merton, *Witness to Freedom: Letters in Times of Crisis (Letters, V)*, ed. William H. Shannon (New York: Farrar, Straus and Giroux, 1994) 97; hereinafter, *WF*.

4. Thomas Merton, *The Thomas Merton Reader*, ed. Thomas P. McDonnell (New York: Doubleday, An Image Book, 1974, 1989) 305; hereinafter, *TMR*.

respect for the sacredness of the Earth. Thus, the prophetic-moral and contemplative-poetic are deeply connected and no more so than when dealing with people so intimately connected to their lands. Or, as Merton said elsewhere, "The ecological conscience is essentially a peace-making conscience."[5] And like Millet's wake-up call to Congress, Merton warned the Church and its theologians that they "ought to take note of the ecological conscience and do it fast."[6]

THE EMERGENCE OF MERTON'S PROPHETIC VOICE

By the late 1950s, Thomas Merton had already established himself as one of the foremost writers on the spiritual life, emphasizing the importance of silence, solitude, and contemplation. Many of his followers and many in the wider society and Church were unprepared for the emergence in the 1960s (with some hints earlier) of a strong, sometimes "loud" prophetic voice. The genius of Merton was to hold the contemplative and prophetic in a healthy, mutually beneficial tension in which growth in one would contribute to growth in the other (sometimes after a period of adjustment and self-reflection). Even as he moved closer to an eremitical life in the woods, Merton increasingly spoke out on issues of the Cold War, war and peace, violence and nonviolence, human and civil rights. He wrote passionately about African-Americans and their struggles for equality. His writing on eco-justice and social justice issues included their interconnection in the history of Euro-American treatment of Native Americans and of the American land or earth. His increased involvement in social issues included hosting meetings at his monastery, giving conferences, and corresponding voluminously with political and religious dissidents. He was pushing Christians to heed the call to a more critical and sometimes unpopular "prophetic" vocation.

While this essay will not detail the history of Merton's growing interest in indigenous peoples of the Americas, there is a glimpse of his interest's movement in his correspondence with Ernesto Cardenal. The Nicaraguan had been a novice under Merton from 1957-1959. They developed a unique friendship which continued in their sharing of ideas and ideals in letters and through their public

---

5. Thomas Merton, *Preview of the Asian Journey*, ed. Walter A. Capps (New York: Crossroad Publishing Company, 1991) 107; hereinafter, *PAJ*.
6. Thomas Merton, "The Wild Places," *The Merton Annual 24* (Louisville: Fons Vitae, 2015) 26; hereinafter, *WP*.

writings long after Ernesto, a poetic and persuasive writer himself, had left Gethsemani for health reasons in 1959. One of their mutual interests and a passion of Cardenal's which affected his mentor was the history, religious traditions, and plight of indigenous peoples of the Americas. Merton had already during the 1950s exhibited an interest in the religions of Native North Americans, in this case, the Lakotas (Sioux) of the Plains. "The book I showed you here," Merton reminded Cardenal, "was *The Sacred Pipe by Black Elk* . . .. It was a very fine book . . .."[7] Joseph Epes Brown had recorded Black Elk's oral recounting of the seven major rites of the Oglala Sioux. Black Elk, a visionary in his own right, revealed the richness of his Oglala tradition. In the book, Black Elk speaks of religious experience and personal spiritual transformation as well as on ceremonial actions and attitudes, including several rites of passage.

After he had left Gethsemani, Cardenal became a passionate and prophetic voice through poetry, political and social tracts, and speeches as well as through direct action for the rights of indigenous people and the poor especially of Central America. Merton kept abreast of his work and admired it immensely. Merton obviously took their mutual interest in "Indians" seriously. In one letter Merton makes the following comments: "Yes I have received your *Epigrams*: they are magnificent" . . . "Your poems about the Indians have been simply superb" . . . "I am sure your whole book will be splendid and look forward to seeing it." And in a touching as well as a revealing comment he reminds Cardenal: "I have not forgotten about the Indians and all that they mean to us both."[8]

Ernesto Cardenal went on to study for the priesthood in Mexico and was ordained a priest in 1965 in Granada. Merton had a few special words of advice for the seminarian. They provide an insight into the critical spirit with which Merton judged the Church's past actions towards Native Peoples. His words also evidence a deep theology concerning who Christ is and what that should have meant to centuries of conquerors, colonists, and missionaries.

[R]ather than becoming purely and simply a conventional priest, you should think in terms of this strange kind of mission in which you will bring to the Church knowledge

7. Thomas Merton, *The Courage for Truth: Letters to Writers (Letters, 4)*, ed. Christine M. Bochen (New York: Farrar, Straus and Giroux, 1993) 142; hereinafter, *CT*.
8. *CT*, 136.

of these [indigenous] peoples and spiritualities she has so
far never understood. This has been a factor in the lives of
the greatest missionaries, however: to enter into the thought
of primitive peoples and to live that thought and spirit as
Christians, thus bringing the spirituality of these people
into the light of Christ where, indeed, it was from the start
without anyone realizing the fact.[9]

Cardenal later fought with the Sandinistas and later became Minister
of Culture in the Nicaraguan government after the Sandinistas took
power. As late as 1968 Merton was still considering the possibility
of visiting Cardenal at Solentiname (a contemplative and artistic
community founded by Cardenal) to "see if it seems to be where
God wants me" though he had some doubts about that option by
that time.[10]

Merton's interest in the Native Peoples of both continents grew
during the 1960s; his readings and reflections led to a deeper grasp
of their cultural riches as well as their ability to blend the ecological and cosmic with the religious and contemplative. Certainly,
his own deepening experience of the natural world assisted in his
appreciation for it as an integral material/spiritual reality and as a
sacred presence to Native Americans. They sought its power and
guidance in their religious ceremonies. The natural world provided
artistic and verbal symbolism for their prayers, their mythic and
sacred stories, and poems. Its presence and through the presence of
"spirit-persons" affected spiritual transformations both at a communal and individual level.

Merton's correspondence with poets, activists, anthropologists,
and historians familiar with and sensitive to the plight of indigenous
peoples stoked the flames of Merton's prophetic ire against the unjust and inhumane treatment of indigenous people and their natural
habitats. These dialogues contributed to his sympathetic understanding of the many cultural and spiritual riches of Native Peoples,
to which most European immigrants and subsequent Americans
(including Christians in a special way) had been blind and deaf.
Merton appears to have quickly grasped the inner spiritual dynamics and even mystical experiences of Native Americans owing to
his extensive study of religious experience in many traditions. His

9. *CT*, 143.
10. *CT*, 162.

own experiences and his widening understanding of the meaning and manifestations of "natural contemplation" (*theoria physike*) bolstered his awareness of the immanent presence and creativity of the divine (as Word/Logos or Wisdom/*Sophia*) in the natural world.

THE PROPHETIC CALL: TAKE IT SERIOUSLY

During a series of conferences conducted at Gethsemani in December 1967 and May 1968 for contemplative nuns, Merton made it clear that their contemplative vocations implied taking the call to the "prophetic vocation" seriously. "Now an essential thing about a prophetic vocation is *awareness* of factors behind the facts."[11] Picking up on the terminology of Herbert Marcuse, Merton claimed that our "one-dimensional" society, "doesn't want this." Knowledge of these factors would "complicate life too much; they could create problems." They might force us to struggle with real issues and to make real changes. Some of the difficulties that the popular mind has in locating these "factors behind the facts" are due to a widespread loss of historical consciousness, a lack of appreciation for both the historical content and context of the facts. This loss of historical consciousness began when the first wave of immigrants made an explicit separation of their identity and their mission from Europe and its history. For Puritans and like-minded Euro-Americans, this was "the end of history as far as they were concerned." They had convinced themselves that their mission was the start of "a whole new life, a new creation, the kingdom."[12] The truncating of a genuine historical consciousness makes it difficult for subsequent generations of Americans to identify in their times those ideological, social, political, religious, and economic factors that lurked behind the mistakes made and tragedies inflicted on others in the past. Thus the pattern repeats itself. He agreed with Herbert Marcuse that today the widespread and abusive manipulation of language by powerful interests via the mass media makes it difficult for people to get "any kind of accurate perspective on what's happening."[13] He pointed out the self-justifying rhetoric that Americans have used to hide or trivialize the seriousness of the destructive violence inflicted on both the Earth and those peoples

11. Thomas Merton, *The Springs of Contemplation: A Retreat at the Abbey of Gethsemani*, ed. Jane Marie Richardson, SL (New York: Farrar, Straus and Giroux, 1992, 2010) 156; hereinafter, *SOC*.
12. *SOC*, 156.
13. *SOC*, 152.

living close to it, whether in North America or Vietnam.

In the mid-1960s, Merton continued to research the roots and patterns that were foundational to the history of American cultural pathology. Evidence of his research is grounded in his reflective reviews of such seminal works as *Wilderness and the American Mind* (1967) by Roderick Nash, *The Shoshoneans* (1967) by Edward Dorn and Leroy Lucas (African-American Photographer), and *Ishi in Two Worlds* (1965) by Theodora Kroeber.

WILDERNESS AND THE AMERICAN MIND

As with many of his book reviews, Merton's 1968 review of Roderick Nash's *Wilderness and the American Mind*, provides him with an opportunity to reflect on the work itself as well as on issues Merton considers crucially connected to it. Patrick O'Connell has edited the complete original text of this review, "The Wild Places," drawing on a typed carbon copy located at the Thomas Merton Studies Center.[14] Merton's original review underwent minor changes when it appeared in *The Catholic Worker* 34 (June 1968) 4, 6, but a little more extensively when it was published by *The Center Magazine* (1968). This latter version is best known since it also appeared in *Preview of the Asian Journey*.[15] My discussion of the review includes ideas Merton expressed in his original draft reproduced in *The Merton Annual*.

One of Nash's themes that Merton highlights in his review is the ironic nature of American attitudes and actions towards the continent's natural world. While Americans loudly proclaim their love for the land and wilderness ("America the Beautiful"), they concurrently embrace a political ideology and economic system that depend on destroying America's natural legacy and thus that on which their own identity and survival ultimately depend on many levels. They continue the tradition embodied by the frontiersman who was at once "a product of wilderness" and "a destroyer of the wilderness." The success of the pioneers depended on their ability to be victorious in his battle against wild nature and to turn the wilderness into "a farm, a village, a road, a canal, a railway, a mine, a factory, a city – and finally an urban nation."[16]

---

14. Thomas Merton, "The Wild Places," *The Merton Annual* 24 (Louisville: Fons Vitae, 2011) 15-28; hereinafter, *WP*.

15. Thomas Merton, "The Wild Places," *PAJ*: 95-107.

16. *PAJ*, 96.

Merton found it disappointing that Nash barely touched on the "really crucial issues of the present moment in ecology." Although Nash "does not develop the tragic implications of the nation's inner contradiction concerning wilderness," he does present them "clearly enough for us to recognize their symptomatic importance." In the present, as in the past, America confesses its "love and respect for wild nature" while being firmly attached to values that "demand the destruction of the last remnant of wildness." Merton pointed out that Americans, not often blessed with the ability to recognize their self-contradictions, have labeled people like Rachel Carson "fanatics" for suggesting that there is something pathological about poisoning the natural world on which they depend for their health. This penchant for unconscious irony extends to modern western Christianity where "a certain popular, superficial, and one-sided 'Christian worldliness'" carries implications that are "profoundly destructive of nature and of 'God's good creation' even while it claims to love and extol them."[17]

Merton's review cautioned that although this "ambivalence towards nature" might be rooted in the "Biblical, Judaeo-Christian tradition," one should be careful about making hasty judgments as to what its genuine teachings are regarding creation and its relationship to the Creator. Unfortunately, what is often presented as the real Christian teachings on wilderness are drawn from recent politically and culturally self-serving pronouncements. Nevertheless, Merton seemed to agree with many of the observations that Nash made about the deep repugnance for wilderness and the Indians often displayed by the Puritans and later adopted by capitalists influenced by them. The Puritans hated wilderness as if it were a person, Merton wrote, even as "an extension of the Evil One."[18]

Native Americans were likewise considered evil because they lived in this evil milieu. They were full of nature's evil contagion. Wilderness was "the domain of moral wickedness" because, among other things, "[i]t favored spontaneity – therefore sin." The Puritanical mind, "haunted by repressed drives," fantasized that all kinds of "wanton and licentious rites" were taking place in those wild places. Judging Nature as fallen and corrupt, the basic duty of the Christian was "to combat, reduce, destroy, and

17. *PAJ*, 96-97.
18. *PAJ*, 98.

transform the wilderness." This duty was "God's work."[19] In the
original draft of his review, Merton added: "The elementary duty
of the Puritan settler was to attack the forest with an axe and to
keep a gun handy in order to exterminate Indians and wild beasts,
should they put in an appearance."

The Puritans considered success in their battle against wilderness as a sign of their predestined salvation. Their reward from
God was "prosperity, real estate, money, and ultimately the peaceful
'order' of civil and urban life." Merton mentioned Max Weber's
classic study of "the influence of the Puritan ethos on the growth of
capitalism." Hence, the culture of American capitalism "is firmly
rooted in a secularized Christian myth and mystique of struggle
with nature." This mystique, like its religious counterpart, has a
central "article of faith" the belief "that you prove your worth by
overcoming and dominating the natural world." Your existence is
justified, and the promised bliss is attained (in the here or hereafter)
"by transforming nature into wealth."[20] Merton pointed out that,
according to the exchange value and use value theories of both
Adam Smith and Karl Marx, nature is "useless and absurd" unless
and "until transformed." Any individual who disagrees with this is
dismissed as a "half-wit – or, worse, a rebel, an anarchist, a prophet
of apocalyptic disorders."[21]

Not mentioned by Nash or Merton are William Strickland's
rich insights into the attitudes and values behind the abuse and at
times destruction of the American earth and its native inhabitants
along the Hudson River in 1794 and 1795. Strickland noted that
the settler exhibited "an utter abhorrence for the works of creation
that exist in the place where he, unfortunately, settles himself."

In the first place he drives away or destroys the more hu-
manized Savage, the rightful proprietor of the soil; in the
next place he thoughtlessly, and rapaciously exterminates
all living animals, that can afford profit, or maintenance to
man; he then extirpates the woods that clothe and ornament
the country, and that to any but himself would be of greatest
value; and finally he exhausts and wears out the soil, and
with the devastation he has thus committed usually means
his own ruin; for by this time he is reduced to his original

19. *PAJ*, 98.
20. *PAJ*, 98-99.
21. *PAJ*, 99.

poverty; and it is then left to him only to sally forth and seek on the frontiers, a new country which he may again devour.... The day appears not too distant when America so lately an unbroken forest, will be worse supplied with timber than most of the old countries of Europe.[22]

However, as both Nash and Merton pointed out, there arose a "cult of nature" in the nineteenth century that viewed the Indian as Noble Savage. Leaders of this movement displayed a different set of attitudes and values concerning wilderness and indigenous peoples. Poets like William Cullen Bryant, novelists like James Fenimore Cooper, and mystically inclined preservationists like Henry David Thoreau and John Muir, as well as the Transcendentalists, warned the nation of the terrible consequences, not only to the natural world but to the human spirit, in the campaign to destroy all that was deemed "wild." The Transcendentalists, especially, sought to "reverse the Puritan prejudice against nature." They taught that God was more accessible in the wilderness than the city and that humans, rather than being evil by nature and hence easily corruptible by the wilderness, were good by nature – and in nature. "The silence of the woods whispered, to the man who listened, a message of sanity and healing," Merton wrote, reflecting his own experience as well as that of the Transcendentalists. The cities were more likely than not to corrupt human goodness, while "contact with nature" could help a person recover his or her goodness and "true self."[23]

Merton calls Thoreau's work "prophetic" because it went much deeper into the reality of the natural world than the popular "enthusiasm for scenery and fresh air." Thoreau already realized that "American capitalism was set on a course that would ultimately ravage all wild nature on the continent – perhaps even in the world." Thoreau "warned that some wilderness must be preserved." If it were not, humans would destroy themselves "in destroying nature." Contrary to the Puritans, Thoreau held that to overly domesticate a human being, to tame the wildness within him would "be to warp, diminish, and barbarize him." Hence, "the reduction of all nature to use for profit would end in the dehumanization of man." The "passion and savagery that the Puritans had projected onto nature turned out to be" within humans themselves. Meanwhile, today's

---

22. William Strickland, *Journal*. Quoted in Thomas Berry, *The Great Work* (New York: Bell Tower, 1999) 42.

23. *PAJ*, 100.

urbanites were busy turning the green living wilderness into "asphalt jungles." Absent the discipline of the wilderness, the savagery of urban humanity became "savagery for its own sake."[24]

Merton agreed that the natural world is not responsible for the violent crimes perpetrated daily in urban centers; they are an expression of what lies in supposedly "civilized" souls. John Muir's Scotch Calvinist father regarded it "as a feminine trait" in his son to enter wilderness without an axe to cut down trees or a gun to hunt down and kill wild animals. "To leave wild nature unattacked or unexploited was, in his [father's] eyes, not only foolish but morally reprehensible." The American male had to prove his virility through an "aggressive, compulsive attitude toward nature." This attitude among most American males did not reflect "strength," but manifested a deep "insecurity and fear." Beneath the American "cult of success" there lies a "morbid fear of failure" which results in "an overkill mentality" that has "been costly not only to nature but to every real or imaginary competitor."[25]

An important statement on eco-philosophy by Merton based on Muir that also implies much about the Native American view of nature appeared in the original draft of his review.

> Muir's basic insight was not simply romantically religious ... but the realization that man needed to feel a part of wild nature. He needed to recognize his kinship with all other living beings and to participate in their unchanged natural existence. In other words, he had to look at other living beings, especially wild things, not in terms of whether or not they were good *for him*, but as *good for themselves.* Instead of self-righteously assuming that man is absolute Lord of all nature and can exterminate other forms of life according to his real or imagined needs, Muir reminded us that man is *part of nature.* He must remember the rights of other beings *to exist on their own terms* and not purely and simply on his [and] *unless man learns this fundamental respect for all life, he himself will be destroyed.*[26]

The historical conflict between the wilderness mystique and the mystique of "exploitation and power" continues to act itself out

---

24. *PAJ*, 101-102.
25. *PAJ*, 101-102.
26. *WP*, 23.

in the American mind at a "tragic depth." For example, "[T]he ideal of freedom and creativity that has been celebrated with such optimism and self-assurance runs the risk of being turned inside out if the natural ecological balance, on which it depends for its vitality, is destroyed." And, what happens to the "pioneer mystique?" In some American ghettoes, the pioneer has become a policeman ready to shoot every black who looks at him in the wrong way. And, today's "pioneer in a suburb" is a tormented man always on the prowl for "projects of virile conquest."[27]

Merton, following Muir, saw an overlap and a deep connection between the objectification, abuse, and violence of human beings toward nature and the violence of human beings upon their kind. The cultural and psychological roots of the ecological tragedy are based upon the "profound dehumanization and alienation of modern Western man" who has substituted "the artificial value of inert objects and abstractions (goods, money, property) for the power of life itself." Thus, human beings and nature have become defined as mere resources. If Aldo Leopold's arguments for an ecological conscience and consciousness are to become effective, we must realize that at its heart, "the ecological conscience is essentially a peace-making conscience." The absence of an ecological conscience in the early history of America was obvious in the lack of a "peace-making conscience" towards both Native Americans and their habitats. Nor does the recent record of hot and cold wars bode well for the "ecological conscience." Merton was hopeful that the connection between the ecological conscience and the peace-making conscience would become more clear as people woke up to "the very character of the war in Vietnam – with crop poisoning, the defoliation of forest trees, the incineration of villages and their inhabitants with napalm." Merton ends his review by pointing out that some people – like himself – are wearing "the little yellow and red button 'Celebrate Life' and bearing witness as best we can to these tidings."[28]

THE SHOSHONEANS – FROM CONTINENT TO RESERVATION: FROM FREE, ESSENTIAL IDENTITY TO IMPOSED IDENTITY

In a May 1967 letter to Jonathan Williams, Merton announced: "I just finished a piece on Ed Dorn's Indian book. Thought you might

27. *PAJ*, 104.
28. *PAJ*, 106-107.

like it."[29] Here again, Merton uses the opportunity that writing a review of a recent work offers him to include his reflections on certain themes as well as certain literary or artistic values expressed in the work itself. He often develops his thinking on issues and spots new avenues that he might want to explore later. In his essay, "The Shoshoneans,"[30] Merton reviewed *The Shoshoneans: The People of the Basin-Plateau,* a book written by Edward Dorn but graced with rich photos by Leroy Lucas. Lucas was an African-American who, according to Merton took part in a Shoshonean Sun Dance for Peace in Vietnam. He "danced for the full three days, fasting, in the hot sun."[31] Lucas' participation in the ritual dramatically illustrated for Merton the connections he had and would make between the treatment of "Indians" and "Negroes" by the dominant American society.

Merton introduced his review with an excerpt from a mimeographed government document concerning the Indians of Fort Hill Reservation, Idaho: "Indians who are now principally on the reservation were the aboriginal owners of the United States. Placing them on reservations was an act to protect the white settlers from acts of depredation, which became more common as the Indians were pushed further back out of their original holdings." At this legalese, Merton began to exercise his sarcastic wit in several places in his review. He suggested that this "modest production of some very minor bureaucratic mind" not only deserved attention but "perhaps an international prize for crass and impenetrable complacency." Since the government document purportedly has to do with "Indians," Merton asked, "What are Indians?" They seem to be those people the government says are living "principally" on "reservations." Merton admitted that, of course, Indians could choose to leave their reservation and live in a ghetto. If they stay on the reservation, they are considered "wards of the government."[32] Once upon a time (long ago), they might have been considered "property owners" in a laughable way, Merton quipped. They seemed to own the whole continent, "until we arrived and informed them of the true situation." Their real status was that of "squatters on land which God had assigned to us." The government document referred to them as "*aboriginal* owners," Merton pointed out, but *everybody* (tongue in cheek) knew "how much of an owner

29. *CT*, 268.
30. Thomas "The Shoshoneans," *The Catholic Worker* 33, no. 6 (June, 1967) 5-6.
31. *IMM*, 8.
32. *IMM*, 5.

that is." In reality, it means that the Indian was "no owner at all." European Christians who took over Indian land realized "from the first [that] it was quite evident that the manifest destiny of the Indian was to live 'principally' on reservations as wards of the true owners of the land. The European Americans were those for whom legal title had been prepared in some mysterious fashion from the beginning of time, or drawn up perhaps in Noah's ark." And, of course, one must not forget the "depredations" initiated by those sneaky *aboriginal* owners just when the white man started to "develop the neighborhood, to make a little money on his investment."[33]

In a 1965 letter to Alejandro Vignati who was lamenting the brutal history of conquest in Latin America, Merton noted how this history of conquest had already played itself out in North America. "I agree with what you say about the religious values of the Indians. You are right a thousand times over. The history of the conquest was tragic, but not as tragic as that of this continent here in the North, where almost all (sic) of the Indians were exterminated. Some remain in silence, as an accusation; and each year the white people try to steal from them another piece of the reservation that remains theirs."[34]

Merton might be thinking of his earlier protest about a "recent violation of a very old treaty with the Senecas." They were forced to leave so-called "inviolable" land which was now to be "flooded by a big dam." A newly elected John F. Kennedy had refused to listen to the Seneca's many-sided objections to approval of the building of the Kinzua Dam on the Allegheny River which would destroy the historically and culturally significant Cornplanter's Village and many other villages as well as rich farmland. This area was a revered place to the Seneca which was also located in the Allegheny National Forest. Merton pointedly asked: "If we have no concern for rights and freedom in the concrete, how can we expect the world to respond to the perfunctory mouthing of our ideals."[35]

In his review of *The Shoshoneans*, Merton realized that forcing Indians onto reservations, an act of enforced physical confinement pointed to the even more violent act of restriction and confinement directed at the Indian as a human being. America had attempted to reduce the Indian's sense of inherent self-worth, "the reduction to a definition of him not in terms of his essential identity, but a defini-

---

33. *IMM*, 6.
34. *CT*, 234.
35. *WF*, 97.

tion of him in terms of a relationship of absolute tutelage imposed on him by us. Such a drastic and demeaning act "is of course extremely significant not only for the Indian (against whose human identity it is an act of systematic violence) but for ourselves." For by this action, "we are also expressing a definition and limitation within ourselves, we are in fact defining our own inhumanity, our own insensitivity, our own blindness to human values."[36]

We try to salve our conscience and express a bogus political largesse by giving the Indian the freedom to leave the reservation and to become like us, "by manifesting business acumen and American know-how, by making money, and by being integrated into our affluent society." Merton sarcastically quipped, "Very generous indeed."

The monk then asked what all of this meant: "IT MEANS THAT AS FAR AS WE ARE CONCERNED THE INDIAN (LIKE THE NEGRO, THE ASIAN, ETC.) IS PERMITTED TO HAVE A HUMAN IDENTITY ONLY IN SO FAR AS HE CONFORMS TO OURSELVES AND TAKES UPON HIMSELF OUR IDENTITY [Merton's emphasis]." But given the fact that the Indian, like the "Negro," differs from us in skin color and many other traits, "he can never be like us and can therefore never have an identity." Oh, we can announce that, in theory, he is human, but in practice, the Indian is, "like the Negro, at best a second-class human." And, despite his efforts to dress and act like us, he "never quite manages to make the grade." "In one word 'the ultimate violence' exerted on Indians and other races of color, especially the Negro, by Europeans and Americans "has been to impose on them *invented identities*" and place them in a position of powerlessness where they believe that their actual identity is the one "conferred upon them."[37]

There was one last effort by some Indian nations to reverse the complete takeover of their land, the loss of the great bison herds, and the push towards confinement on reservations and cultural re-education through "Indian schools." The famous Ghost Dance of the nineteenth century (ca. 1870-1890) as an act of resistance began in the far west, swept across the Plains, and made some Americans very nervous. The Ghost Dance was the last great attempt by Native Peoples to liberate themselves (with the aid of "supernatural powers") from American imperialism. The movement was dealt a great blow in 1890 with the massacre by the U.S. military of 152 Lakota

36. *IMM*, 9-10.
37. *IMM*, 10-11.

(mostly women and children) in their encampment along Wounded Knee Creek on the Lakota Pine Ridge Reservation in South Dakota. Merton quoted Ed Dorn who had written that the massacre "registered another small installment in the spiritual death of America."

Seeking access to traditional sources of power and vision, and hence identity, some Native Americans, including some Shoshonis, had embraced the Peyote Cult – but not all. Dorn reported that one man who spoke for the many abstainers told him that "'It [was] very important for his people to work for their cosmic identities within the unaltered material of their own being, without the agency of an hallucinogen.' His point was that a man has as much potential as a plant and should grow by virtue of his own roots."[38] Merton noted that peyote had only been among the Shoshoni for about fifty years. He went on to remark that "the Indian is still conscious, or able to be conscious, that he is close enough to his own roots to return to them in spite of the violence exercised upon his spirit by the white man." And Merton insisted that "in so far as a man returns to his own roots, he becomes able to resist exterior violence with complete success and even, after a certain point, invulnerably." However, in a footnote, Merton asserted that the peyote cult "grew up as a desperate spiritual reaction against the policies of genocide and cultural destruction." It was not merely an attempt at a psychological escape but a spiritual adjunct that could help the Indian recover "his identity and spiritual roots in a ground of messianic and apocalyptic vision." Many Indians, as well as Merton, objected to peyote's trivialization and abuse.

Merton ends his review with an extensive quote from a young Ponca Indian, Clyde Warrior. The whole document comprised the last four pages of Dorn's book and was a speech drafted for a conference on the War on Poverty. Merton introduced it with these words: "Its wisdom effectively balances the unwisdom of our opening quotation and makes us feel that America would be better off if we had a few more articulate Indians." I invite the reader to read the bulk of the speech as presented in Merton's review.[39] Here are a few passages on poverty and powerlessness:

> [T]he indignity of Indian life, and I would presume the indignity of life among the poor, in these United States, is the powerlessness of those who are "out of it," but who

---

38. *IMM*, 12-13.
39. *IMM*, 13-16.

yet are coerced and manipulated by the very system which excludes them . . ..

When I talk to Peace Corps volunteers, they tell me that the very structure of the relation between the rich and poor keeps the poor poor; that the powerful do not want change, and it is the very system itself that causes poverty. I hope that men of good will even among the powerful are willing to have their "boat rocked" a little in order to accomplish the task our country has set itself . . ..

As I say I am not sure of the causes of poverty, but one its correlates at least is this powerlessness, lack of experience, and lack of articulateness.

I do not know how to solve the problem of poverty, but of this I am certain, when a people are powerless, and their destiny is controlled by the powerful, whether they be rich or poor, they live in ignorance and frustration because they have been deprived of experience and responsibility as individuals and communities.

In the old days, the Ponca people lived on the buffalo, and we went out and hunted it. We believed that God gave the buffalo as a gift to us. And we felt ourselves to be a competent, worthy people. In those days we were not "out of the system." We were the system, and we dealt competently with our environment because we had the power to do so.

Democracy is just not good in the abstract, it is necessary for the human condition, and the epitome of democracy is responsibility as individuals and communities of people. There cannot be responsibility unless people can make decisions and stand by them or fall by them.[40]

Merton's final comment: "The speech was never given. This was not permitted. The ideas come too close to the nerve."

Ishi: The Last of the "Wild Indians"

Michael Mott, Merton's biographer, reported that in early January 1967, Merton was visited by John Howard Griffin and a friend, Doris Dana who was a literary executor of the late Chilean poet Gabriela Mistral, the only Latin American woman to win the Nobel Peace prize (1945). Ms. Dana knew South America quite well and

40. *IMM*, 14-16.

was well versed in the Indians of South America of whom Merton had an interest, partially through Ernesto Cardenal. But it was their conversation about a new book on Ishi, the last of the Yana peoples of California, that peaked Merton's interest. She promised to send him a copy of the book.[41] In a letter to John Howard Griffin, Merton wrote: "Doris Dana's visit here was very worthwhile from many points of view, and I profited by it. Many ideas and new leads for work, reading, and so on."[42]

Throughout most of the 1960s, Merton increased his reading and writing on the indigenous peoples of the Americas. He read with great interest anthropologist Theodora Kroeber's *Ishi in Two Worlds: A Biography of the Last Wild Indian in North America.* She based her biography of Ishi in part on the work of her late husband Alfred L. Kroeber. Ishi was a member the Yahi sub-tribe of the Yana people of California. Merton produced a reflective reading of the biography, "Ishi: A Meditation," which appeared first in *The Catholic Worker* (1967) and was reprinted in other volumes, including *The Nonviolent Alternative* and *Ishi Means Man.*

"Genocide is a new word," Merton observed. This reflects the heightened power and effectiveness of today's technology which makes it easier to destroy "whole races at once."[43] This does not mean genocide itself is new, but "– just easier." "A century ago white America was engaged in the destruction of entire tribes and ethnic groups of Indians," making little or no distinction between "good" and "bad" Indians, "just so long as they were Indians." Because they were a proud, fearless, and able to make themselves hard-to-find, the Yana Indians of California "were understood to be completely 'savage.'" Gradually moving further into the hills, they took up raiding instead of their traditional hunting and fishing economy. Reprisals by whites were "expected" and "ruthless." The Yahi or Mill Creek Indians "were marked for complete destruction."[44] This mentality was bred earlier in American history by the Puritans who believed this new land to be another biblical "Promised Land," and proceeded to "clear out" the modern equivalents of the idolatrous Canaanites, identifying themselves

41. Michael Mott, *The Seven Mountains of Thomas Merton* (New York: Houghton Mifflin, 1984) 474-75; hereinafter, *SMTM*.
42. Thomas Merton, *The Road to Joy: Letters to New and Old Friends (Letters, 2)*, ed. Robert E. Daggy (New York: Farrar, Straus and Giroux, 1989) 135.
43. *IMM*, 25.
44. *IMM*, 26.

and their mandate with that of the ancient Israelites. Theirs was a divine mission, as was that claimed by the Conquistadores in Latin America.[45] Finally, a small group of the Yahi or Mill Creek Indians in 1870 promised peace and withdrew into the "the hills without a trace." To preserve their identity, they had to stay clear of the white man. Commenting on the Yahi group's solitary plunge into the forests and hills, Merton imagines their impulse to be monastic: "To anyone who has ever felt in himself the stirrings of a monastic or solitary vocation, the notion is stirring. It has implications that are simply beyond Speech."[46]

"Actually, the Indian lived by a deeply religious wisdom which can be called in a broad sense mystical, and that is certainly much more than a 'mystique.'" Although *Ishi Means Man* doesn't deal with specifically religious matters in any depth, Merton gets a strong impression that Ishi was a person "sustained by a deep and unassailable spiritual strength which he never discussed."[47]

Merton refers his readers to the works of William Faulkner, especially his hunting stories like "The Bear," for insights into Native American wisdom. Merton had written elsewhere that Faulkner understood that "[t]he wisdom of the Indian in the wilderness is a kind of knowledge by identification, an intersubjective knowledge, a communion in cosmic awareness and in nature." Faulkner identified indigenous wisdom "as a wisdom based on love: love for the wilderness and for its secret laws. [As] love for the 'spirits' of the wilderness and the cosmic parents (both Mother and Father)."[48]

Given Merton's recognition of the indigenous Americans' intimate and varied relationships with wilderness and its inhabitants, he judged the wanton genocide and biocide unleashed across the continent by Euro-Americans as a great crime committed against both this land's ecological and human communities. "Why do we always assume the Indian is the aggressor? We were in *his* country, we were taking it over for ourselves, and we likewise refused even to share it with him." What myths justified a Euro-American approach to the Indians as "others?" One conceit was that "We were the people of God," quipped Merton, "always in the right, following a manifest destiny." The Native Peoples of America deflected

45. *TMR*, 306.

46. *IMM*, 28.

47. *IMM*, 30.

48. Thomas Merton, *The Literary Essays of Thomas Merton*, ed. Brother Patrick Hart, OCSO (New York: New Directions, 1985) 108; hereinafter, *LE*.

this divine vocation of Euro-Americans. They were categorized as devils obstructing this divine mandate.

A mixture of pseudo-biblical and secular-nationalistic justifications still permeates American rhetoric surrounding war, whether with human enemies or nature. Given the indefensibly violent and brutal history of government treatment of Native Americans, we should have learned something, but "Unfortunately," Merton lamented, "we learned little or nothing about ourselves from the Indian wars!" We certainly haven't adopted the indigenous peoples' sense of a sacred earth with its accompanying morality of respect. Merton asserted that those labeled "savages" often turned out to be the more culturally advanced humans, while those who called themselves "civilized" frequently showed themselves to be the real "barbarians."[49]

> In contrast to the Forty Niners whose morality and morale had crumbled, Ishi and his band remain incorrupt, humane, compassionate, and with their faith intact even unto starvation, pain, and death. The questions then are: what makes for stability? For psychic strength? For endurance, courage, faith?[50]

One is reminded of Merton's 1958 letter to Pablo Antonio Cuadra where he states: "We have an enormous debt to repay to the Indians, and we should begin by recognizing the spiritual richness of the Indian genius."[51] One great source for the "endurance, courage, faith" of Ishi and his people was their mystical or spiritual relationship with the "land," opined Merton. "The Yahi were on their home ground," in Merton's phrasing. He suggested that we "should reflect a little on the relation of the Indian to the land on which he lived. In this sense, most modern men never know what it means to have a "home ground."[52] Merton's use of "home ground," of course, brings us back to the notion both of *oikos* (eco-home) and of "Place" as an ecological value meant to counter the homogeneity of Space and spaces and also of the constant mobility that is characteristic of modernity.

And not coincidentally, a great source of inner strength for the

---

49. *IMM*, 27.
50. Theodora Kroeber quoted in *IMM*, 29.
51. *CT*, 180.
52. *IMM*, 29.

Yahi (and for many indigenous peoples) was the ability to resist and grow from the unjust suffering inflicted on them by the outside invaders. The Yahi, like many, "found strength in the incontrovertible fact that they were in the right. They were not guilt-ridden."[53]

Merton then linked his insights into these paradoxical effects of America's war on its indigenous peoples with the war it was exercising at the time in Vietnam. "Every bomb we drop on a defenseless Asian village, every Asian child we disfigure or destroy with fire only adds to the moral strength of those we wish to destroy for our own profit." And even if the Vietcong have their own flaws, "by an accumulation of injustice done against innocent people we drive them into the arms of our enemies and make our own ideals look like the most pitiful sham." As is evident from this essay on Ishi, Merton recognized an older page in American history in the metaphors associated with "clearing" the jungles of Vietcong and "cleaning out" "hostiles" or "vermin" from a forested area. He noted how settlers and frontiersmen spoke about the *necessity* of "clearing" the woodlands and the plains of savage and hostile Indians. The use of images associated with acts of "cleansing," "purifying," and "clearing out" makes the aggressor seem like someone engaged in a hygienically beneficial task.[54]

Of course, such language glosses over the fact that it is often innocent men, women, and children who are the objects of this "housecleaning" or sanitizing work. At first, this killing of women and children, whether in the Old West or Southeast Asia, was justified as an unintended "side effect" or "consequence" of "something more important" that simply had to be done. Over time, Merton pointed out, there is "more and more killing of civilians and less and less of the 'something more important' which is what we are trying to achieve." Today's modern military weapons make the bombing of areas "infested" with civilians easier than cleaning out the frontier of "dirty injuns." Nevertheless, acts of "ethnic cleansing" whether of "dirty injuns" or "gooks/dinks" are acts of genocide. In many ways, the Vietnam war "seems to have become an extension of our old western frontier, complete with enemies of another, 'inferior' race," concludes Merton. Among the Forty Niners, the saying went that the "only 'good injun,' is a 'dead injun.'"

Myths and images centered on the American "Old West" con-

---

53. *IMM*, 30.
54. *IMM*, 30-31.

cerning the frontier, the land, and "the injuns" were still alive and well in American popular culture in the 1950s and 1960s whether in movies or textbooks or on television. (One could argue that many persist, like giving the code name "Geronimo" to Osama bin Laden when planning his assassination.) As a new frontier, Vietnam allowed us "to continue the cowboys-and-Indians game which seems to be part and parcel of our national identity." Merton then lamented the fact that "so many innocent people have to pay with their lives for our obsessive fantasies." Ishi, true to his peoples' tradition, "never told anyone his real name." The California Indians apparently referred neither to the living nor the dead by their "real," i.e. secret tribal name. Americans never learned the true names of any other member of his "vanished community." It is fitting that, given our blindness to their humanity, "Ishi means simply MAN."[55]

BLACKS, INDIANS, WILDLIFE, AND NATURE

We have looked at only a few examples of places where Merton has spoken with a prophetic voice, criticizing and condemning both the environmental and human destruction wreaked by Euro-Americans, both secular and religious. The focus of this essay is not Merton's dedicated writings on the civil rights movement of the 1950s and 1960s. Merton's involvement in these civil rights movements was multidimensional and multi-cultural. His range of interests included a book on Gandhi (*Gandhi on Non-Violence*), to some direct advice on bringing about social justice like "Letters to a White Liberal" in *Seeds of Destruction*, and to poems reflecting racial violence and tragedies such as "The Children of Birmingham" (*The Collected Poems*). Merton greatly admired Reverend Martin Luther King, Jr., whom he mentions in a letter written to Agnes Smith, a Native American, in April 1968 just weeks after the assassination of King.

In his letter to Smith, he expressed his regret over the past harshness and continuing violence, systemic and physical, towards the Indian and the Black. "Believe me, I understand." He felt "very close" to her "because recently I have been doing some work on the Indians of the Northwest – working on the Ghost Dance movement [*The Geography of Lograire*] . . . I think I have some idea of the suffering and bewilderment of your people out there."[56]

America's moral sickness is evident everywhere if one opens

---

55. *IMM*, 32.
56. *WF*, 339.

one's eyes to its history and current condition. "The sickness is in this country itself, in the injustices committed against the Negro, the Indian, against the wildlife of the country, the beautiful nature God made."[57] Once again, as he did in his letter to pioneering environmental scientist Rachel Carson,[58] Merton identifies a pervasive and deep "sickness" that runs like a root "pattern" throughout much of our culture. This sickness erupts through the surface manifesting its effects in a history of violence and injustice to other races and to "the beautiful nature God made" including its "wildlife." The hermit-monk pointed again to the "awful force for destruction" that lives within us. Though this force is directed outwards towards other humans and nature, at the same time it proves to be "self-destructive."

Merton observed that because of the historical and ideological connections that have existed between the sufferings inflicted on "the black and the red" people, the two groups have the motivation, reason, and opportunity to unite to change the situation. Just as Blacks are in the process of freeing themselves from their internalization of bad images projected onto them by whites, so Agnes and her people must "recover a real sense of your worth" and "see yourself" not through the eyes of whites whose effort has been to degrade and negatively change the Indian, but "as God made you." Indians have to believe in themselves again "as really fine people." Merton suggested that Martin Luther King, Jr.'s message must be taken to heart not only by the Black community but also by Native Americans. "He understood better than anyone that the whole country is sick." Including himself among those concerned with this injustice, Merton insisted that "[w]e cannot afford to be just passive and negative." Action must be taken with love and awareness, an action whose aim is "helping people to remedy their lot."[59]

Martin Luther King, Jr. was killed on April 4, 1968, in Memphis. Merton revealed in a January 1968 letter to Vincent Harding that, while details were still fluid, MLK wanted to come to Gethsemani in the spring for a retreat. In the same letter, Merton mentions his present self-education on civil rights and African-American history, but also on the history of the American Indian. He finds "the idea of a history that is lily white . . . just monstrous." Merton

---

57. *WF*, 339.
58. *WF*, 70-72.
59. *WF*, 340.

tells Harding that "I am with you in wanting to see it all through the eyes of the black and the red."[60]

PART II

VISIONS, DREAMS, AND CALLINGS:
ILLUMINATION AND GROWTH

We have an enormous debt to repay to the Indians, and we should begin by recognizing the spiritual richness of the Indian religious genius.

There is great hope for the world in the spiritual emancipation of the Indians.

Thomas Merton, *The Courage for Truth*

In 1967 Merton studied a newly published work, *Two Leggings: The Making of a Crow Warrior* by Peter Nabakov (1967). Merton would meet Nabakov in person on a rare trip to the southwest in May, 1968.[61] Nabokov's work was the inspiration for one of Merton's reflective reviews: "War and Vision: The Autobiography of a Crow Indian" (*The Catholic Worker,* 1967), also collected with other essays in *Ishi Means Man.* Merton had high praise for the work, considering it "one of the most fascinating autobiographies published in this century." Nabakov's text presented a series of conversations fifty years earlier between Two Leggings and an interpreter. He had edited and given the exchange historical context.

We can assume from Merton's lengthy opening remarks that he already had a basic understanding of the importance of visions and dreams to most indigenous peoples of North America. For Two Leggings, the meaning of biography or a human life, "consists primarily in a series of visions," Merton observed. As a result, "his life is his 'medicine.'" His biography in some sense is a tale of how over the years his medicine bundle was put together under spiritual guidance.[62]

"The practice of 'fasting for a vision' was once almost universal among North American Indians for whom a certain level of 'mysticism' was an essential part of growing up." "The Indian"

---

60. *WF*, 242-243.
61. *IMM*, 17.
62. *IMM*, 21.

would base his or her future "on a spiritual illumination beyond
the ordinary conscious level of psychic experience." While the
initial vision-fast was usually a feature of a rite of passage from
childhood to adulthood, ritual fasts "and solitary retreats" were
frequently undertaken throughout one's lifetime. "Such visions
were taken for granted as a normal part of life in archaic culture."
In fact, "a well-integrated and purposeful existence could hardly
be conceived" without them.

The one fasting initially "sought a personal encounter with a
clearly recognizable spirit-friend, a protector whom he felt destined
to meet . . . not just any spirit [but] his spirit, his 'vision person.'"
Such an encounter was more than an act of seeing or knowing,
more than just an "experience." It "changed the course of the seer's
entire life" or perhaps more accurately "it was what gave his life
a 'course' to begin with." Throughout his life, the seer would be
alert for signs or messages sent by his own or other spirit-persons in
dreams, in encounters with certain animals or through unexpected
events, etc. Their content could be positive, containing advice to
assist him as hunter or warrior, or cautionary, warning him about
certain actions or places or individuals. A seer might seek additional
power or guidance from his vision-person through fasts, the Sun
Dance (for Plains Indians), or other traditional means including
ecstatic dancing.[63]

Discerning the meaning of the often complex messages from
and behaviors of a vision person was rarely left to the seer alone.
This was especially the case during the initiatory vision but also
when a later vision or dream seemed to contain a warning that could
affect the well-being of the whole community. The seer, usually
anxious, had to seek out further "comment and approval from the
more experienced men of the tribe, the elders, the medicine men and
the chiefs [who] had a better and more accurate knowledge of the
language of vision." What was revealed on the mountaintop or in the
forest or on the plains was open to several levels of interpretation.

"Medicine balls" were a feature of the vision-quest of many
tribes. The contents of these bundles "had been assembled under
the explicit direction of the vision person" to empower, protect, and
heal the visionary. The medicine ball was an extension or embodi-
ment of the vision-person and in some cases might be considered a
"person" itself. A bundle might contain "fragments of animal skin,

63. *IMM*, 17-18.

bone, rock or herbs."[64]

As for dreams, Irving Hallowell noted that "Whereas social relations with human beings belong to the sphere of waking life, the most intimate social interaction with other-than-human persons is experienced chiefly, but not exclusively, by the self in the dream."[65] Some peoples unite the spiritual presences in the bundle (usually associated with the sacred figures who exist in the Bush) with their own night time experience of entering the world of dreams. This world is at a level "spatially" that corresponds to the temporal mythic time and hence with the sacred animals and plants that one can encounter in the bush when one's mind or spirit is receptive.

A classic example, according to Robin Ridington, can be found among the Beaver Indians where men traditionally slept with their heads pointing towards the east. A medicine bundle usually hung above a man's head, tied to one of the poles of the lean-to. At night it might provide both protection and informative dreams. During the day it remained in its place and children were warned about touching it, and some who did touch it claimed to feel something alive and powerful move from within the bundle.[66] And although children undergo an experiential shift into adulthood with help from the medicine animal they encounter in the vision-fast in the forest, they "do not find their medicines then, but they do find the path that will lead them to this discovery later on. It is a path of dreaming and singing." "The Beaver word for medicine is *mayine*, his or its song," explains Ridington, "and the central symbol of a man's medicine dream is a song given to him by his medicine animal."[67] The song goes back to mythic times.

Merton found a special spiritual resonance with stories or accounts of visions from the mouths of individuals who have experienced the personal and life-altering effects of visions and ongoing encounters with their "vision-person." These storied experiences make one realize that there "was really a deep psychological validity to this way of life" which cannot be adequately understood or explained away by notions of superstition, magical thinking, or mental

64. *IMM*, 119.

65. Irving Hallowell, "The Role of Dreams in Ojibwa Culture," *The Dream and Human Societies*, eds. G. E. von Grunebaum and Roger Callois (Berkeley: University of California Press, 1966) 274.

66. Sam D. Gill, *Native American Traditions: Sources and Interpretations* (Belmont, CA: Wadsworth Publ. Co., 1983) 22; hereinafter, *NAT*.

67. *NAT*, 24.

fantasies. These people "inherited an archaic wisdom which did somehow protect them against the dangers of a merely superficial, willful and cerebral existence [and] did somehow integrate their personality in such a way that the conscious mind was responsive to deep unconscious sources of awareness."[68]

VOCATION, CALLING, AND VISION

During one of a series of conferences that Merton gave to contemplative nuns at the Abbey of Gethsemani in December 1967, he refers to an article on "the primitive concept of vocation." He wove together some interesting similarities between Native American rituals and the Christian concept of a "calling" to the Religious Life.[69]

"In Native American societies there are built-in rituals for young people." Generalizing a bit, Merton claimed that when a boy "in an Indian tribe" is approaching maturity and is deemed ready to take the step into official adulthood or manhood, "he has to go through a difficult experience." All alone, he climbs to a mountaintop or the top of a cliff or to some other remote and often "desolate and perilous place." He abstains from food. Although Merton claimed he went without human support, this was not always true, even if the support was from a short distance behind a rock or other barrier.

The young man marked off a certain area with "talismans" to mark the boundaries of his sacred space. Ideally, the young man would fast and pray for several days and nights until he had a vision or a powerful message. Merton then went on to "translate" the vision-quest in language that aimed for an inter-religious understanding. "The young man is supposed to come into contact with what is called his 'vision-person,' that is to say, not only his true self, his transcendent self, but almost what we would call his guardian angel, a spirit-being who will henceforth guide him in his hunting, his fighting, and everything." From then on, throughout his life, the young man would be expected to obey his spirit-being. Elders of the tribe would work with him. Merton emphasized that it is "all very serious." Merton suggested that the visionary undergoes a "death." He died to his shallow self, becoming humble and open to his deeper or true self. It is at the moment when the visionary

---

68. *IMM*, 20.
69. *SOC*, 68.

"died" that he experienced the "spirit-person."[70]

SOMETHING WITHIN NEEDS RELEASE:
THE DEPTHS OF NATIVE AMERICAN SPIRITUALITY

Merton spent a couple of weeks in Alaska (September 17-October 2, 1968) on his way to India and Thailand during his Asian journey. Among other activities, such as looking for possible hermitage sites in the incredibly majestic and rich landscape, he gave conferences to nuns and priests. During a workshop that touched on prayer, tradition, and the importance of religious experience, Merton turned again to Native American spirituality and practices. He discussed the importance in the western monastic tradition of men of the spirit or spiritual mentors who were able to wield a profound influence on the spiritual growth and development of young monks. Found among the early Desert Fathers, these mentors were part of Asian traditions such as Hinduism and Buddhism, and among certain indigenous traditions of North America. The effective dynamic of the spiritual practices that were mentored by spirit men and women drew upon universal themes connected with self-renunciation and illumination, the death of the superficial self, and the birth of a new deeper identity. While Christian spirituality related these experiences to participating in the Christ-Mystery of the Cross (or Death and Resurrection), Merton found a similar dynamic present in the spiritual training and disciplines found in Native American religions.

> I have studied some of our own Indians' spiritual training. In almost any tribe the young Indian had to go through a kind of novitiate. He was sent off into the mountains, into some rugged place perhaps on the top of a cliff, to fast and pray. He was given instructions beforehand on what to do and he would mark out an area with the points of the compass, which made it into a cross-shaped place, and he had to stay within that area. While he was there fasting and praying he was supposed to have a vision (that was the object of his being there), and this vision would be of his own spirit-person. It was really a discovery of one's own deeper self. There was something in himself that had been released by this period of fasting and praying alone.

---

70. *SOC*, 69.

He had access to a deeper level of his own being, a sort
of sixth sense.[71]

Merton claimed that this type of spiritual practice should be "really
interesting" to monastics "because we don't have anything like this
anymore." Nor did much remain of the tradition of the "spiritual
father" who would work with, mentor, and serve as an example for
a younger monk or novice. What such a tradition offered is an elder
or spiritually mature monk or seasoned member of an indigenous
community who "knows intuitively how to bring out what is deepest
in a person." "Believe me, that is what we really need." Merton
asserted that religious orders, especially the strictly contemplative
ones, no longer needed more information and theology. Like the
Indians, monastics needed "a release from all that is deepest in us
that we would like to have access to." "We know it is there, and
yet we can't get it."

Merton's insights in Alaska resonate with the studies of sensitive anthroplogists like Robin Ridington:

I cannot tell you what "really happens" to children in the
bush, just as they cannot tell other people their experience
directly. I was told that, if a child has the right thoughts, if
his head is in the right place, a medicine animal will come
to him. There is a moment of meeting and transformation
when he is in a dream-like state. In this experience, he can
understand the animal's speech, and the animal speaks to
him. It may seem to him that he stays with the animal for
days or weeks. The animal usually tells him when to leave.
. . .. It is clear that the experience . . . is fundamentally
the beginning of a path of seeking to understand his own
humanity.[72]

Merton's use of the death-rebirth and Cross symbolism reso-
nates with the findings of Joan Halifax. For her, this discovery of
one's humanity or move into a deeper state of consciousness and
awareness and a religiously important status in one's culture (perhaps even as a shaman) often involves a "death/rebirth" experience.
She sees it as common to all serious spiritual traditions, whether the

71. Thomas Merton, *Thomas Merton in Alaska: The Alaskan Conferences,
Journals, and Letters*, ed. Robert E. Daggy (New York: New Directions, 1988)
121-122.
72. Robin Ridington, "Beaver Dreaming and Singing," in Gill, *NAT*, 23.

experience occurs suddenly or gradually. In her valuable anthology, *Shamanic Voices*, she notes that:

> Certain potential shamans are given explicit instructions that, if properly carried out, will surely transform his or her awareness so dramatically that an experience of death and rebirth is inevitable. The spontaneous experience of death and rebirth is also found among the Plains Indians of North America. It can occur during the Sun Dance, in which flesh is given or pierced, or on the occasion of a vision quest associated with puberty or other important passages in a person's life. All such events include a period of purification, isolation, and frequently body mortification.[73]

Piers Vitebsky, drawing upon a study of shamanism in polar and sub-polar areas, especially in Siberia, states that "The symbolism of transformation and rebirth is often very clear." Many candidates come to understand "the true nature of things by being dismembered and reassembled as someone greater and more complete than before."[74] The symbolism and experience of dismemberment/ rememberment can be quite dramatic especially in the call to become a shaman. The "old self" is literally pulled apart and a new self is formed from the remnants but enhanced with new and richer spiritual power.

In a mid-January 1968 letter to Eugene Setiore, Merton noted that there is a level of Native American spirituality and mythology where a human being . . .

> is represented in his existential nakedness, helplessness, loneliness, and in which the ambiguities and shortcomings of his culture are emphasized. The chaotic, the evil, and the mendacious in cultural establishments are made clear. But then other, deeper initiations are proposed and man discovers his helplessness in order to transcend it with the help of the spirits and gods. In so doing he transcends the limits of his present culture, renews himself, and in so doing renews his culture.[75]

---

73. Joan Halifax, editor *Shamanic Voices: A Survey of Visionary Narratives* (New York: Viking Penguin Books, 1991) 7.

74. Piers Vitebsky, "Shamanism," in *Indigenous Religions: A Companion*, ed. Graham Harvey (London: Cassell Publishers, 2000) 60.

75. *WF*, 339.

It might be problematic, then, to reduce primitive or aboriginal or indigenous religious life to the purely material and cultural level, in effect, projecting western functional and materialistic values onto all rites of passage, vision quests, shamanistic callings, etc. Merton (and to some extent Hallowell, Ridington, Halifax, and others) are not afraid to suggest that individuals can "transcend" their culture and their ego-self, to renew themselves and through their guiding, healing, invoking activities to renew their culture. Merton's rich knowledge of the spiritual life in its many forms and within many traditions, as well as his own experience, helped him break through the western anthropologically conservative descriptions and interpretations of the spiritual life and experiences of Native Americans. He located them within the "wisdom traditions" with which he was becoming more familiar and finding more universal.

NATIVE AMERICAN WOMEN AND "CALLINGS"

Merton focused on the initiatory visions among young men in his remarks on Nabakov's book as well as when he compared them with the spiritual journey of monks. He realized, however, that there were female puberty rituals as well as "callings" to be healers or to exercise other special arts among almost all Native religions of North America.

During the conference to contemplative nuns in 1967, Merton discussed the topic of women and their experience of a "calling" or vocation. He began by pointing to an article he had read about the "primitive concept of vocation." A vocation "can come along without someone intending it." Furthermore, it might also be the case that the path ahead does not tell one exactly "where it is going to lead." Likewise, the vocation might not be simply carrying out a neatly defined role or leading a life controlled by established norms. It is more like "feeling one's way towards new possibilities in ways of thinking and working." One stage opens out into another. "This reminds us that a vocation is essentially open-ended, not something contained." It is "a creative possibility, leading to things we never suspected."[76]

Merton notes that "normally girls of the tribe do not go through" the type of initiatory rites that boys do, "unless they are going to be medicine women." Merton considered medicine women to be "a contemplative and prophetic elite in the tribe." Usually, the

---

76. *SOC*, 68.

candidates have already exhibited a sensitive – even nervous – disposition because "it's taken for granted that, if you are going to be a contemplative, you are also going to be a very sensitive person." The girl may have "a rough time" on the way to finally accepting "her vocation, her destiny." Merton saw this path as "akin to a deep religious conversion, one of the phenomena of adolescence. It frees the girl from her mother." Merton suggested that the lesson to be learned was that "there's no real freedom unless you go through a serious crisis which delivers you from dependence on other people." Such a crisis for the young Indian woman involved a certain distancing of herself from others so that she will have the time and space to be prepared for "real giving" when she returns.

For the young woman, these first experiences might be full of "great conflict." As she accepts and "surrenders to her vocation," the conflict subsides. Having experienced conversion and transformation, "her psychic energy is now focused on new interests and tasks." She seems to be more "self-possessed," more "dignified" and her actions are "marked by charity." Her interest in other people grows as she exercises her "power to allay and cure their ills."[77]

One example of what Merton was alluding to concerning an Indian woman's call to a role as a particular kind of healer, can be found in an illuminating work by John Grim.[78] Dr. Grim relates the story of a young Ojibway named Sky Woman whose beloved adopted grandmother was very ill. One night as Sky Woman was sleeping, a vision-person appeared to her in a dream, reminding Sky Woman of the time when she was young and distraught, lost and wandering alone in the forest. It was then that her vision-person appeared to her and "called" her to become a medicine woman, more specifically, a *nanandawi* (one who cures by sucking out the evil disease). Unfortunately, Sky Woman had forgotten all about that dream-vision call. Aware of that, the vision-person repeated her instructions on the techniques and implements to use during a healing ceremony. Not coincidentally, the sick elder-woman had been a member of the search party that found Sky Woman those many years ago. She subsequently took such loving care of the forlorn young woman that Sky Woman adopted her as her grand-

77. *SOC*, 69-70.
78. John Grim, *The Shaman: Patterns of Religious Healing Among the Ojibway Indians* (Norman, OK: University of Oklahoma Press, 1983); hereinafter, *SPRH*.

mother. As Grim notes, her calling and initiation into becoming a *nanandawi* had two stages. The first was when, as a girl wandering in the forest, she met her vision-person in the initial dream-vision, was called to the vocation of a *nanandawi* healer, and was instructed on its method of healing. The second was the "spontaneous dream initiation" which occurred when her grandmother was ill, and Sky Woman was called upon and offered the knowledge, power, and skills taught to her years ago.[79]

As Grim noted, the performance of this shamanic ritual by Sky Woman went deeper than merely a display of magical techniques. These were "the actions of an individual aggressively evoking unique personalistic powers in which she trusted." She assumed "the heroic qualities of a shaman" and the sacrificial ethos that would empty her of self and fill her with sacred power to be mediated to her people. All of this expressed "a worldview of personalistic contact with sacred power that is accessible for healing."[80] Sky Woman used a rattle, chanted *Manitou kazo* (talking like a Manitou or Manitou-talking) and performed sucking techniques to remove the illness.

Other rites also describe a change in consciousness and identity among young women. *The Sunrise Dance* is a beautiful and power-ful rite of passage to womanhood among the Mescalero Apache (a similar ceremony is called the *kinaalda* among the Navajo). According to Ines Talamantez, a pubescent girl becomes a woman by uniting with and embodying the power of Isanaklesh (Earth Mother, or Changing Woman among the Navajo). In addition to increasing her life-giving fertility (connected to the Earth also), the ceremony endows her with the powers of Isanaklesh that can be used for the well-being of the wider community whether to grow crops, to heal illness or to assure a long life-span.

> Mescalero Apache believe that, as each initiate is trans-formed into Isanaklesh, our mother, the earth, the world itself is again created. Each time a girl's life is celebrated through the ceremony, the earth is celebrated as well. The Mescaleros view the initiate's changing body in the same way they view the changes that occur in the springtime in the natural world. What is important in both cases is that the balance, symmetry and harmony seen in the natural world

---

79. *SPRH*, 123-124.
80. *SPRH*, 125.

are the most important criteria for the ways in which human bodies, and especially the bodies of the female initiates are intimately related and seen as one.[81]

Four days of ritual activity (like the four seasons) are followed by four days of meditative isolation. It is a lengthy and richly symbolic period during which the girl goes through three stages: *separation* from family and usual activities; *transition* or entering into a "State of liminality" during which traditional Apache wisdom and knowledge are "inscribed in her;" and *incorporation,* where she returns to the tribe but now with new status, new powers (exercised first by blessing members of the community who so desire it). In short, through "sacred songs which generate *dye,* power," the girl "is transformed into the deity and finally into a new Apache woman."[82] The young women experience a shift in consciousness and identity similar to that experienced in a different context by young men. Since Merton had read *The Sacred Pipe*, he would have been long familiar with Black Elk's description of the Lakota (Oglala) "Preparing a Girl for Womanhood" ceremony.[83]

PROPHETS, VISIONS, AND THE GHOST DANCE

Although Merton did not deal at length with the history and variety of Native American "prophets" whose "call" usually came from a high deity who had the power to direct actions for a whole tribe or even for a pan-Indian movement, he studied one of its dramatic revitalization movements: The Ghost Dance.

As was mentioned in Part One, John Howard Griffin and Doris Dana visited Merton for a couple of days in early January of 1967. New interests arose from his conversations with Professor Dana who later sent the monk a book on Ishi by Theodora Kroeber. Importantly, he was also to receive from anthropologist Cora DuBois a copy of her study, "The 1870 Ghost Dance."[84] For one of his long poems, Merton borrowed events, names, and some

81. Ines Talamantez, "In the Space Between Earth and Sky: Contemporary Mescalero Apache Ceremonialism," *Native Religions and Cultures of North America, Anthropology of the Sacred*, ed. Lawrence E. Sullivan (New York: Continuum, 2000) 143; hereinafter, *NRC*.

82. *IES*, 158-159.

83. Joseph Epes Brown, *The Sacred Pipe: The Seven Rites of the Oglala Sioux* (Norman, OK: University of Oklahoma Press, 1953) 116-126; hereinafter, *SP*.

84. Cora DuBois, "The 1870 Ghost Dance," *Anthropological Records*, vol. 3 no. 1 (Berkeley: University of California Press, 1939); hereinafter, *1870GD*.

direct quotes from DuBois' informants and visionaries. Merton creatively integrated theses with comments and background notes into short stanzas of verse and prose into sections III. GHOST DANCE: Prologue and IV. GHOST DANCE of the final canto "WEST" of his long experimental work of poetry and prose, *The Geography of Lograire.* In a letter dated November 7, 1967, Merton excitedly announced: "I have been working on the Ghost Dance Canto of Lograire. Goes like a charm! Everything there in Cora DuBois mimeograph report from Berkeley. Beautiful, haunting, sad stuff. All you have to do is quote the Indians' own words!"[85]

Although Merton's untimely death in December of 1968 prohibited him from writing the final revision of *Geography of Lograire,* it was, nevertheless, published in 1969. Patrick F. O'Connell, at the beginning of his wonderful treatment of *Lograire* in *The Thomas Merton Encyclopedia,* calls it "a single unified work, epic in scope, alternating sections of verse and prose." He also points out that the work's overall theme "is both the global unity of humanity and the ways in which that unity has been violated, particularly by Western assertions of cultural and moral superiority."[86] In the "Author's Note" preceding this first draft of *Lograire,* Merton's cautionary comments should be taken to heart by the reader who plans to launch into the poem, including "West," containing the two sections on the Ghost Dance:

> This is a purely tentative first draft of a longer work in progress, in which there are, necessarily, many gaps. This is only a beginning of patterns, the first opening up of the dream.
>
> . . . In this wide-angle mosaic of poems and dreams, I have without scruple mixed what is my own experience with what is almost everybody else's. Thus "Cargo" and "Ghost Dance," for instance, cease to be bizarre anomalies and are experienced as yours and mine as well as "theirs." But for this to be true, what is given in "Cargo" and "Ghost Dance" is most often literal and accurate quotation with slight editing and with of course much personal rearrange-

85. *SMTM,* letter in "Restricted Journal," 638, n. 15.

86. Patrick O'Connell, *The Thomas Merton Encyclopedia,* eds. William H. Shannon, Christine M. Bochen, and Patrick O'Connell (Maryknoll, NY: Orbis Books, 2002) 169.

ment. And where more drastic editing is called for by my dream, well, I have dreamed it.[87]

If one looks at just a few passages from letters in which Merton gives some clues to when and how he is structuring *Lograire*, one sees both the agony and ecstasy and a bit of the parody. As early as April 1967, Merton tells Nicanor Parra that "I keep working – I am busy with a long poem." (This was obviously before he had the DuBois article.)[88] The prior day he had written: "I am also in the middle of a new long and mad poem . . .."[89] In October he sent an enthusiastic but cautionary note along with a tape of *Lograire* to his much admired former Columbia University Professor and friend, Mark Van Doren.

> Today I am mailing you a tape. Mysteries of all kinds. On the top side is the new work I am doing, *The Geography of Lograire*, a big poem about every thing under the sun. . . . It may take some getting used to!! I don't expect this to do much more than bewilder the reader when in print, but myself I do feel there is something going on here. What, God knows.[90]

In November he wrote "Lately I have been drawn into some absorbing work on the cargo cults and other apocalyptic movements which spring up here and there and everywhere . . . a long poem which is growing and evolving all the time. Perhaps an apocalypse of our own."[91]

Merton has explained (partially) why his treatment of the Ghost Dance will require both some context building and some tough decisions as to how he will shape the stanzas, what quotes he will include and which ones he will exclude, as well as how to order the whole work. Those individuals with little understanding of The Ghost Dance Movement (whether the 1870 or 1890 phase or some hazy forerunners), or of the study by Cora DuBois, will understandably find themselves scratching their heads at times. Although Merton's treatment is short and challenging, he obviously

---

87. Thomas Merton, *The Collected Poems of Thomas Merton* (New York: New Directions, 1977) 457; hereinafter, *CP*.
88. *CT*, 214.
89. *CT*, 230.
90. *WF*, 138-139.
91. *CT*, 108.

considered it important to his efforts at encountering and understanding religious movements from many traditions and seeing both their similarities to and sometimes borrowings from one another. He certainly recognized that the visions and messages of these "prophets," as well as their efforts to grasp a new view of history, resonated with the Biblical ideas of the prophet and of the "end times." According to Ake Hultkrantz, the title *Ghost Dance* itself "refers to the ritual round-dances that were thought to imitate the dances of the dead and were performed to precipitate the renewal of the world and the return of the dead."[92]

Merton's first part, III. GHOST DANCE: Prologue is historically out of synchronization with the second section, IV. GHOST DANCE but it does provide a poignant insight into the spirit of the movement and hopefully stokes the reader's interest. The statement in Section III, made by a Sioux, American Horse, to the government agent of Pine Ridge Reservation, originally occurred in conjunction with the 1890 Ghost Dance. American Horse spoke just a month before the horrendous massacre of Sioux men, women, and children by the U.S. military at Wounded Knee and which, while it didn't end all outbursts of the Dance, did send the overall movement into a much more modest last phase.

Among other things, American Horse in Merton's poetic rendering complains that . . .

We were made promises by the Commissioners but
We never heard from them since.
They talked nice to us and after we signed they took our
Land cut down our rations.
They made us believe we would get full sacks if we signed
But instead our sacks are empty . . .

When we were in Washington the President
The Secretary the Commissioners promised
We would get back a million lbs. of beef . . .
But the Commissioner
Refused
To give us
Any meat.[93]

---

92. *NRC*, 201.
93. *CP*, 587.

These words spring out of a history of betrayals, out of desperate conditions marked by the slaughter by whites of the last herds of bison; by an all-out assault on northern Plains cultures and religions; and by the condescending and demeaning treatment of the newly reservationized Sioux. These betrayals included residential boarding schools which ripped children from out of their native culture and sought to indoctrinate them into the ways of the dominant culture (and almost always its dominant religion).

IV. GHOST DANCE takes us back to the 1870 Ghost Dance, concentrated West of the Rockies. Merton's "Dr. Sam" (an informant of Cora DuBois') claims that "Wodziwob was the real Starter" of the 1870 Ghost Dance movement. However, during the 1850s and 1860s, an earlier version of the Ghost Dance was initiated by Smohalla (1815-1895), a dreamer and prophet. He was a Wanapum who operated near the Columbia River in the present day Washington state.[94] The indigenous peoples of that area were already suffering from economically and culturally destructive forces. After having disappeared from his tribe for a couple of years, Smohalla returned with messages given to him in dreams and visions. He took a leadership role in a revivalist or revitalization movement called "The Dreamers." He preached a return to traditional ways, a rejection of the ways of the whites (including the blasphemous digging into Mother Earth through farming) and a refusal of their corrupting goods (including alcohol). He predicted "an impending destruction and renewal of the world during which the dead would return" and whites and others would be removed. His followers were to perform a ritual with drums, bells, and dancing in which ecstatic feelings and visions would occur. Many sought guidance through "dreams," hence, their name "The Dreamers." His following increased during the 1870s.

Among his admirers were Chief Joseph and the Nez Perce. Smohalla and his admirers had borrowed some Christian eschatological and apocalyptic views probably because they resonated with what felt to them like the end of their "world" and their being cast in a new linear view of history. "The Dreamers" movement was relatively small but probably had some influence on the rise and spread of the 1870 Ghost Dance movement. It was effective for decades in keeping Indian removal and hence the influx of white

---

94. Sam D. Gill, *Native American Religions: An Introduction*, 2d ed. (Belmont, CA: Wadsworth/Thomson, 2005) 121.

settlers down even after Smohalla's death.

Around 1869, Wodziwob, a Northern Paiute or Paviotso from the Walker Lake Reservation in Nevada, had a series of visions prophesying the destruction of the present world, including whites, through a severe earthquake, and the return of the Indian dead along with the game animals, and the entrance of Native Peoples into a new age.[95] Merton's poem quotes one of Cora DuBois' informants: "Dr. Sam said Wodziwob was the real Starter. Four Paiute men from Surprise went to hear him."[96] Wodziwob's messages had their skeptics, and in response to opposition or a waning of belief, he experienced other visions, some of which modified or clarified his teachings and others that intensified his warnings to those who did not believe. He predicted, for example, that only those Indians who believed in his message would be spared in the upcoming destruction, while the unbelievers would perish with the whites.[97] Later, Wodziwob, or perhaps his disciple Weneyuga, who is also mentioned in DuBois and *Geography of Lograire*, added prophecies about a train coming from the east within four years, carrying the dead.[98] Wodzibwob is quoted in *Lograire*: "There are a lot of people telling the new, but they are not telling it right." (This might also indicate the fact that some of the "messages" connected with previous visions had been superseded or that there might also have been some twisting of his teachings.) Wodziwob affirms: "What I said was: 'A train is coming' and my real dream was about that train."[99] But there arose differences over whether the dead would come in a train.

Before his death in 1872, Wodziwob also altered his message concerning the end times to emphasize racial equality. "All peoples, including white people, would be granted eternal life after the destruction of the world and the return of the dead."[100] "The Starter said the dead were on their way with the Supreme Ruler . . . all coming in a group. There was to be '[n]o distinction . . . any more between races.'"[101] The Starter also encouraged much dancing in

95. *NRC*, 201.
96. *CP*, 588
97. James Mooney, *The Ghost Dance Religion and Wounded Knee* (New York: Dover Publications, 1896) 702; hereinafter, *GDR*.
98. *1870GD*, 3-4.
99. *CP*, 588.
100. *GDR*, 203.
101. *CP*, 589.

anticipation of the return. For some this dancing involved contact with the dead. There were to be five nights of dancing with bodies painted but with "no preaching against the whites." The songs to be sung had been acquired in dreams by men who journeyed to the "Land of the Dead." Dancers went into trances and many "fainted."

But the messages were still changing. Weneyuga ("Dr. Frank", i.e. Frank Spencer) continued preaching and may have been the one who revived the prophecy that whites would indeed disappear when the dead appeared. When the train carrying the dead failed to appear, "The Washo doctors said Dr. Frank was an imposter. He headed north with one disciple." Weneyuga simply returned to his status as a shaman/medicine man. But, as Merton's stanzas indicate, there were other "doctors" and prophets, and the other dances (Warm House Dance, etc.) to continue the tradition.

By 1880 much of the movement begun by Wodziwob had died out. Merton seems to end his poem's relation of events on a pessimistic note. First, in Stanza 30: "Annie Peterson (an informant) said Coquille Charlie (a later sponsor of the dances) carried the dance around only to make money. He did not say the dead would return or tell what would happen to the whites. Nobody had any visions at Charlie's dance." Then in the final Stanza: "After a while the dreaming stopped, and the Dream Dance turned into a Feather Dance. It was just a fun dance. It was mostly a white man's show."[102]

As already noted, Merton only deals with the 1890 Ghost Dance in the "Prologue," quoting a speech given by the Sioux, American Horse. We shall briefly place that speech in some historical context. The 1890 Ghost Dance was sparked by the prophetic visions of Wovoka (1856-1932), a Northern Paiute living in Nevada. His father may have been a follower of Wodziwob and a shaman or medicine man among the Paiutes (a "calling" that Wovoka would also answer). Wovoka was also known as Jack Wilson, a name given by the Wilson family on whose ranch he had worked since childhood. The Wilsons also gave him instructions in the Bible and Christian thought. By the late 1880s, Wovoka was notable among his people for his extraordinary shamanic powers, especially regarding the weather. Wovoka's knowledge of the Biblical tradition was also important to his message and status as a prophet.

During the solar eclipse of January 1, 1889, he had a visionary experience out of which came the message that the Indian dead

---

102. *CP*, 593.

would be resurrected and return and that there would be peace with the whites. But for this to happen, warned Wovoka, not only his people but all Indians had to reform their lives and perform the Ghost Dance, a five-day ceremony during which the dead would be called back to life and participation in the creation of a new era if not a new world. The center of this ceremony was the familiar "round dance." Many recognized Wovoka's message and the "Ghost Dance" like Wozdiwob's.[103]

The Lakota and other Plains Indians had recently suffered devastating losses to the bison herds (nearly extinct by 1884), the loss of much of their freedom and mobility through the military and governmental take-over of their lands, and victimization by broken promises, as White Horse had mentioned. The Lakota and other nations sent delegations to hear the prophecies and advice of Wovoka as more and more of the Northern Plains peoples were caught up in the movement. Wovoka's message and the Ghost Dance, claims Hultkrantz, "spread like fire among the Plains Indians."

There were some modifications to Wovoka's message, especially among the more militant Lakota, inferring that the Indians would be given the power to drive the whites out. Their own visionaries revealed that the wearing of special white ghost shirts (possibly a Mormon borrowing) would protect the Sioux from the bullets of the white soldiers and settlers. Fear rose among whites. The over-reaction of white soldiers included the massacre of 200 men, women, and children in a camp along Wounded Knee Creek on the Pine Ridge Reservation. This might well have brought the end to the Ghost Dance movement, but it continued for a bit longer. And its legacy was not as dispiriting as some suggest. According to Sam Gill:

> The 1890 Ghost Dance movement played a major role in bringing together and unifying people that had previously had little association. It diffused among them new religious patterns, which were adapted in a variety of ways to maintain some continuity with the old religious traditions. [Other changes] in the 1880s . . . promoted the rise of an Indian distinct from a tribal identity among the Plains people.[104]

---

103. Abe Hultkrantz, "Ghost Dance" in *NAR*, 202.
104. *NAR*, 123.

CONCLUSION: MERTON'S VISION: INDIAN LIBERATION
AS GROUNDS FOR WIDER HOPE

"Let me be quite succinct," Merton warns in "A Letter to Pablo Antonio Cuadra Concerning Giants," "the greatest sin of the West is above all *its unmitigated arrogance toward the rest of the human race.*" And the ironic result of this has been the West's slide into barbarism, a barbarism that is now springing "*from within itself.*" At root, this condition is due to a "twofold disloyalty: to God and to Man." For the Christian who fully understands the meaning of the Incarnation, "this is not two disloyalties but one." Why is this so? Because to state that, "the Word was made flesh," is to say not only that God is in humankind, but that "God is in *all [humans].*" Therefore every human being is "to be seen and treated as Christ."[105]

Merton did not object to Christian Europe's desire to "bring Christ to the Indians." Their real failure "was in their inability to *encounter Christ* already potentially present in the Indians." Instead of entering into dialogue with them, "they imposed their own monologue, and in preaching Christ, they also preached themselves." By utilizing this monologic approach, they ruled out listening to the other, which also meant that they "omitted to listen to the voice of Christ in the unfamiliar accents of the Indian, as Clement had listened for it in the pre-Socratics."[106] This dual act of *listening* and *hearing* for and to the voice of Christ in the stranger was almost totally missing among missionaries and Church leaders. The spiritual riches thereby ignored hurt the Church in the Americas and closed America off from something essential to its ecological and human well-being and sustainability.

Merton believed, as did Clement of Alexandria, that God speaks unpredictably and in unpredictable places. "The Holy Spirit is 'blowing where he pleases' (*John* 3:8) and he is everywhere." The sad truth is that "if we cannot see him unexpectedly in the stranger and the alien, we will not understand him even in the Church." Merton asked, "How can we reveal to others what we cannot discover in them ourselves?"[107] "Our task now is to learn that if we can voyage to the ends of the earth and find *ourselves* in the aborigine who most differs from ourselves, we will have made a fruitful pilgrimage." At the end of this long journey, we will see "that the stranger we meet there is no

---

105. *TMR*, 305.
106. *TMR*, 307.
107. *TMR*, 307-308.

other than ourselves – which is the same as saying that we find Christ in him." "If the Lord is risen, as He said, He is actually or potentially alive in every man."[108]

As early as 1958 in a private letter to Antonio Pablo Cuadra, Merton worked out the terrible implications of Christian violence towards Native Peoples or aborigines. He suggested that the Cross is a powerful symbol of the pain and suffering inflicted on the Christ already present in Native Peoples of both hemispheres for nearly 500 years. This fact should be a call for Christians to become prophets who proclaim, work for, and in their hearts trust that a Resurrection of that crucified Christ will manifest itself through the vital outflowing of Indian culture and spirituality. In powerful words, Merton proclaimed that we have . . .

> a tremendous and marvelous vocation, the vocation of being *Americans*, that is to say, of being and of forming the true America that is the Christ of the Americas: the Christ that was born among the Indians already many centuries ago, who manifested himself in the Indian culture, before the coming of official Christianity: the Christ that has been crucified for centuries on this great cross of our double continent; the Christ that is agonizing on this same cross; when will the hour of the Resurrection of the Christ of our Americas come? We can and should be prophets of its advent.[109]

It would have made a huge difference if the Conquerors and Colonizers who claimed to be Christian would have believed and acted on Merton's affirmation that "God speaks, and God is to be heard, not only on Sinai, not only in my own heart but in the *voice of the stranger*."[110] Listening with our whole being is to hear not only the stranger's voice but even more importantly to hear those truths lurking within the silence of the Indians, whether voluntary undertaken or forced. Listening to Indian voices or their silences is essential:

> It is first of all important to listen to the silence of the Indian and to admit to hearing all that has not been said for five hundred years. The salvation of our lives depends on

108. Thomas Merton, Thomas "From Pilgrimage to Crusade," *Mystics and Zen Masters* (New York: Farrar, Straus and Giroux, 1967) 112.
109. *CT*, 182.
110. *TMR*, 307.

it . . . to realize the full dimension of our priestly calling in the hemisphere . . . a redemptive and healing work, that begins with *hearing*. We begin already to heal those to whom we listen.[111]

The early conquerors and colonists were sure that their superiority gave them a monopoly on wisdom and truth. Only through preaching, and the "Indians" listening would come the latter's redemption.

But the Native Peoples were not stupid. They recognized that "whites" neither listened to their voices nor to the voices in nature, (which Merton might say are united in the Spirit which speaks in unpredictable places). These words of a Stoney Indian Tatangi Mani (Walking Buffalo) deserve to be listened to by us moderns as they bear witness to the "voices" through which nature speaks:

Did you know that trees talk? Well, they do. They talk to each other, and they'll talk to you if you listen. Trouble is, white people don't listen. They never listen to the Indians, so I don't suppose they'll listen to other voices in nature. But I have learned a lot from trees: sometimes about the weather, sometimes about animals, sometimes about the Great Spirit.[112]

"White people" over the centuries have missed numberless opportunities to be educated by listening to others. "We have an enormous debt to repay to the Indians, and we should begin by recognizing the spiritual richness of the Indian religious genius."[113]

Deepening one's communion with nature's concrete realities, whether animals, plants, streams, or hills is at the center of most Native American spiritual traditions. And developments in Merton's own intellectual, aesthetic, and spiritual life had made him increasingly sensitive to the presence of Wisdom both in nature and within many cultural traditions. He was discovering "a relation between all 'wisdoms.'"[114] He was being educated by "the others."

Joseph Epes Brown, recorder and editor of Black Elk's words in *The Sacred Pipe*, a book Merton was familiar with in the 1950s, allowed the Lakota understanding and relationship to the Great

---

111. *CT*, 146.
112. T. C. McLuhan, *Touch the Earth: A Self-Portrait of Indian Existence* (New York: Simon and Schuster: a Touchstone Book, 1971) 23; hereinafter, *TE*.
113. *CT*, 180.
114. *LE*, 100.

Spirit to inform Merton's view of "the real" and its implications for contemplation. Interestingly, Joseph Epes Brown (*The Sacred Pipe*) reported that a bird gave a young man on a vision quest these words of wise advice: "Friend, be attentive as you walk!"[115] This message – "Be Attentive" – well expresses a spirit which is central to the Indian peoples; it implies that in every act, in everything, and in every instant, the Great Spirit is present and that one should be continually and intensely "attentive" to this Divine presence.

> This presence of *Wakan Tanka*, and one's consciousness of it is that which Christian saints have termed 'living in the moment,' the 'eternal now,' or what in the Islamic tradition is termed the *Waqi*. In Lakota this presence is called *Taku Skanskan,* or simply *Skan* in the sacred language of the holy men.[116]

As theologian Christopher Pramuk points out, Merton was primarily a contemplative. As such he was more concerned with "*religious experience*" than with "doctrinal formulas." The divine was often spoken of and experienced in its mode as "*presence.*"[117] Frequently this presence of the divine was experienced within the natural world.

In the summer of 1968 in a talk to a group of Gethsemani monks, Merton discussed this experience of the immediacy of the "Now," this sense of "Presence," and in general, this genuinely contemplative "penetration" of reality. In whatever tradition, the immediacy of the "Now" goes beyond dualisms, whether ontological or linguistic. There are not two separate realities: the visible/invisible, material/spiritual, natural/supernatural, but One Reality.

> Contemplation does not mean prescinding from present material reality for some other reality. There is only one reality. Here it is – we haven't got any other. Contemplation does not mean discarding the only reality we've got. It means *penetrating* the only reality we've got. God is not absent from the material world. God appears through the material world. He's right there. The reality that we've got is matter and spirit together, and so, the only way of contemplating

---

115. *SP*, 64.
116. *SP*, 64n, 65n.
117. Christopher Pramuk, *Sophia: The Hidden Christ of Thomas Merton* (Collegeville, MI: Liturgical Press, 2009) 3.

anything is to contemplate what's real, what's right there. But we have to see it in the right way.[118]

If one would substitute *Wakan Tanka* (The Great Spirit) for "God," Merton would be close to the underlying ethno-metaphysic of the Lakota. The bird's advice to be attentive draws a person back to the reality that is here in the moment but which is "heard" or "seen" in a deeper and more direct way. Merton might have also suggested the term "sapiential awareness." "Sapiential awareness deepens our communion with the concrete" and is not "an awareness of the abstract or esoteric."[119]

Merton's contemplation and his sapiential awareness helped him commune with his brothers and sisters of the Earth community. Had the opportunity arisen, he would have been able to sit on the ground with a Lakota and join in meditation (each nuancing their experience differently given their culture but with a deep spiritual brotherhood). Chief Luther Standing Bear said: "The man who sat on the ground in his tipi meditating on life and meaning, accepting the kinship of all creatures and acknowledging unity with the universe of things was infusing into his being the true essence of civilization." Even the Native Americans were losing contact with this ancient spirituality: "And when native man left off this form of development, his humanization was retarded in growth."[120]

For Merton, because Christ and one's deeper self are in communion, one's deeper spiritual sensitivities can resonate with the equally deep qualities in indigenous spiritualities. Becoming open to and appreciating the Lakota or Ojibway intersubjective communion with the myriad forms of creation can at the same time awaken the Christ within one's being to the Cosmic Christ or *Sophia* (Wisdom in creation). One not only "brings the spirituality of these people into the light of Christ," as one has come to experience it, but one fosters a recognition of that Spirit or Light as already present within the Ojibway or Lakota or Iroquois religious culture and practice. It is out of these deep experiences of nature that so many great chants and prayers and poems (especially among the Inuit) emerge. Listen to Basho the great Japanese Zen poet: "Your poetry issues of its own accord when you and the object become one – when you have

118. Thomas Merton, "Aesthetic and Contemplative Experience – James Joyce," *The Merton Annual 27* (Louisville: Fons Vitae, 2015) 41.
119. *LE*, 100.
120. *TE*, 99.

plunged deep enough into the object to see something like a hidden glimmering there."[121]

The resurrection of Christian contemplative practices, such as *theoria physike* (natural contemplation), might open the modern Christian's "inner eye" to the light shining through Native spirituality and the natural world. Practicing "natural contemplation" is a desperate need for a peaceful globalization of religious dialogue and the recognition of a deeper religious unity. "Natural contemplation" is basic for an ecologically-imbued spirituality and morality-embraced, lived, and acted upon by adherents to the world's religions.

How should one go about establishing such relationships and learning from another wisdom tradition? In a letter to Ernesto Cardenal, written the day after the assassination of John F. Kennedy, we hear the voice of Merton as prophetic-teacher. He spoke as a contemplative/spiritual mentor to Cardenal who had also liberated his own mind, heart, and voice from the script set down for priests by the Catholic hierarchy:

> Rather than becoming purely and simply a conventional priest, you should think in terms of this strange kind of mission in which you will bring to the Church knowledge of these [indigenous] peoples and spiritualities she has so far never understood. This has been a factor in the lives of the greatest missionaries, however: to enter into the thought of primitive peoples and to live that thought and spirit as Christians, and thus bringing the spirituality of these people into the light of Christ where, indeed, it was from the start without anyone realizing the fact.[122]

Many "traditionalists" in the past and today have found and would find such a priestly mission "strange." But Merton's version of universalism (truly "catholic") neither denys nor displaces Christ. He assumed that Christ had been present "in the spirituality" of indigenous peoples from the beginning. As for the *thought* of Native Peoples, one is to "enter into" it, not simply study it academically. Merton challenges Cardenal (and us) to both "live" that thought

---

121. Matsuo Basho, *The Narrow Road to the Deep North and Other Travel Sketches*, trans. with an introduction by Nobuyuki Yuasa (London: Penguin Books, 1966) 11.

122. *CT*, 143.

and be enlivened by its permeating "spirit."

In his "Letter to Antonio Pablo Cuadra Concerning Giants," Merton suggests that one of the major assets of American indigenous peoples is their "spiritual outlook" on life that is "concrete" rather than abstract, "hieratic, intuitive, and affective, rather than rationalistic and aggressive."[123] Unfortunately for them (and now the rest of us) the Conquerors and Colonizers set out either to seal up "the deepest springs of vitality in these races" or to poison the waters. But displaying his profound grasp of this deep and vital spirituality, Merton expressed the hope that "if the stone is removed from the spring perhaps its waters will purify themselves by new life and regain their fructifying power."[124] This fructifying power can inspire and vitalize precisely the new energy and vision that the world needs. Therefore, we let Merton's words encourage us all for he promises that "there is great hope for the world in the spiritual emancipation of the Indians."[125]

OTHER REFERENCES

St. John, Donald P. "Handsome Lake," *The Encyclopedia of Religion,* 2nd ed. Farmington Hills, MI: Cengage Gale, 2005.

————. "Neolin," *The Encyclopedia of Religion,* 2nd ed. Farmington Hills, MI: Cengage Gale, 2005.

————. "Tecumseh," *The Encyclopedia of Religion,* vol. 14. New York: Free Press, 1986. 361-363.

————. "The Regeneration of Time: Indian Prophets and Frontier Pressures, 1760-1812," *Unitas Fratrum,* Heft 21/22. Wittig, 1988. 49-60.

---

123. *TMR*, 305.
124. *TMR*, 305.
125. *CT*, 172.

SEEKING TRUTH ELSEWHERE: THOMAS MERTON AND ENTHEOGENS

William Torres

When I experimented with LSD-25 in Seattle between 1957-1960, I invited the late Thomas Merton, Trappist monk and distinguished theologian, mystic, writer, to join me for a series of sessions. We had five sessions together, lasting an average of eight hours each. During the peak (between 4 and 5 hours from ingestion), as we were listening to Henry Purcell's Ode on Saint Cecilia's Day, Merton said "Look, you and I are now one, numerically."[1]

I urge you, the reader, to pause, take a deep breath, and spare a few moments of awareness for what you are experiencing in the part of your brain in which Thomas Merton, his writings, and perhaps more importantly, your attachment to said writings reside. Let us take stock of what one might be feeling upon learning that there is at least the possibility that Thomas Merton chose to ingest Lysergic Acid-25 (LSD) not once but several times. In fact, it is my opinion that one's reaction to this "news" directly correlates with the relationship the reader feels she or he has had with Thomas Merton; in other words, what role Merton has fulfilled in that reader's life.

I stumbled upon Thomas Merton amidst the spiritual angst of my early twenties. As a member of a generation to which the psychedelic exploration of our forefathers has always held much allure, I viewed the possibility of his having used drugs with great excitement as well as a strong sense of "I knew it!"

For those of you for whom Thomas Merton has become a sort of Christian Buddha or prophetic monk, very different emotions might be coursing through you. First, you might be experiencing a strong sense of disbelief. Maybe even a little shock pulses through

---

1. Bharati Agehananda, "That Which Shows Itself," *The Language of Mysticism and the Mystics* (Stonybrook, NY: Institute for Advanced Studies of World Religions, 1982) 232-233.

you as the pedestal on which Thomas Merton has been placed during your spiritual search begins to crumble a bit. If you are one who lived through those psychedelic times and yet recalls them with a bad taste in your mouth, perhaps this knowledge of Merton has caused an irrevocable shift in how you view him as a whole, though I sincerely hope not.

If you were one fortunate enough to interact with Merton beyond the edited pages of his writing, I imagine very different emotions are being felt. Perhaps a sense of intrigue or of quiet humor at what Merton "did" this time. After all, for a Trappist monk known to sneak out to visit Louisville Jazz clubs, is the idea of Merton "dropping acid" really that foreign of a concept? Perhaps my favorite reaction to this quote came from one of Merton's fellow monks and former students, Brother Paul Quenon.[2] Brother Paul listened intently to my reading, paused a moment, and then laughingly commented how Merton never went to Seattle and the whole thing was just an incredulous notion.

While perhaps a bit incredulous and for a whole host of reasons improbable, the important part of all this is that it highlights something Merton readers want to know more about, something that the global Merton community has perhaps always wanted to know. For a man who wrote prolifically on just about every subject even remotely spiritual, the fact that Merton did not write extensively on drugs, psychedelics, or entheogens proves an interesting discrepancy. Furthermore, given that Merton lived through not only the birth pangs but also the maturity of what is now called the "counterculture" movement of the 1960s, the absence of any extensive commentary on the substances themselves transcends the label of interesting and begs to be explored.

I intend to approach this question as it stands and shed some light on Merton's thoughts on entheogens or substances ingested for the specific purpose of "generating the divine"[3] in an individual's psyche. Like many of Merton's writings, his thoughts on entheogens and psychedelics are best perceived with a view that transcends the "right" vs. "wrong" and the "spiritual" vs. "material" dichotomies through which humans

---

2. Brother Paul Quenon, OCSO, Abbey of Gethsemani. Interview with author, June 9, 2014.

3. Rick Strasman, *DMT: The Spirit Moledule* (Rochester, NY: Park Street Press, 2001) 30; hereinafter, *DMT*.

are so apt to look at things, particularly spiritual things.

For Merton, any topic he explored would eventually come to be understood as either an authentic path of deepening contemplation or a less authentic path. However, this is not to say that Merton viewed every possible topic he explored as a route authentic in its own right. On some topics, such as the influence of technology on society, he had very firm opinions (Shannon et al., 2002: 466-470).[4] I am calling upon readers to view the matters I shall discuss as Merton would have viewed them. The reality of the situation is that our culture has a very narrow understanding of "good" drugs and "bad" drugs, choosing to vilify some and approve others. It is the unfortunate situation that what this writing will reference has been demonized by many and thus presented to all of us, and indoctrinated into some of us, as evil, hedonistic, and spiritually devoid of meaning. I urge you, as we delve into this subject, to temporarily shrug off these societal shackles and, as Merton did, enter into the search for authentic contemplation and a profound experience of the divine.

WHAT DO WE MEAN BY "DRUGS"?

In exploring Merton's musings on the matter, we need a working definition of what exactly is meant when one utilizes the word "drug." Few words have been victim to as many different euphemisms as this one, with perhaps death remaining the reigning champion. Thus far, I have already deployed three words: "drugs," "psychedelics" and "entheogens." Each one more specific than the last, and all with the purpose of attempting to both expand and yet limit what exactly I am attempting to communicate. When the word "drug" is used within the context of this essay, it is meant to encompass the entire classification of substances which, when present in the human body, either through ingestion or intravenous means, causes a change of perceptual state, an altered state of mind.

The words "entheogen" and "psychedelic" are an attempt to be more specific. Drawing on the work of Dr. Rick Strassman and his book *DMT: The Spirit Molecule*, an Entheogen is a substance which generates the divine or experiences of the divine. Similarly, and perhaps a bit broader, a psychedelic is a substance which gener-

---

4. William H. Shannon, *The Thomas Merton Encyclopedia*, eds. William H. Shannon, Christine M. Bochen, and Patrick O'Connell (Maryknoll, NY: Orbis Books, 2002) 466-470.

ates a manifestation of the mind. Meaning that psychedelics "show you what's in and on your mind, those subconscious thoughts and feelings that are hidden, covered up, forgotten, out of sight, maybe even completely unexpected, but nevertheless imminently present."[5]

It is important to note the difference between an entheogen and a psychedelic. A psychedelic simply manifests, whether we are conscious of it or not, whatever it is that we have buzzing around in our minds at the time of its use. Entheogens, although they might have the same amplifying effects as psychedelics, produce a more specific and direct experience of the divine. I now explore Thomas Merton's opinion on drugs and, specifically, the nuances of his views on entheogens and the validity of the experiences they have produced in recent decades for Western Europeans and since time immemorial for many indigenous cultures worldwide.

How did Merton view drugs? To discover his perspective, I turn to the most reliable Merton resource, his writings. His writing, particularly his letters, evidence Merton's first engagement with the subject matter. On November 27, 1958, Merton wrote Aldous Huxley in response to a piece which appeared in *The Saturday Evening Post*. In his article, Huxley had made the argument that entheogens such as Peyote or LSD are viable vehicles for what he calls a "temporary gratuitous grace" which takes the form of an authentic transcendental mystical experience:

> When administered in the right kind of environment, these chemical mind changers make possible a genuine religious experience. Thus a person who takes LSD or mescaline may suddenly understand not only intellectually but organically, experientially the meaning of such tremendous religious affirmations as "God is love," or "Though he slay me, yet will I trust in Him."[6]

To head-off any counter-arguments rooted in asceticism, Huxley quickly goes on to further argue:

> Those who are offended by the idea that the swallowing of a pill may contribute to a genuinely religious experience should remember that all the standard mortifications –

---

5. *DMT*, 30-31.

6. Aldous Huxley, "Drugs That Shape Men's Minds," *The Saturday Evening Post* Issue 231, October 18, 1958; hereinafter, *DSMM*. https://www.brainpickings.org/2014/03/25/aldoushuxley-moksha-drugs/ Consulted 4/4/2019.

fasting, voluntary sleeplessness and self-torture – inflicted upon themselves by the ascetics of every religion for the purpose of acquiring merit, are also, like the mind changing drugs, powerful devices for altering the chemistry of the body in general and the nervous system in particular.[7]

Here, I cannot stress enough how revolutionary Huxley's claims are or how controversial. By stating that drugs cannot only produce genuine religious experiences but also are but a different way to accomplish what traditional ascetic practices attempt, Huxley is not only challenging traditional notions of contemplation but, in a roundabout way, the very need for organized religion itself. If we can take a pill and experience a relationship with God first hand, the necessity of going to Sunday mass, or receiving the Eucharistic host, could lose their appeal.

Merton's response to Huxley's article is characteristic of his approach to religion and specifically Catholicism. Merton chooses inquiry over inquest and dialogue over diatribe, which simultaneously cements his theological stance while it also creates space for the exploration of this new topic. In his letter of response, Merton prefaced his remarks:

> I am in no position to dispute what you say about the effect of drugs. Though occasionally fortified by aspirin, and exhilarated by coffee, and even sometimes using a barbiturate to get to sleep (alas), I have no experience of the things you speak of. Perhaps I shall make a trial of them one of these days so that I will know what I am talking about. But since I feel, as you do, that this is a matter which merits discussion and study, I would like to put forward the things that occur to me after my first encounter with the subject. I hope by this to *learn* rather than to teach, and I can see that this is your attitude also.
>
> • 1. Are you not endangering the whole concept of genuine mystical experience in saying that it is something that can be "produced" by a drug? I know you qualify the statement, you say that a drug can induce a state in which mystical experience can be occasioned: a drug can remove obstacles in our ordinary everyday state of mind, and make a kind

---

7. Huxley, *DSMM*.

of latent mysticism come to the surface. But I wonder if this accords with the real nature of mystical experience?

I think this point must be studied carefully, and I suggest the following:

- 2. Ought we not to distinguish between an experience which is essentially *aesthetic and natural* from an experience which is *mystical and supernatural*. I would call aesthetic and natural an experience which would be an intuitive "tasting" of the inner spirituality of our own being – of an intuition of being as such, arrived at through an intuitive awareness of our own inmost reality. This would be an experience of "oneness" within oneself, and with all beings, a flash of awareness of the transcendent reality that is within all that is real. This sort of thing "happens" to one in all sorts of ways and I see no reason why it should not be occasioned by the use of a drug. This intuition is very like the aesthetic intuition that precedes the creation of a work of art. It is like the intuition of a philosopher who rises above his concepts and their synthesis to see everything at one glance, in all its length, height, breadth and depth.[8]

Merton established the crux of his argument about drugs, entheogens, and the like. It is not a matter of choosing this or that, but an issue of definition. His argument does not center on contradicting Huxley, since he freely admits to being a neophyte in these matters, but rather focuses on categorizing the nature of the "tasting" in question as being a mystical experience or not. Differentiating between the inspiration of an artist or philosopher and the mysticism of a contemplative, he further argued that:

- 3. It seems to me that a fully mystical experience has in its very essence some note of a direct spiritual *contact of two liberties*, a kind of flash or spark which ignites an intuition of all that has been said above, plus something much more which I can only describe as "personal," in which God is known not as an "object" or as "him up there" or "him in everything" . . . But what I mean is that this is not the kind

8. Thomas Merton, *The Hidden Ground of Love: The Letters of Thomas Merton on Religious Experience and Social Concerns*, ed. William H. Shannon (New York: Farrar, Straus and Giroux, 1985) 437; hereinafter, *HGL*.

> of intuition that smacks of anything procurable because it
> is a presence of a Person and *depends on the liberty of that
> Person* . . . from the moment that such an experience can
> be conceived of as *dependent on* and *inevitably following
> from* the casual use of a material instrument, it loses the
> quality of spontaneity and freedom and transcendence
> which makes it truly mystical.[9]

In short, for an experience to be anything other than a personal
rave show, the mystical experience in question must involve the
"direct spiritual contact of two liberties," in this case to mean the
liberties of God and said entheogen user. Furthermore, the impetus
for such a meeting does not rest with the drug user but rather with
God. Therefore, if an authentic mystical experience is dependent
on the will of God, then it cannot be dependent on any substance
for its occurrence. It is pure and simple, an intentional gift from
"that Person." Thus, in Merton's argument, the very idea that one
can use an entheogen and be relatively well assured to authenti-
cally experience the divine is flawed, and thus this idea by its very
conception has already corrupted much, if not all, of the mystical
potential of the experience.

Merton argued for a view of mysticism which, while having
his flavor, is not necessarily original. What Merton reflects here is
a school of mystical thought perhaps best described as apophatic
and best represented by the well-known fourteenth-century mystical
text entitled *The Cloud of Unknowing*. Grounded in the idea that
God is so unknowable that any concept of his majesty falls short,
a mystic of this flavor would see any conceptualization, image,
colorful manifestation, etc. as not only inauthentic but a sure indi-
cator that he or she was "going the wrong way." Merton explored
apophatic mysticism in great depth and accepted "not knowing" as
his standard mark for an authentic mystical experience.

> In these pages, I have decided to ignore the complexities
> of this now defunct argument, and simply assumed the
> existence of a supersensory intuition of the divine which
> is a gift of grace for which we can, to some extent, prepare
> ourselves by our own efforts. In this I am basing myself
> on a distinction made by the Greek Fathers: that between
> natural contemplation (*theoria physike*) and theology

9. Shannon, *HGL*, 438.

(theologia), or the contemplation of God. *Theoria physike* is the intuition of divine things in and through the reflection of God in nature and in the symbols of revelation . . . *Theologia*, or pure contemplation ("mystical theology" in the language of Pseudo Denis [Pseudo-Dionysius]), is a direct quasi-experiential contact with God beyond all thought, that is to say, without the medium of concepts. This excludes not only concepts tinged with passion, or sentimentality, or imagination, but even the simplest intellectual intuitions that require some sort of medium between God and the spirit.[10]

To dispel even the semblance of doubt of where his mystical orientation lay, Merton, after an appropriate quote from St. John of the Cross, further states, "But this theology has one other characteristic that must not be overlooked. It is a contact with God in Charity, yes, but also and above all in the *darkness of unknowing*" (emphasis added).[11]

The question now arises, dear readers, in what direction do we go? If Thomas Merton does indeed fall on the apophatic/*theologia* side of the mystical divide, which I believe is supported, then what next? Do we hammer this point home with quote after quote of evidence from his extensive volumes? Do we attempt to prove the accuracy of this conclusion, pointing out the parallels existent between apophatic mysticism and where Merton's interests lay in Zen Buddhism? Or, do we accept that perhaps this is as far as Merton went intellectually on the matter, and in doing so free ourselves to explore where Merton's spiritual confidence allowed him to go? It is this latter question that this essay now explores.

ILLUMINISM

One such direction Merton's spiritual confidence led him to was an expansion on the views of entheogens about which he first wrote to Huxley. He equated the use of drugs for spiritual experiences as a form of "illuminism," a contemplative orientation that he saw as one of the most hazardous pitfalls to any seeker's development.

---

10. Thomas Merton, *The Inner Experience: Notes on Contemplation*, ed. William H. Shannon (New York: Farrar, Straus and Giroux, 2003) 67-68; hereinafter, *IE*.

11. Merton, *IE*, 69.

Illuminism essentially means the "taking of one's subjective experiences so seriously that it becomes more important than truth, more important than God. Once spiritual experience becomes objectified, it turns into an idol."[12] It is this potential for the idolatry of the experience induced by drugs that Merton most feared. Merton did not dislike entheogens in and of themselves. He freely admits that there is medicinal potential in them, further acquiescing that maybe one can experience the divine through their use. Nevertheless, the ends do not justify the means as Merton explains:

> Whatever may be the final outcome of these experiments, they are to be viewed with extreme caution. Assuming that the facts are correct, and there is no reason to doubt the reported experiences, there is still no reason to conclude that because such things are possible, therefore they ought to be done. On the contrary, it seems to me that we would run the risk of organized and large-scale illuminism.[13]

Merton inspected the bigger picture. He challenged us to consider what society would spiritually look like if anyone could meet God with no more effort or discipline required than what it took to take a drug. Merton's opinion is that there is no true contemplation and no mysticism without contact initiated by the divine.

> . . . what really matters in spiritual experience is not its interiority, or its natural purity, or the joy, light, exaltation, and transforming effect it may seem to have: these things are secondary and accidental. What matters is not what one feels but what really takes place beyond the level of feeling or experience. In genuine contemplation, what takes place is a contact between the inmost reality of the created person and the infinite Reality of God.[14]

The questions surrounding drugs and religious experience point to the greater question of the role subjectivity has in contemplation. For the psychedelic culture, both recreational and mystical, then and now, subjectivity reigns supreme; it is all about the experience, the trip. Merton's emphasis is opposite: the subjective is to be shed in hopes of transcending to something more, something utterly

---

12. Merton, *IE*, 106.
13. Merton, *IE*, 107.
14. Merton, *IE*, 108.

incomprehensible. For Merton, "the true contemplative is a lover of sobriety and obscurity,"[15] and everything else is just white noise.

Let us now pause for a moment and survey the journey of Merton's writing concerning drugs and entheogens. He at first seemed anti-drugs because they reflected a mysticism oriented differently than his own. He was not comfortable with the concept of readily com- modifying the divine. In developing his ideas around illuminism, he argued it was not so much the value of entheogen use per se that provoked his questioning of their place in active contemplation.

In light of his judgments, how should we understand Merton's clear affinity for indigenous cultures, both Central, South, and North American? These are cultures within which the use of entheogens was not only an accepted but a recommended practice with which to interact with the divine. The key I believe lies in intimately understanding the underlying theme of Merton's writings on indigenous contemplative practices. While contradictory at a glance, Merton's fascination and deep appreciation of indigenous culture and religion do not counter his stance on entheogens. In fact, for Merton, delving into the past offered an alternate vision for how drugs could be safely integrated into society.

Merton often wrote of his admiration and interest in indigenous spirituality when writing to his contacts in South America. To his friend and former postulant, the now famous Nicaraguan poet, Ernesto Cardenal, he wrote:

> I am very happy to hear of your visit to the Cuna Indians on San Blas Islands . . .. The more time you spend with them, the better. I think indeed that this is a really important aspect to your vocation, and that rather than becoming purely and simply a conventional priest, you should think in terms of this strange kind of mission in which you will bring to the Church knowledge of these peoples and spiritualties she has so far never understood . . . thus bringing the spirituality of these people into the light of Christ where, indeed, it was from the start without anyone realizing the fact.[16]

---

15. Merton, *IE*, 109.
16. Thomas Merton, *The Courage for Truth: The Letters of Thomas Merton to Writers*, ed. Christine M. Bochen (New York: Farrar, Straus and Giroux, 1993) 143; hereinafter, *CT*.

He explored the necessity for appreciating indigenous spiritualities in several essays such as "The Sacred City" and "War and Vision" both of which were later compiled into the work, *Ishi Means Man*.

In reading the introductory paragraphs of "War and Vision," it is almost as if Merton realizes that there is the potential for these writings to appear contradictory to his other thoughts. Therefore he began the essay with the following disclaimers:

> The practice of "fasting for vision" was once almost universal among North American Indians for whom it might almost be said that a certain level of "mysticism" was an essential part of growing up. The term mysticism is here used broadly. I am not here concerned with the religious content or value of the visions in themselves, but with the fact that such visions were taken for granted as a normal part of life in an archaic culture.[17]

Merton did not mean to reflect on the validity of indigenous mysticism. Using a very anthropological approach, the indigenous spiritual would be explored through the lens of the indigenous societal framework. Merton additionally dispelled what he viewed as a myth about Native American mystical life:

> Fasts and solitary retreats were multiplied throughout life and other "psychedelic" expedients were resorted to: ecstatic dancing, self-torture, and drugs, which are now well known, all might be called upon to stimulate the "vision" without which a well-integrated and purposeful existence could hardly be conceived. However, we must not generalize: the use of drugs was far less widespread than dances and fasts for vision.[18]

(I note here that the rituals Merton claimed to have occurred most frequently are the rituals that either have exact duplicates or counterparts in Western mysticism and monasticism.)

Merton saw stark differences between the entheogen use in Western culture and that of indigenous North Americans. These differences transcended the simple comparison of drug preference. In the practices of the indigenous North American cultures, Merton

---

17. Thomas Merton, *Ishi Means Man* (Greensboro, NC: Unicorn Press, 1976) 17; hereinafter, *IMM*.

18. Merton, *IMM*, 17-18.

found an approach to contemplation that addressed everything that the current entheogen and experience-grounded Western paradigm lacked. These differences, while several and nuanced, can be understood when considered within the following categories: desired outcome, discipline, and interpretation.

The desired outcome category above all is important because it addresses one of the fundamental differences between both cultures' contemplative practices, i.e. motivation. For the Native American, the primary motivation behind various spiritual practices was to attain a vision in which a practitioner meets his "spirit guide." This vision was hoped to instigate a lifelong relationship:

> This protector was not just any spirit. It was his spirit, his "vision person." And the encounter was not just a matter of seeing and knowing. It was not just "an experience." It changed the course of the seer's entire life: or rather it was what gave his life a "course" to begin with. However, guidance was not automatic. Protection and other forms of help could be completely withdrawn if the Indian was not careful if he disobeyed, and if he was not extremely attentive to every hint or suggestion from his vision person.[19]

It is not hard to see why these practices appealed to Merton. They were less concerned with the immediate experience and more with the relationship it initiated. When entering into these rituals, the desire was for something beyond an impressive or deeply symbolic "trip." The more important desire was to cultivate what Merton labeled the "direct spiritual contact of two liberties."[20] This direct contact was more dependent on the actions and will of the "vision person;" it was not directly produced by any action of the practitioner. Conversely, it is also important to recognize that although these beliefs resonated deeply with Merton, this does not mean they were perfectly compatible with his mystical vocation. I believe that even Thomas Merton would have trouble accepting a God that was as demanding as the "vision people" are portrayed.

Merton recognized motivation as an important distinction in spiritual experiences with or without drugs. If one reads closely it is abundantly clear that Merton aimed his criticism at the likes of Huxley, Leary, and other entheogen aficionados:

---

19. Merton, *IMM*, 18.
20. Merton, *HGL*, 438.

The nature and content of the vision were not left entirely to chance. It was not just a matter of removing the block of everyday automatisms and the flowering of deeper psychic awareness. The Indian who fasted for vision sought a personal encounter with a clearly recognizable spirit-friend, a protector whom he felt himself destined to meet, one to whom he felt himself providentially entrusted.[21]

Merton appreciated Native American spiritual practices, such as "fasting for a vision." He assumed that Native American disciplines and dedication were unmatched in the entheogen use of Western practitioners. Many in the psychedelic movement, such as Huxley. Leary, and Huston Smith, regularly combined entheogen usage with fasting, meditation, holy reading, and other ascetic practices. Since few of his correspondents on the topic of entheogens emphasized their other spiritual disciplines, Merton might have had little or no exposure to this hybrid-concept of their practical inter-spiritualities. Furthermore, his respect for Native American mysticism over drug-induced mysticism was biased by his judgment of the hedonistic nature of Western entheogen usage.

We need to look no further for evidence of this than one of the books Merton himself read and referenced in his research, *Two Leggings, The Making of a Crow Warrior* by Peter Nabokov. Originally documented by William Wildschut, an ethnologist from the Museum of the American Indian, it narrates the life of the Crow Indian warrior, Two Leggings. A moving glimpse into the indigenous culture of the Plains people, for Merton it provided primary documentation as well as powerful firsthand accounts of the lengths one would go in search of a vision. For example in the excerpt below Two Leggings describes his search for his "medicine":

> As I walked around, I found a root-diggers stick. I turned toward the sun and drew out my long knife. On the ground, I crossed the knife and the stick and then raised my left index finger. I called the sun my grandfather and said that I was about to sacrifice my finger end to him. I prayed that some bird of the sky or animal of the earth would eat it and give me good medicine because I wanted to be a great chief some day and have many horses.[22]

21. Merton, *IMM*, 18.
22. Peter Nabokov, *Two Leggings: The Making of a Crow Warrior* (New

While undoubtedly ascetic in the extreme, accounts such as this struck a chord with Merton's monastic values. Offering a faith and ascetic discipline on par with any Cistercian, Two Leggings provided a strong counterexample of discipline to the sensationalized contemplation becoming increasingly popular during Merton's time.

This brings us to the aspect of Native American contemplative practice, which undoubtedly spoke to Merton the most: interpretation. Much like a young postulant would receive spiritual direction as he first began entering into the life of a monk, so too did indigenous traditions offer guidance to their neophytes:

> However, the Indian was not left to deal with his vision person alone: the visions and indications required comment and approval from the more experienced men of the tribe, the elders, the medicine men and the chiefs. In other words, they had a better and more accurate knowledge of the language of vision. The young Indian might interpret his vision one way, and the elders might proceed to show him that he was quite wrong. He remained free to disobey them and follow his own interpretation, but if he did, he ran the risk of disaster.[23]

It is this deference to hierarchy, to the spiritual tradition of one's people, that appealed to Merton. Despite being one the most independent and prolific writers of his generation, it is important to remember that Merton still very much enjoyed being part of a monastic tradition that stretched back into the ancient deserts. Hand in hand with this joy was a deep respect for the spirituality of those who came before and a recognition that much, if not all, of his contemplative development, was made possible by his spiritual predecessors.

Once again it is not hard to see why Merton identified much more with the contemplative practices of North American indigenous culture than with the solely entheogen-grounded psychedelic movement. Indigenous traditions, much like his own, not only encouraged the use of a wide variety of contemplative practices but had found a way to both encourage yet limit the influence of subjectivity, something which solely entheogen based contempla-

York: Crowell, 1967) 50.
    23. Merton, *IMM*, 19.

tion seemed unable or unwilling to do. In works like *Two Leggings*, Merton found a template for what contemplation had been and could be again, integrated, essential, and accessible to everyone.

I would like to offer some of my thoughts on the subject of entheogens and Merton. It is important to remember that Thomas Merton was a human being and thus, like all human beings, was dramatically shaped by his surroundings, history, parents, language, etc. Merton deployed natural and nurtured biases when he related entheogen use to mystical experiences. One of the most important biases was the traditions of monasticism. From the moment he entered the Abbey of Gethsemani, Merton was dramatically shaped by a monastic culture. Although Gethsemani provided the space and structure that Merton needed to flourish, the cost of his development was a certain amount of necessary conformity, a prominent feature of Trappist monastic living.

Furthermore, Merton's monastic training cemented a distrust of subjectivity, which had already begun to take root before he entered the monastery. Merton's early years had been by no means tame, especially his time at Cambridge University in particular:

> Then I was proud and selfish and denied God and was full of gluttony and lust. I was so filled with all these things that even now the unhappiness of them does not leave me at all but keeps forcing itself back upon me in thoughts and dreams . . .. But all these things were much stronger because I did not resist them at all.[24]

Any Merton reader need not search very far in *The Seven Storey Mountain* or any of Merton's early letters and journals to find similar dramatic statements of self-loathing for who he was "in the world." While much of the severity can be attributed to the spiritual zeal of a recent religious convert, it is not a far intellectual leap to argue that Merton pursued monkhood, at least in the beginning, to escape the personal subjectivity he felt ill-equipped to master. Given the dark depths to which his subjectivity had taken him in his youth, and then the "shedding" of one's subjectivity encouraged by monasticism, the real surprise in all this is not that Merton disliked drug-based mysticism but that he gave it the thought he did.

---

24. Thomas Merton, *The Intimate Merton: His Life from His Journals*, eds. Brother Patrick Hart, OCSO and Jonathan Montaldo (San Francisco: HarperSan-Francisco, 2001) 5.

Why did Merton write about drugs and mystical experiences at all? While by no means a defining theme of his intellectual pursuits, repeatedly throughout the 1950s and 1960s the subject was brought to his attention and in each case, he took the time to address the topic with a thoroughness that is intriguing. In a journal entry for November 27, 1965, three months after he had entered his hermitage full time, Merton summarized his stance to counter-cultural movements:

> Yesterday I read some articles on psychedelics. There is a regular fury of drug-mysticism in this country. In a way, I am appalled. Mysticism has finally arrived in a characteristic American mode. One feels that this is certainly it. The definitive turn in the road taken by American religion. The turn I myself will not take (don't need to!). This leaves my own road a lot quieter and more untroubled, I hope. Certainly, the great thing, as I see it now, is to get out of all the traffic: peace movement traffic, political traffic, Church traffic, "consciousness-raising" traffic, Zen traffic, monastic reform traffic. All of it![25]

What is most interesting about this entry is not the reiteration of Merton's views on entheogens, nor the obvious shift in his writing towards further withdrawal from the world. Rather, here we see Merton making an important prediction. For better or worse, the drug mysticism of the 1960s would mark a definitive point in America's conception of religion. Merton's prediction has largely held true. For although the psychedelic movement, when considered in its original form is no longer existent, the fact that it occurred at all has forever marked the spiritual map of our nation.

Traversing the religious, linguistic, and even fashion realms of our society, the core belief that there is another way, another choice, a personal subjective decision that is an option in the face of the overwhelming force of society's institutions continues to live today. It is because Merton eventually came to recognize the potential magnitude of drug mysticism's impact on society that he rarely passed up an opportunity to write on it. Scholars can find much to critique about Merton, much to poke and prod, and yet one undeniable fact is that Merton was acutely aware of how influential

---

25. Thomas Merton, *Dancing in the Water of Life: Seeking Peace in the Hermitage*, ed. Robert E. Daggy (San Francisco: HarperSanFrancisco, 1997) 318-319.

his writings would be, not only in his life's time but also for later generations. It is this knowledge, which I believe motivated Merton's writings on drug use, entheogens, etc. He did not write for the contemplatives of the day, but for those of tomorrow.

A strong example of this is evidenced in Merton's 1967 correspondence with psychedelic advocate and activist, Lisa Bieberman. Merton first wrote Bieberman after reading an article written by her entitled "On Getting the Message" published in the magazine *Innerspace*. Written at a time when the psychedelic movement was first beginning to stumble, the article addressed the challenges of communicating the LSD experience and analyzed much of the miscommunication about drug experience that Bieberman felt had already occurred. Her article possessed a contemplative tone about drug mysticism rarely found outside the work of Leary, Huxley, or Cohen:

> The purpose of making explicit the possibility of a religious commitment to that which is revealed in the psychedelic event is to suggest to the person whose attitudes are still unformed that this is something to be open for. I think, too, that this concept may help us understand in what way a psychedelic experience can be a force for good in a person's subsequent life, and why it sometimes fails to be . . .. If LSD has any power to help a person change, it is by that person's <u>active commitment</u> to something he has recognized in the LSD state, which inspires him to exert his <u>own</u> efforts toward changing his way of life.[26]

The buzzwords here are what Bieberman herself underscored, "active commitment" and "own." Before we quickly label her as another subjectivist, let us pause a moment and ask ourselves what exactly is she urging an active commitment to? LSD experiences? Ourselves? Our own personal growth? In reality, it is probably a combination of the three and yet what is important to note is that we see here a break from what up until now readers might consider as a subjectivity drenched personal hedonistic experience. Yes, Bieberman acknowledged that for many, illuminism would be their experience but points out that to a degree it is also their choice. Some, like herself, have chosen otherwise and tried to "listen" to

---

26. Lisa Bieberman, "On Getting the Message Out," *Innerspace Magazine* (Spring, 1967).

what was being communicated in the experience, through the experience. Cannot this listening, this active commitment to seeking something higher than oneself, this meeting of two liberties, be a form of contemplation? I think so.

We have but to read Merton's opening lines to Bieberman to quickly see that he also felt the same way. He writes, "I have a great deal of respect for what you are doing, and I can see from your article that you are completely on the level and what is happening with you is like a lot of things that have happened in another way and in another context for me."[27] Can these be the words of the same man who claimed that a true contemplative is a lover of quiet and sobriety? The answer is a most definite yes and I believe that his words articulate an evolution in his thinking and an acknowledgment of the definitive turn in American religion mentioned above. He states:

> I honestly think you people need more than anything else a *disciplina arcani* (like the first Christians – they did not talk about the sacraments). You need to get a good sane group of you underground fast because with the public emotion and fury about it this whole thing may dissolve fast into something it need not be. I think you really need an element of silence, of loneliness, of non-communication in order to make the whole thing more valid and keep it so.[28]

Merton saw what he perceived as a monumental shift approaching, and he attempts shaping it rather than suffocating it. Thus, in the end, he offers not criticism but encouragement, and by fanning the contemplative embers he sees in Bieberman's motivation, he hopes to refine what she and others sought.

When I first began exploring this topic, my primary question was "did Merton ever drop acid," and I will be honest in stating that I sincerely hoped to find supporting evidence of this. I wanted to believe that Merton truly did not leave a single rock unturned in his pursuit of an authentic experience of the divine and thus gain some confidence for my limited forays into the world of entheogens. However, this was not the case, and I now recognize that his reasoning for why he chose not to use entheogens and the intellectual

---

27. Thomas Merton, "Dear Lisa Bieberman." Undated correspondence, The Thomas Merton Center, Bellarmine University, Louisville, KY; hereinafter, *LB*.
28. Thomas Merton, *LB*.

labyrinth this reasoning led him down has proven to be so much more interesting and important. For in disagreeing with the basic principles of the psychedelic mystical movement, Merton, in fact, lent it an authenticity far greater than any session he could have been a part of in Seattle. In disagreeing, he authenticated. In challenging, he prompted discussion, and in exploring he influenced the lives of people for generations to come.

In moments of clarity, I have realized that Merton can never truly be for us what we ask him to be, a gatekeeper to our salvation. He cannot do all the spiritual labor for us; we must each in our way explore, challenge, and fail in our spiritual pursuits for any real growth to come. So let us leave no rock unturned, no path untaken and remember that in even the most ironclad of our beliefs is a little wiggle room.

> I have no criticism of anyone who seeks truth elsewhere and by some other way of life, provided that they really seek truth. There are all kinds of ways to God, and ours is only one of many.[29]

---

29. Thomas Merton, *A Life in Letters: The Essential Collection*, eds. William H. Shannon and Christine M. Bochen (New York: HarperOne, 2008) 8.

THE SPIRIT OF THE TLINGITS

Kathleen Witkowska Tarr

INTRODUCTION TO KATHLEEN W. TARR'S
WE ARE ALL POETS HERE AS EXCERPTED BELOW

In September 1968, Thomas Merton journeyed far off his conventional monastic path to undertake a spiritual reconnaissance to California, New Mexico, and Alaska, prior to his departure for Asia. Merton's developing interest in the plight and oppression of America's First Peoples coincided with his extraordinary visit to Alaska, an important but often overlooked journey in the biography of Merton's last few months.

During 17-day sojourn to Alaska, while also exploring for a possible location to establish his future, more secluded hermitage, Merton covered a vast swath of territory, mostly by private airplane charter, under the auspices of the Anchorage archdiocese. In Alaska, the inquisitive monk witnessed unimaginable landscapes of glaciers, volcanoes, mystical mountains, and desolate and lost little towns not connected by any roads. He visited or flew over small settlements and villages such as Dillingham, Eklutna, Copper Center – many places inhabited historically by Alaskan Native Peoples. (Approximately 15-20% of Alaska's population is classified as "Native.")

Merton spent time on the ground in Cordova (home to Eyak) and traveled further south into the Southeast Alaska region, the center of Tlingit culture – specifically to Yakutat and Juneau. The monk predicted that one day he would return to Alaska. He would have welcomed the opportunity to absorb as much as he could from indigenous cultures for whom he felt a deep spiritual bond.

The following Chapters 4 and 5 have been excerpted from Kathleen W. Tarr's memoir, *We Are All Poets Here: Thomas Merton's 1968 Journey to Alaska, A Shared Story about Spiritual Seeking.*[1]

1. Kathleen W. Tarr, *We Are All Poets Here: Thomas Merton's 1968 Journey to Alaska, A Shared Story about Spiritual Seeking* (Anchorage, AK: VP&D House, Inc., 2018). A review by Patrick F. O'Connell appears in *The Merton Annual 31*, 215-220.

ABYSS OF SOLITUDE

The truest solitude is not something outside you, not an
absence of men or sound around you; it is an abyss opening
up in the center of your own soul.

Thomas Merton, *Seeds of Contemplation*

. . . If I trust You, everything else will become, for me,
strength, health, and support. Everything will bring me
to heaven. If I do not trust You, everything will be my
destruction . . .

Thomas Merton, *Thoughts in Solitude*

Jim drove us to our FAA government housing five minutes from
the Airport Lodge. Our second-floor apartment was practically on
the direct flight path of Alaska Airlines, not far from the runway.

"Every day, you'll be able to see the jet on its final approach,
and right from your picture window, you'll have a good view of
Mount Saint Elias, *if* and *when* it's clear," Jim said with a grin as
he turned the key to open the door.

The one-bedroom apartment came with an orange, yellow, and
brown plaid couch, scratched up pine end tables, two oversized
olive green lamps, a bed, and a chest of drawers. We didn't own a
single piece of furniture and had nothing to supplement the décor
except one dried up African violet. Michael also brought a piece
of wood with strange Chinese symbols he had carved into it. For
a long time, he had a fascination with Lao Tsu whom I had not
heard of before and said the carving was supposed to represent the
Tao te Ching. I feigned understanding who he was talking about.

Time passed slowly over the next few months, especially in
the days before satellite television, computers, and the Internet.
Through the mail, I ordered a copy of a thick hardcover book, *The
Norton Anthology of Literature by Women,* to entertain myself
during the monotony of staying in the apartment alone while Michael worked shifts at his aviation job, filing pilot flight plans and
learning about weather systems.

To force myself outdoors, I wandered around the small boat
harbor with my camera, often loaded with infrared film, to take
pictures of aging fishing boats and the piles of empty, rusted crab
pots strewn on the gravel bank. (Thomas Merton stood on this
very same spot in 1968 with his camera. He couldn't resist taking a

black and white photo of an old fishing boat named Tommy Boy.)

Lots of new words filled my head. *Muskeg* – something Yaku-tat was full of – a bog of organic material in poorly drained areas. *Moiety* (moy-uh-tee), a word meaning one of two equal parts, two Tlingit social groups, either Raven or Eagle. And *toion*, a word of Russian innovation that translated to Tlingit "chief."

My life had become so different from what I had imagined, that all I could do for the first six months was cry and feel sorry for myself. I had gone and done it. I'd be forgotten before I was ever discovered and die a slow death in obscurity.

I wasn't someone who knew what to do with real solitude – the kind of solitude you have to face day in and day out, solitude born in geographic isolation you can't run from, solitude that forces you to take a good, hard look at yourself. But for all the serenity and inner stillness my new quiet wilderness surroundings might bring, I wasn't the least bit grateful. I fought against it. Striving for this or that, to get ahead, setting goals, making money, building careers and reputation – I bought into the predefined picture of what success should be.

Even after I had met Jim's wife, Sue, and she shared some much-appreciated household advice, I moped around the apartment and wallowed in self-pity. The days dragged on.

I stared at the cardboard boxes of personal belongings but couldn't bring myself to unpack them. Relocating as we did in the dead of winter made it far worse. Fast food restaurants, video rental places, ski trails, movie theatres, or medical offices were nonexistent. Isolation suffocated me.

It was winter, and it was dark, or it was dark, and it was pouring rain, or it was dark and spitting snow.

A few months passed, and we still didn't know very many people. I can't remember the precise moment when my friendship with Jennie Pavlik and her family began. She was the daughter of a Tlingit woman and white father. They were a large, eccentric family and the subject of much local gossip. Now and then, one of the Pavliks would show up at our apartment with Rudy Pavlik's famous canned, smoked king salmon or fresh caught Dungeness crab. Everyone, including the Pavliks, heard we were the *cheecha-kos,* newcomers in Alaska, and people felt a little sorry for us.

Rudy was one of Jennie's five brothers, a friendly guy who whenever we bumped into him even when the rain was battering every square inch of Yakutat, never wore any rain jacket or hat.

I wondered about this awe-inspiring mountain view Jim had told us about. Because of the mountain's trickery, the downpours and the gloomy days, I had not yet seen any full views of Mount Saint Elias. Though Mount Saint Elias supposedly dominated the horizon, most of the time, the peak remained cloaked in clouds or was only partially visible.

Some days were better than others during my self-imposed wilderness exile. Eventually, I set up a darkroom in the basement of our building. On April days when conditions slightly improved, I drove down to the small boat harbor to shoot photos and kept trying to capture Mount Saint Elias, but no matter what I did, the pictures I produced were always lacking.

The Jensens lived directly behind our apartment in a modest ranch house, one of the privileges of being aviation chief. This made it easy for me to show up unannounced in Sue's kitchen after Michael left on his one-mile walk to work. I'd stand near her crowded pantry full of jarred salmon, 25-pound bags of flour and sugar, boxes of powdered milk, case lots of mayonnaise, tomato sauce, and Pilot Bread that had all been delivered via barge from Seattle. Sometimes I'd watch her prepare moose meat. She and some of the wives of the U.S. Weather Service employees showed me how to make bread, how to roll and stretch the dough and pound it into the counter a few times until it was elastic and smooth enough to be covered for its first rise.

It was odd that I should meet my first *Yu'pik* woman in the midst of a Tlingit Indian village so far from the treeless, north-west arctic coast in Kotzebue where Sue Jensen had spent most of her life. All I knew about Alaska Natives was what I'd seen on television growing up. Eskimos dressed in real fur parkas and lived in igloos surrounded by polar bears and they traveled by dog sled pulled by huskies. Public school didn't teach details about the 49th state; there were no lessons about Aleuts, Athabascans, Eskimos (Inupiaq and Yup'ik), Tlingits, Haida, and Tsimpshians, not when there were so many other Indian tribes in the Lower 48 and closer to home.

It didn't matter when I showed up at Sue's. She always welcomed me with my lists of culinary questions about how people usually cooked sockeyes and kings, which became our primary food sources, along with moose, and how to make "Poor Man's Lobster" by dropping halibut chunks into boiling water sweetened with a little sugar. Sue answered my nagging questions so cheerfully that I thought all locals must be as good-natured, and generous about whatever they knew.

But Mr. Pavlik shattered that initial impression. The notorious patriarch of the Pavliks, Jennie's father, Mike Pavlik, kept a wealth of trade secrets about how to live off the land. He believed his knowledge and wisdom should be guarded like a rare family heirloom and not shared, especially not with anyone outside of his immediate family and never with those "bastards who don't give a damn about the land."

Alaska existed as an icon of untouchable wilderness, a vast land of impenetrable ice. The superficial view of history mostly revolved around its boom-and-bust days in gold mining, fish processing, military expansion, oil exploration, and drilling. Alaska was a detached mountainous enigma. The state was not thought of as a state, but as a gigantic piece of tundra way up there on the top of the globe, a whopping cold wasteland even though *less* than 20 percent of it sits *above* the Arctic Circle. In contrast, Alaska also attracted young backpackers, adventurers, loner artists and wandering monks who wanted to lose themselves in the Land of the Midnight Sun. No matter how Alaska was imagined, it was never an accidental destination.

Days for Sue Jensen centered around cooking, cleaning, or washing clothes even though most of their brood of fourteen children had left the roost. For a little fun, she went to the Alaska Native Brotherhood Hall to play bingo on Friday nights. Occasionally, we'd see one another at the Glacier Bear Lodge. Sometimes, when she had a few beers, she would repeat the same old lines about her marriage to Jim.

"Kathy, you know what's funny? I've spent twelve years of my life pregnant! You can count it up yourself. You will never pass me in this with your man," she'd say. And we would burst into laughter.

We ate a lot of frozen hamburger and jarred spaghetti sauce procured from Mallott's General Store since the summer salmon season was months away, and I didn't yet know how to cook. Part of what held me together was the daily drive down the one-and-only paved road to the post office. I was desperate for packages and letters and mail order deliveries from Outside. Michael started playing basketball at the elementary school gym. He befriended

George "Chunky" Henninger and Jimmy Bremner, both Tlingits who had grown up in Yakutat, and both performers with the St. Elias Dancers.

Yakutat is an ocean town, a forest town, a glacier town, a rain town. It's north of Juneau and situated 220 air miles southwest of Cordova on latitude 59°61' N, along the north Pacific coast, or on the shores of the Gulf of Alaska. The northernmost border of the Tongass National Forest reaches Yakutat, part of the world's largest temperate rainforest, comprised of the greenest, tallest, thickest Sitka spruce and hemlock you've ever seen. The Tongass National Forest covers 16.9 million acres and stretches almost 600 miles south, to below Ketchikan.

Except for those few, hardy steelheaders, most people bypassed the town altogether. The reason was simple: weather. Yakutat's average precipitation was over 130 inches per year compared to Anchorage's 15 inches. The tedious rain kept people out. And that's the way Mr. Pavlik and his whole family liked it.

Approximately 70 miles northwest of town stands Mount Saint Elias, the third highest mountain in North America. Imagine a peak dramatically rising out of the ice and snow like a gleaming all-white Egyptian pyramid. From sea-level, it shoots up to 18,008 feet, higher than any peak in the Rockies. As mountains go, it doesn't quite look like any other precisely because of its singular, dominating appearance. Mount Saint Elias stands alone and aloof from its many glacier covered brothers and sisters. Technically, the border splits this triangular, trowel-shaped mountain down the middle – half of it lies in Canada and half within Alaska's legal boundary.

Two things happened when summer finally arrived. First, we bought an all-terrain vehicle, a Honda three-wheeler to ride the backcountry logging roads and down the shoreline and out to Ocean Cape – it was delivered as airfreight aboard Alaska Airlines.

And I finally landed a job to make Gloria Steinem proud: I became a fish slimer.

When the commercial fishing season began in June, I reported for duty down at the docks at 8:00 a.m. to work in the fish cannery.

Six or seven days a week, from early-to-mid-summer, cannery workers stood in an assembly line against a long, plastic counter to gut and clean salmon. The whole place reeked of raw fish and entrails. Thousands of pounds of salmon were piled high in white plastic fish totes that looked like garbage dumpsters. If I arrived at the cannery for the morning shift on an empty stomach or with the slightest feeling of a hangover from being out with Michael the night before at the Native-owned Glass Door Bar, the overpowering odor of fish waste would make me gag.

Once the morning shift began, those totes had to be emptied, every one of them, and quickly. Scraps of fish intestines, fish scales, salmon eggs, and streaks of blood splattered everything, even forklift blades, and the unformed cardboard boxes stacked high in nearby flats. Fish scraps stuck in between the wooden planks of the floor.

Large, steel freezer doors continually slammed shut, and hundreds of pounds of crushed ice went tinkling and pelting like a waterfall. Manual labor stretched for eight or ten hours at a time. Sometimes we traded stations on the slime line to relieve the drudgery of standing in the same place. Within a few weeks, a fish slime camaraderie developed as I got to know some of my fellow workers. Nikko, a Japanese man, gave the white glove treatment to salmon eggs, handling each sac as if it were a crystal vase. All the salmon eggs were saved for export to Japanese seafood markets.

One by one, the salmon were beheaded, their organs stripped, and the main artery which runs along the fish's spine scraped clean. Carcass after carcass slid down the assembly line. I firmly gripped a metal tablespoon and scraped out any remaining blood or slime, then heaved the red salmon, often weighing up to ten pounds, down to the next group of workers who would then give it a quick rinse and toss the sockeye into its holding container. There were no conveyor belts; everything was done by hand.

Most of the cannery workers showed up from the Lower 48 either as lost souls bumming around the Pacific Northwest, as college students who hoped to make fast cash or as perpetual seasonals who migrated around wherever they could find work.

But not Barbie. She was a veteran, one of the regular cannery workers, a local who had grown up in town. Barbie seemed to enjoy her role as one of the strongest and most dependable fish handlers. I knew her only casually as the sister of someone else I knew in the village. I watched her wield a knife with the speed and agility that won her the first position on the assembly line. Her shoulders and biceps bulged; she was firmly sculpted, as if she built houses for a living. Barbie spent all day cutting off salmon heads, and she was proud of it. She had never married, never even had a boyfriend that anyone knew about, and didn't order any pretty clothes from the Sears & Roebuck catalogs. Although she was my age, it was hard to talk to her because Barbie didn't like "girl talk" like my pre-Alaska girlfriends did. During her off time, she hung around anything with motors: rusty pickup trucks, ATVs she could race down the beach, skiffs, Zodiacs, and even her brother's dirt bike. Whenever I saw her at the Glass Door, she sat at the far end of the bar and rarely spoke more than four or five words in an evening. She stayed to herself and sipped her drink.

At the morning break from the slime line, or when it was quitting time, we all ran to the hoses to wash off the salmon blood and guts from our massive, army green bib overalls and brown rubber Xtra-Tuff boots. A stream of cold water mixed with fish blood swirled to the floor; rivulets of maroon waste flooded the drain. But Barbie was apparently in no hurry to rinse off. At the end of the shift, she hung back from the hoses for a few minutes, grabbed a pack of smokes, and smirked at the rest of us who jetted to the hose and sprayed a full blast of water down our front sides. I started wondering if life in the bush had put that hard, smelly crust on Barbie and if that kind of hardening up would happen to me in this surreal and primitive place the world had forgotten.

Generations of Tlingits had built their Southeast Alaska culture in the fjords and bays and rivers next to the North Pacific Ocean, subsisting on salmon for their very survival for thousands of years. One of the Tlingits' early fishing methods involved trapping fish in tidal estuaries, or in small ponds called *ishes*, where salmon would rest after their tremendous migrations. Once the salmon collected in their tidal paradise, clever Tlingit fishermen would direct them into their nets. Tlingits caught and hand-processed and smoked the salmon into dried strips, each family in their particular way and for their own tribal and family needs, without the benefit of modern canning machinery, vacuum sealers, or Ziploc bags.

The Libby Packing Company opened Yakutat's first salmon cannery in 1905. Half a world away in bustling New York City or London restaurants, customers dined on salmon cakes from fish caught and canned in places like Yakutat.

Six weeks passed on the slime line. It was the most physically grueling, smelliest, most unconventional job of my life. I tried to console myself. I'm not some wayward city woman who's simply biding her time in this male-dominated fishing town until her husband saves her and they transfer out. Steel Town Girl wanted to show how tough she was. And I wanted to be liked and to fit in.

But for the time being, feminist fish slimer or not, I still cared about *appearing* feminine, about being sensual and sexy. I complained to Michael about the stench in my hair – it smelled like dead fish. And how much my wrists and lower back ached – as if I had been lifting spruce logs all day. How I never dressed in anything nice anymore – except in Yakutat tennis shoes,

B. F. Goodrich, Xtra-Tuff knee-high rubber boots and in dirty, red bandanas. I wore baggy sweatshirts that advertised the "Yakutat Rain Festival from Jan. 1 to Dec. 31."

I stopped wearing mascara, eyeshadow, skirts, or anything remotely feminine, as none of it worked anymore. In less than six months, I had become a parody of the self I had been striving to be. From every angle, my current situation was full of paradoxes that I didn't quite understand.

In the beginning, I never considered where the salmon I was gutting had migrated from. Nor who the men were who risked their lives season after season out in the dangerous breakers in small skiffs to haul those thousands of pounds of sockeyes. Or why the bay outside the cannery, Monti Bay, and the beaches beyond, the Ankau Lagoon system, and Ocean Cape, and the great fanfare of mountains – too numerous to name – were so much in the blood of these Yakutat Tlingits. For millennia, they nourished themselves with fish and kelp covered in herring roe and with all the delicious edibles the sea provided.

I knew nothing about wild salmon as a species, or about fishing as a means of food gathering. I knew nothing about beach rye grass and skunk cabbage or that the blueberry bloomed in August, or that pink salmon fed the bears, or that ravens were among some of the smartest birds alive. Of bald eagles that scavenged for fingerlings, I knew nothing. Nor of potlatch, pewter skies, Disenchantment Bay, seal hunting, glacial moraines, plate tectonics, coho, brown bear, Devil's Club, salmonberry, williwaws, moieties, or the *teet kwanni* – spirits of the sea in Tlingit.

"Being Tlingit is *knowing who you are*. Being Tlingit is living in partnership with the land." I heard these words spoken, but I had no real concept of what a close relationship to the land meant.

I had little direct, in-depth knowledge of mountains, streams, forests or any closeness to nature from anywhere I had lived before. Not in the close physical and spiritual sense that the Yakutat people had. The Tlingits – they weren't merely subsisting on the land. They were embodied and *inspirited* by it.

I grew more interested in my ancestry. The indigenous peoples of Alaska had lived for 10,000 years without Western religion. They lived in deep awareness of the sacred landscape surrounding them, and they did it without a church or book. What sacred rituals and traditions had been passed down to me? What traditional clothing or dress to mark my family's heritage? What prayers, stories, or songs had my family ever shared?

I recalled how a few longtime Alaskans had erroneously warned us as we prepared to move to the village: "Remember, don't ever shoot a raven, or say anything negative about those noisy, black-birds, either. That would be a very offensive thing to do because to the Tlingit Indians, ravens are like God: they hold the spirit of their ancestors."

What city people often repeated about the "*Click-it*" Indians was often nothing but pure speculation and stereotype. It's not that the Tlingits perceived Raven as God, or as a special deity to be worshipped. Tlingits saw ravens as creatures to be greatly respected. They believed in One Spirit Above, without written doctrines, syl-logisms, theology books, or Scriptural references.

The spirit of their ancestors . . . the spirit of their ancestors. Those words, when I first heard them, repeated through the drooping vine of my soul. I was a drifting boat, unsure of where my moorings were, and could not speak with any authority about my ancestors.

The relentless gray of winter came around again, and we weren't going anywhere. It was time I had a heart-to-heart talk with myself, a clearing of the mind. Maybe there was a Creator at work in the universe.

Finally, I caught my first unobstructed views of Mount Saint Elias from our living room window, and again from the boat harbor. The mountain appeared as white as a piece of paper – the whitest white triangle dominating the horizon. I took out the blank leather journal I had packed in with our meager belongings, and for the first time in a quiet moment, I sat down to scribble a few quick words.

I wrote: "Mount Saint Elias is the most beautiful mountain I have ever seen. Petty ambitions will die on mountainsides."

SPIRIT OF THE TINGLITS

It was a bright day, and the sea was calm, and I looked out over the glittering blue water, realizing more and more that this was where I belonged. I shall never forget it. I need the sound of those waves, that desolation, that emptiness.

A Note from Merton's *Alaskan Journals*, 1968

In trying to get more acquainted with my new home, I studied maps and realized the Pacific was one mother of a big damn ocean. Everyone knows it's the biggest body of water on earth. I knew this much at least, but I hadn't thought about its actual scale or dimensions until I moved to Alaska. I first laid eyes on the Pacific Ocean, not from sunny Santa Monica or Hawaii, but from the uninhabited, cold, and blustery beaches of Yakutat. I wondered how many Gulfs of Mexico would fit into it, and why we rarely saw vessels on the cloudy horizon.

The northern rim of the Pacific – the open Gulf of Alaska – is an 850-mile arc extending from the Kodiak archipelago south to Ketchikan near British Columbia's border. It was fun to imagine that if I had a sailboat, and if I could sail it straight out into the horizon and head due west from Yakutat and south without ever changing longitudinal direction, I wouldn't see a trace of land again until I reached the Marquesas Islands over 4,000 nautical miles away, below the equator and deep into the South Pacific. In equatorial climes, we tend to associate the ocean with turquoise seas, sparkling sunshine, coconut palms, and bronzed women walking through warm sands in hot pink or yellow strapless sundresses. But in those early years, from where I first saw the Pacific, every nuance of its tropical, *pacific* persona was cast away. I stood chilled to the bone, covered head to unpolished toes in drab olive green rain gear and pants three sizes too big, without a Tiki hut in sight.

The Yakutat people deal in everything that is wet or about to become so. Historically, Tlingits are ocean-going people – *low tide people* – a name that suits them well. Harvesting marine resources remains a central part of their culture. "When the tide goes out, the table is set," as the old Tlingit expression goes. An estimated 16,000 to 20,000 Tlingits live in Southeast Alaska, with five Eagle and Raven clans calling Yakutat home – Yakutat being the northernmost territory in the Tlingit region.

For centuries, Tlingits constructed sturdy canoes out of spruce and hemlock logs and became experts at handling them. To save their rowing muscles, they often improvised by turning their canoes into prototype sailboats and attached canvas material to poles and paddles to increase propulsion across bays and fjords. In more modern times, Tlingits became adept at launching and running skiffs as set-net fishermen in the choppy seas, as all five of the Pavlik sons had learned to do as commercial and subsistence fishermen.

I spent as much time as I could investigating the beaches on my ATV. I rode with Michael from our apartment down the gravel road to Canon Beach and hugged the shoreline for miles until we reached Ocean Cape. The name refers both to the beach and to the bluff above it where the long expanse of natural beach temporarily halts, and the indentation that forms the mouth of Yakutat Bay begins. From our apartment the whole one-way trip by three-wheeler to Ocean Cape took about thirty minutes, depending upon how fast we zipped through the pebbly sand, and how many times we stopped along the way. On most days, especially in the fall, I donned full rain suit regalia and wore gloves to cut the chill.

At Ocean Cape, the surf was loud and booming. Swells could reach twenty feet. The Pacific whirled up, converged with the twenty-mile-wide mouth of Yakutat Bay, and relentlessly broke over boulders as it pummeled the shore. Ocean Cape was, and is, spectacular. More so than the great Gulf Island National Seashore near Pensacola.

The memories I had of north Florida beaches all seemed like another life after I moved to Alaska. My college girlfriends and I hung out on those hot, sugar white beaches, and as the Jimmy Buffet song went, we saw tourists covered with oil, living on sponge cakes, watching the sun bake. We wore bikinis and slathered with baby oil mixed with iodine and enjoyed the gentle, blue-green waters. Sprawled on frayed blankets with our portable radios blasting Lynnard Skynnard, we baked, too, under an intense, glaring sun. I lived under the hopeful delusion that fair, freckled skin like mine might darken to another tint besides pinkish-ivory.

At Ocean Cape there could be snow pellets in early September, and if I saw anyone at all at the beach on a fairly decent day – one with periodic drizzle instead of rain that fell by the barge load – it would be the Tlingit kids on their ATVs with an uncle or auntie, zipping down the shore. It was mostly about the thrill of the ride, but the kids, too, inspected the wrack line for whatever marine treasures washed up. A few of them were bundled in hooded sweatshirts and gathered around a small fire made from the sticks and driftwood scattered across the sands. By the sheer force of nature, the Gulf of Alaska would deposit whole spruce trees, 30 to 40 feet long, onto the beach, as if they were nothing but large Tinker Toys wedged in the sand.

Less than 20 miles north, the world's largest piedmont glacier, the Malaspina, extends its lobe down to the Gulf of Alaska between Icy Bay and Yakutat Bay. The Malaspina completely dominates the western side of Yakutat Bay, an area known as the Grand Wash where the ever-resourceful Mr. Pavlik and his sons frequently explored. If this were southern California, every sliver of this virgin beach and waterfront would be clogged with pricey condominiums, crowded boardwalks, and seafood restaurants. But in the isolated North Pacific, Yakutat's coast is a lonely place.

From this vantage point, the ocean rolls into an unbroken shore, part of an undisturbed strip of rainforest and coast that could technically extend uniformly without interruption for almost 200 miles, except for the mouths of streams and rivers that empty into the sea, and a few scattered fish camps near those rivers.

A dense, but narrow, band of tall Sitka spruce mixed with western hemlock and thick underbrush grows parallel to the Gulf of Alaska beach. Brown bears of all ages and sizes roam these pristine shores. Sandhill cranes and trumpeter swans fly overhead on their annual spring and fall migrations along the Pacific Flyway. Bonaparte's gulls and Great Blue Herons search the shallow waters and tidal outwash. Harbor seals occasionally bask on one of the large boulders. Succulent wild strawberries and purple lupine grow in sandy margins along the open greenbelt before dense Sitka spruce, and hemlock forest begins. In a matter of minutes, you can walk from the waves straight into the shadows of the rainforest, thick with salmonberry, lily-of-the-valley, twin flowers, ferns, lichen, and green walls of extra-thorny Devil's Club that only a bear can move through. The shrub thrives in Yakutat's fertile coastal environment growing well over 12-feet tall.

In this most tumultuous region of the North Pacific, a 60-foot wave is often a ripple. From Cape Fairweather 130 miles to the southeast to Cape Yakataga due northwest from Ocean Cape, the sea is often driven by over 100 miles per hour winds. The wind battered the shore, and the boulders that were carried downward by glaciers would be reduced to grit in no time.

Tumultuous. Fleeting. Dramatic. Seismically off the charts. A good place for restless women. The "turbulent crescent," the geologists called it, a land of widespread metamorphism. When it came down to it, Ocean Cape was not a beach to dabble your toes in. Instead of striped beach towels and coolers of chilled iced tea and sodas, you might see a rotting salmon, pieces of fishing net, a trail of bear footprints in the sand – or a brown bear ambling toward you. The north Gulf of Alaska coast is where other Alaska Native People – the Eyak – from Copper River in the north near Cordova had settled. The Eyak would portage across ice fields and streams to make their passage southward into Yakutat. The Tlingits who lived closer to Sitka ventured north to Yakutat in their canoes for trading.

Frederica de Laguna was a well-respected Bryn Mawr anthropologist who spent much time in the Yakutat region during the 1940s and 50s. She believed that *Yakutat* was likely derived from an Eyak Indian word meaning "the place where the lagoon is forming." Tlingits sometimes interpret its name to mean "the place where the canoe rests or bounces."

The Russians, European explorers, and other traders made initial contact in the region over two centuries ago. The explorations of Cook, LaPerouse, Malaspina, and Vancouver drew new nautical charts of the Southeast Alaska coastline. The ships' naturalists studied the inlets, coves, and islands, recorded the abundant wildlife they saw and collected botanical specimens. They made sketches of Tlingit women adorned in labrets – dramatic piercings of their lower lips where pieces of bone were inserted.

At the start of the twentieth century, the lands which the Tlingits and Eyaks had called home would be "discovered" by gold panners, drifters, East Coast museum collectors searching for finely woven Native spruce root baskets and Chilkat blankets.

Swedish missionaries bent on introducing God to the frontier's Godless tribes with their devil dancing and totem painting followed. The zealous Christians, the ones with the "million dollar missionary smiles" as some Natives later described them, came to evangelize *the heathens* who must be converted to the way of The Word. The Tlingits did not possess any guides to "Godly Living" and didn't keep Bibles around.

I wondered how they knew what they knew, if not from words printed in a book. In the Yup'ik culture, they spoke of *ella*, a deep awareness of the world, and a more selfless way of living. With the Pavliks, and with other Tlingits I befriended, they said the land itself was their Holy Prayer and Holy Spirit. They were grateful for the raven, the salmon, and for the mighty forces of the glacier. They felt a presence of a unifying creative spirit, perhaps, in the rains that endlessly fell on their heads and in the challenges forever thrown their way by Nature in this land of metamorphosis.

The human voice speaking to you, especially by an Elder, was a consecrated act. They paid close attention to another's voice. In the Tlingits' way of life and cultural values, attending to another's speech meant you obeyed the traditions of your ancestors when they spoke to you individually or in a group. You showed respect for self and elders. You were to be strong in mind, body, and spirit. You were to listen well and always try to hold each other up. These were fundamental Tlingit values passed down from one generation to the next. Put another way, as Native People believed, it was important to "stay inside the drum" in language and culture.

Compared to my family upbringing – so much of my youthful cultural awakening had been dependent upon what I heard and learned from the media – all of this sounded completely foreign. In my first few years of living in Yakutat, I was reminded daily of how disconnected I was to the natural environment, to my family, and to my ancestry.

Once, while on a visit to the Carnegie Museum, I came across a poem displayed as part of an exhibit in the American Hall of the Indian. I recognized the name of its author, Walter Soboleff, a well-known Tlingit elder with a Russian last name. I once him heard speak in Juneau. Soboleff's untitled poem reads:

> Nature is like people.
> Nature is alive.
> Mountains are like people.
> Trees are like people.
> Fish are like people.

If my mother were to meet a brown bear in the woods, she would say:

> My father's people, don't harm me.
> My father's people, peace, peace, peace.

Historians began making films and researchers took down oral histories. Nora Marks Dauenhauer and Richard Dauenhauer, both linguists and historians, referenced Andrew P. Johnson, a Tlingit language teacher and minister from Sitka. In a 1971 recording, Johnson explained,

A person will say. "I am going to speak to you." Public speaking is akin to a man walking along a river with a gaff hook.

He lets his gaff hook drift over a salmon swimming at the edge of the river. When he hooks on it, the salmon way over there becomes one with him.

Speaking is a flow that forms relationships. Even speech delivered at a distance becomes one with someone.

I started taking more interest in Tlingit practices and beliefs. They adapted the potlatch tradition from their contact with Russians. When any member of a clan dies, it is the opposite clan who makes all the funeral arrangements and assists the grieving family. At the end of forty days of mourning, the grieving family thanks everyone by organizing a potlatch, a large community gathering, where speeches honoring the deceased member and some of the deceased ancestors are made, and people share local foods and come together to support one another up after the sadness of death.

Meanwhile, Michael stayed busy further refining his wildlife viewing skills. He learned to set traps for mink and marten and spent most of his free time steelhead fishing. From a small bridge over the Situk River, he taught me how to spot the elusive steelhead near log jams. He insisted I don hip boots to hike through the brush to his favorite trout holes. Some days he took me practice shooting so I could learn to fire a Smith & Wesson .357 revolver on the side of the road near Harlequin Lake. He had no real adjustment period. Other than learning his FAA job, everything about the lifestyle seemed to bring out the best in his primordial, masculine nature.

Never agitated or second-guessing himself, he didn't question what tomorrow would bring but was content to be who he was, where he was, carrying his fishing rod like a torch as he moved down trails through thick alder and over massive spruce tree roots.

I started to write a different story and pictured myself as the migratory woman, the woman who was not Tlingit or Eyak, who was not of this place, who had no tribal clan, no tribal mask, no Eagle or Raven name.

As often as I could, I rode up and down the shore in my three-wheeler to where the wind meets the Pacific at Ocean Cape.

With each passing day, I started to lose part of myself in its dampness and beauty.

Pieces of my external self slowly emptied in the rain-washed air.

Everywhere I turned, I saw water – water frozen, water free running. Water seeped and spilled into a pattern of glacial streams, rivers, saltwater lagoons, wetlands, bogs, and sloughs.

On the forest floor, I felt spongy layers of moss under my feet.

The weather was miserable. Rains fell hard. Gales blew. Storms swept in. Winds battered. It's rough out there, fishermen said. And then the North Pacific would hurl a few more hemlock logs ashore, and the currents would pound and hammer the boulders to bits.

Long ago, in another life, as another self, my toes curled in fine, hot sand and touched pretty pink seashells. No more.

Tedious rains beat against my heavy, yellow rain jacket. Every day, the same old weather story:

Today: rain. Rain likely again in the evening. Then a chance of rain, late. Southeast winds 15 to 25 miles per hour. Chance of rain: 70 percent.

Tomorrow: rains likely. Windy. More rain.

I sulked and skulked. Every day, I waited for better weather, for the sun to please stay. Come back, sun!

But my friend, Jennie Pavlik, scolded me. "We don't wait," Jennie said. "Grab your jacket! We go anyway! Come on! Who cares about dumb old rain?"

And so I went with Jennie and with her mother, Genevieve. Sometimes, we picked blueberries. Sometimes we walked in silence beneath Sitka spruce trees. On the beach, we usually found something interesting poking out of the sand – bald eagle feathers, frayed rope. Jennie stuffed her pockets with pieces of this or that, some smooth, white rocks, maybe a razor clam shell. She was always collecting objects for her children and her arts and crafts.

Everyone hunted glass balls. I tried to find them, too. Best to go after storms, locals said. They came from Japanese fishing boats used long ago in the Pacific. Some glass floats looked like rolling pins, some like blue-green beach balls. The Pavliks had glass balls hanging everywhere to catch the light.

But me, the migratory woman, I never found a single one. Michael, he found many.

He had a well-thought-out glass ball strategy, a rational method for finding them, a sixth sense about it, as he did with fishing and wildlife.

"Ocean and glacial winds bury the glass balls inside sand dunes," he said. "Storms blow them out again." Glass balls looked like big green eggs tucked in the sands and scrub. When my husband hunted, he left the open beach and patiently searched the margins between sand and coastal forest.

"You are always in too much of a hurry," he said. "You need patience when hunting for glass balls. Search wherever others easily overlook." And then he grew quiet again.

"Okay," I said, "I will try that, except . . . except, I don't like moving slow. You know it's not my nature to sit still and just be. To wait in one place. And not talk. It's hard."

"You see, I have no patience," I said. But with my Tlingit companions, I did take time to listen. For a long time, we women did not seem to be doing much of anything but looking at the beach and waves. They shared stories with me. They told me about Knight Island and how they lived in Yakutat Bay. Jennie spoke about her father and the important knowledge he taught his children about how to live.

We enjoyed each other's company. We listened to many squawking ravens. Bald eagles swooped right by them and flew low over the surf.

The blackbirds never shut up. "Too noisy! Go away, you stupid ravens!" I said.

But the ravens only laughed and paid no mind.

We sat near the surf in unzipped jackets. No hats. The cold Pacific winds blew down our necks. Jennie and her mother made me smile. So many family stories! Her brother Rudy was always chasing or running from brown bears. All of her brothers hunted seals and otters. Her father cooked with seal oil and made her taste porpoise meat and drink rosehip tea.

I liked these Pavlik women. Gentle, quiet women. Women in repose. Women spiritually whole and well-grounded. They knew how to live in wild and free places. They made me feel calmer inside.

"Look, tide's in!" Jennie only said what needed to be said, nothing more, nothing less.

No *talk-talk-talk*. It was enough.

More often, at my favorite place in the world – Ocean Cape – I was with Michael. We traveled on the old dirt logging roads, past lagoons with muskeg and with yellow pond lilies, only occasionally seeing someone else pass by. Along the creeks and estuaries of the foreland, wherever we rode or walked, it was important to check for fresh, brown bear sign. If out on the clear open beach, I always made sure to check. Brown bears also roamed the sands and sniffed the tides.

We climbed the bluff and explored the area where the old World War II radar equipment and bunkers used to be – the White Alice communications site. From there, we paused to look down at the scrolls of waves rumbling to shore. The surf boomed, and the water splashed with immense power as if a great force was purposely announcing its presence.

Wind blew my copper-red hair. I daydreamed. On my three-wheeler, I spun and swerved around, made figure eights in the sand, and made sure Michael was close by on his machine. We circled amber pieces of kelp, tangled clumps of seaweed, and washed-up sculpin bones. With the engine switched off, I listened to rain pelt my jacket. My mind opened to the sand, the nettles, the sweetgrass, the chocolate lilies, and the heavy, steel-gray clouds dancing above.

I rode in rain and felt a rawness that soaked right through to my breasts. As time passed, I didn't mind the rain so much. I stooped down low to pick flowering beach pea and inspect the wrack line. A wave broke across the beach, and I dragged my hand through the bubbles left in the fine gravel and through the swirls of sea foam as Michael approached.

"Michael, Mount Saint Elias – it looks like a seagull on the water," I said.

"Where did you come up with that? It hasn't been out yet."

"I read it. A Tlingit elder once said that about the whiteness of the mountain."

I probably repeated that gorgeous metaphor one too many times when we were out in the elements three-wheeling, but it's a description that runs through my mind to this day. There was something mystical about the sharp, pure air, the steady winds blowing across the mouth of Yakutat Bay, and the fact we were all alone at Ocean Cape without human intrusions. In my imagination, this swath of pristine land and the Pacific Ocean were mine; the wonderful open space and perfection of nature before me, inseparable from my very breath.

But I felt fear. To be in such sublime beauty overwhelmed me as if I was shown a glimpse of some hidden reality that I couldn't begin to articulate. I didn't know where the fear was coming from, but I felt a pang of terror. I looked up and searched gray skies for the great white mountain but was disappointed. The alabaster pyramid was there, but it was not going to show itself for my benefit and pleasure. I looked up two or three more times. No mountain to feast my eyes upon.

Under the imaginary gaze of Elias, my throat tightened, and my stomach churned. "Why did you bring me here? What is it you are trying to teach me? Have I not opened my eyes wide enough?" I said. But I wasn't speaking to Michael who was driving fast, weaving his ATV in and out of driftwood piles. I was dumbfounded. What was I doing talking to a mountain I couldn't even see? I addressed Elias again, my wet fingers growing numb on the handlebars. "Why wait this long to show me such magnificence? What is it I should do with all this whiteness?"

From the rain and crashing of the sea, and from the Pavlik women, I was learning how to live in this world.

DANCING DEEPLY IN THE THICKET OF THE CROSS: THOMAS MERTON'S OPENNESS TO FIRST NATION ARTS AS ICONS OF TRADITIONAL BELIEF SYSTEMS

Allan M. McMillan

In one of the more important works on Native Spirituality edited by Lee Irwin we find a cautionary note:

> The themes in this volume are not necessarily new nor strictly an expression of developments within a particular field of academic study. They are, in many ways, as old as the earliest meetings, misunderstandings, and conflicts between Native and non-Native Peoples that have led, more often than not, to confusion in trying to communicate the respective differences of their alternative worldviews. From the 'other side of the frontier,' these themes have long been woven around the problem of trying to communicate the value and importance of indigenous religious action, identity, and commonly shared lifeways that are not easily or accurately subsumed into standard "western" analytic categories. These themes involve something more than intellectual understanding, aesthetic appreciation, or a fascination for exotic cultural activities. From the beginning of cultural contact, Native religious practitioners have engaged in a struggle to sustain their authenticity in the face of sustained, oppressive cultural denials. This history of contestation requires contemporary non-Native persons to fully recognize the intrinsic worth and value of Native religious beliefs and practices that are, in fact, not simply accessible or publicly available for inspection or study. Any introduction to these traditions requires respect, patience, and commitment to understanding even

the most elementary aspects of Native beliefs as they relate to religious practices and values.[1]

In a further comment, Lee Irwin offers a qualification of the word "spiritual," saying that it is far more than the mere practice of religion.

> This word 'religion' doesn't sit well in such a context either, being as it is a post-enlightenment concept often rooted in a polarity between ideas of the 'sacred and profane.' Such a distinction is an artificial and nonhelpful locus for understanding the primary foundations of Native spirituality. My perception of the interactive spheres of Native communal life is that they have a relatedness through personal relationships that find common expression in mutual, everyday concerns. It is that connectedness to *core values and deep beliefs* that I mean by 'spirituality' – a pervasive quality of life that develops out of an authentic participation in values and real life practices meant to connect members of a community with the deepest foundations of personal affirmation and identity. In this sense, spirituality is inseparable from any sphere of activity as long as it really connects with deeply held affirmative values and sources of authentic commitment, empowerment, and genuineness of shared concern.[2]

Accordingly, each author writing on Native spirituality must self-disclose their connectedness to Native communities to authenticate their relationship to the culture of which they speak. Many writers on Native Spirituality unconnected to Native communities offer no honest benefit to their readership.[3]

---

1. Lee Irwin, *Native American Spirituality: An Introduction.* (Lincoln and London: University of Nebraska Press, 2000) 1.

2. Lee Irwin, op. cit., 3.

3. Because of the sensitive nature of these works, I must confess that I hold no status with any of the First Nations of Canada, that my experience of these belief systems is based on the writings of those I truly respect. As a Roman Catholic priest with some experience of the First Nations across the northern shore of Lake Huron and Lake Nipissing, and a proclivity for collecting the art works of the Woodland Artists, some of whom I count as friends, I have no special association with members of any First Nation Reserve. I have some anecdotal evidence of a possible racial connection but have never been able to substantiate the claims in official records or documentation.

At first glance, it would appear that Thomas Merton's interest in indigenous peoples was cut short by his untimely death in Bangkok, 1968. A subsequent publication of a thin book, entitled *Ishi Means Man: Essays on Native Americans*,[4] shows the promise of what might have been. We can join the chorus of those who, like Dorothy Day in her brief forward to this work, cried out for "More, more!" In one of Merton's letters to Ernesto Cardenal,[5] who had been a novice for a time under Merton's direction, and who shared Merton's concern for the indigenous peoples of America, Merton mentioned that that he had a copy of *The Sacred Pipe,* by Black Elk as early as 1963.[6] But was there more?

As Novice Master, many of Merton's talks to his students were recorded. These recorded conferences give insights into the development of Merton's thought on Native Peoples. An important element to observe in listening to these conferences for glimpses into Merton's teaching style was that he was capable, while discussing one topic, of occasionally jumping to a second topic. Just such a moment occurred when he was giving a talk on the artistic worth and classical values in the writings of William Faulkner.[7] For a moment Merton comments on a possible future study for him in which the writings of John of the Cross could be explored to throw light on Faulkner's. What was the connection he was making in that instant? He does not give details.

The basis for this talk was an essay which he had written as an introduction to *Mansions of the Spirit,* edited by George A. Panichas and which was later published in *The Literary Essays of Thomas Merton*, edited by Brother Patrick Hart.[8] A careful listening to the tape suggests that he has let his eyes drop to the printed page while

---

4. Thomas Merton, *Ishi Means Man: Essays on Native Americans* (Greensboro, NC: Unicorn Press, 1976).

5. Thomas Merton's letter to Ernesto Cardenal, (no date, 1963). Cf. Thomas Merton, *The Courage for Truth: Letters to Writers,* selected and edited by Christine M. Bochen (San Diego: Harcourt Brace & Co., 1994) 141-143.

6. Black Elk, *The Sacred Pipe,* recorded and edited by Joseph Epes Brown (Norman, OK: University of Oklahoma Press, 1953).

7. Thomas Merton, *The Bear* (Credence Cassettes, AA2079); also available on disc in *Thomas Merton on William Faulkner and Classical Literature*, Disc 3: no. 6, "The Classical Values of Faulkner" (1/1967) and "Faulkner's 'The Bear': Spiritual Formation and Mystical Union" (1/1967).

8. Thomas Merton, "Baptism in the Forest: Wisdom and Initiation in William Faulkner," *The Literary Essays of Thomas Merton* (New York: New Directions, 1981) 92-123.

speaking to the novices. "'Baptism in the Forest': Wisdom and Initiation in William Faulkner," provides insights into the concepts he might have used in presenting his thoughts on indigenous people. Even though Merton's point of departure in the essay was Camus' opinion of Faulkner's religious belief, Merton expressed his strong feelings with terms such as "the disquieting, even annoying, popular tendency to look for "conversions . . .."[9] He further alluded to "the prevalence of another critical vice, that of "claiming for the faith."[10] He judged both tendencies as "intellectual imperialism."[11] Admitting that literary and religious categories should not be confused, Merton suggested that "Faulkner's writing (at least in "The Bear")[12] does have a 'spiritual redemptive' view of the world, though it is not necessarily the orthodox Christian view."[13]

Merton's essay connected the spiritual and redemptive qualities in Faulkner with classical Greek thought, which is also subtly embedded in much of Christianity. He asserted that these elements "are embedded in human nature itself, or, if that expression is no longer acceptable to some readers, then in the very constitution of man's psyche, whether in his collective unconscious or his individual character structure."[14] He pointed out how Greek tragedy has a direct impact on the deepest center of our human nature at a level beyond language. Our most fundamental human conflicts are neither explained nor analyzed, but enacted in the artistic way which Aristotle tried to account for in his theories on catharsis, pity, and terror. Merton then reflected on *hubris*, that excessive self-confidence, arrogance, and at times insolence[15] which overpowers the communion or unity that might have been possible with the First Nations of America. "The idea of religion today is mixed up with confessionalism. One's whole experience of life has to be dominated *from without* by a system of acquired beliefs and attitudes and that every other experience first to be tested by the system of beliefs.[16]

9. Thomas Merton, op. cit., 93.
10. Thomas Merton, op. cit., 93.
11. Thomas Merton, op. cit., 93.
12. "The Bear" is one of the chapters of Faulkner's novel, *Go Down, Moses* which was the focus of the two talks Merton was giving to the novices. Cf. William Faulkner, "The Bear," *Go Down, Moses* (Toronto: Random House of Canada Ltd., 1942) 101-331.
13. Thomas Merton, op. cit., 94.
14. Thomas Merton, op. cit., 95.
15. Thomas Merton, op. cit., 96.
16. Thomas Merton, op. cit., 97.

The power of symbols is, I think, fully explicable only if you accept the theory that symbols are more than mere artifacts of a few human minds. They are basic archetypal forms anterior to any operation of the mind, forms which have risen spontaneously with awareness in all religions and which have everywhere provided patterns for the myths in which man has striven to express his search for ultimate meaning and union with God . . . . *At the same time, it must be quite clear that this imaginative and symbol-making capacity in man must not be confused with theological faith* [my emphasis]. But, because faith implies communication and language, the language of symbols is most appropriate in activating the deepest centers of decision which faith calls into play.[17]

The legends of other peoples seem fanciful to those of us who hear them only with the ears of our own time and place. Judging a legend merely imaginary is the fault of the biased reader or listener; not the fault of the legends or in the cultures offering them for instruction and cultural edification. In his talks, Merton was not proving the priority of one system of thought over another but was demonstrating the basic way that humankind relates to the transcendent.

When Merton turned to a consideration of "The Bear" as related in Faulkner's *Go Down Moses,* he reminds us that the boy, Ike McCaslin, was being initiated by Sam Fathers,[18] the mixed-race hunter, part Chickasaw Indian and part black. For Merton, all men are capable of seeking the transcendent and need to be taught or initiated in the search. Not all are successful. Ike McCaslin is one of the few ever to see the bear. The encounters with the bear stretch from the time when McCaslin was a young lad until he becomes a mature hunter himself. But, each moment of encounter is progressively more mystical. "What Faulkner actually celebrates is the primitive wisdom of the American Indian, the man who was *par excellence* the wilderness hunter and the free wanderer in the unspoiled garden of Paradise."[19]

At one point, in his second conference, "The Bear,"[20] Merton

---

17. Thomas Merton, op. cit., 98.

18. The name is emblematic in that old Sam is both prophetic and paternal.

19. Thomas Merton, op. cit., 105.

20. Thomas Merton, *The Bear* (Credence Cassettes, AA2079); also available in *Thomas Merton on William Faulkner and Classical Literature*, Disc 3, no. 6, "Faulkner's 'The Bear': Spiritual Formation and Mystical Union" (1/1967).

suggested there is room for us to explore a parallel between the ever-deepening relationship of the boy to the bear as it relates to the writings of St. John of the Cross. This parallel is not for a theological purpose but for demonstrating something intrinsically basic to the relationship of each of us with that which is supremely divine. It is a matter of love at its deepest level. Merton suggested that only then do the truths and verities of the heart coalesce with honor, pity, pride, compassion, and sacrifice. The "reasons of the heart" are only embraced through living experiences.

In the final moments of the parable of the Bear, McCaslin totally surrenders to the experience. Having left his gun at home, he eventually lets go of the large stick which he had brought to ward off serpents (in paradise?). Next, he surrenders his watch and compass (emblematic of time and space). Suddenly, while water seeps into the newly planted paw prints of the unseen bear, McCaslin surrenders even more to the truth that he is no longer unseen but seen and known by the bear who is very near by in the thicket. Then, and only then does the bear, Old Ben, present himself to the hunter for a moment. A knowing glance is exchanged. The beautiful moment of seeing arrests McCaslin and we do not know whether he is the seeing or the one seen. Silently, the apparition submerges back into the wilderness like an old trout. This metaphoric image chosen by Faulkner suggests ICHTHYS, the emblematic symbol for Christ. But, nothing is certain. Merton left many elements of "The Bear" open to interpretation during his talks with the novices, but insisted on the degrees of awareness necessary for mystical experience.

In spite of the fact that William Faulkner was not a Catholic author, the intuitive mind of Thomas Merton grasped the connections possible between Faulkner's parable of "The Bear," and stanzas 36 and 37 of *The Spiritual Canticle* by St. John of the Cross. With a little connective thinking on our part, I hope to extend the intuitive connection to Black Elk and his description of the Sun Dance as a mystical moment with symbolic parallels to what Merton intuited as resonating in the writings of Faulkner and St. John of the Cross. There is much more than religious, cultural cross contamination between a visionary like Black Elk and a saint like John of the Cross. The significance of suffering as an agent of mystical moments is central to our purpose. It has nothing to do with a conversion experience. But the similarity of experience to that mentioned by John of the Cross speaks broadly to compassion and the necessity of suffering as a way of seeing. We do not need to discuss Christian conversion to substantiate a companionship of ideas.

> The power of symbols is, I think, fully explicable only if you accept the theory that symbols are more than mere artifacts of a few human minds. They are basic archetypal forms anterior to any operation of the mind, forms which have risen spontaneously with awareness in all religions and which have everywhere provided patterns for the myths in which man has striven to express his search for ultimate meaning and union with God.[21]

If we are looking for revelations from above and beyond, we are looking where we might never see:

> Symbols are not, here, ciphers pointing to hidden sources of information. They are not directed so much at the understanding and control of things as at man's own understanding *of himself* [my emphasis]. They seek to help man liberate in himself life forces which are inhibited by dead social routine, by the ordinary involvement of the mind in trivial objects, by the conflicts of needs and material interests on a limited level. Sapiential awareness deepens our communion with the concrete: it is not an initiation into a world of abstraction and ideals. Wisdom, in any case, has two aspects. One is metaphysical and speculative, an apprehension of the radical structure of human life, an intellectual appreciation of man in his human potentialities and their fruition. And the other is moral, practical, and religious, an awareness of man's life as a task to be undertaken at great risk, in which tragic failure and creative transcendence are both possible. Sapiential thinking has, as another of its characteristics, the capacity to bridge the cognitive gap between our minds and the realm of the transcendent and the unknown, so that without "understanding" what lies beyond the limit of human vision, we nevertheless enter into an intuitive affinity with it, or seem to experience some such affinity. At any rate, religious wisdoms often claim not only to teach us truths that are beyond rational knowledge but also to *initiate* us

---

21. Thomas Merton, op. cit., 98.

into higher states of awareness. Such forms of wisdom are called mystical beyond the aesthetic, moral, and liturgical levels and penetrate so far as to give the initiate a direct, though perhaps incommunicable, intuition of the ultimate values of life, of the Absolute Ground of life, or even of the invisible Godhead. Christian wisdom is essentially theological, Christological, and mystical.[22]

If the selection of readings used each year for the Office of Readings was the same in the old calendar as in the new, then the Second Reading for the Feast of St. John of the Cross is taken from the Spiritual Canticle, sections 36 and 37.[23] If not, then there is no reason for Merton not to have known texts of this sort for he had certainly studied the poetic writings of John of the Cross:

> Let us rejoice, Beloved
> And let us go forth to behold ourselves in Your beauty,
> To the mountain and to the hill,
> To where the pure water flows,
> And further, deep into the thicket.[24]

At first glance, these clues seem trivial and incidental until we consider the explication or interpretation of the poem by St. John of the Cross:

> (36-11) The soul wants to enter this thicket and incomprehensibility of judgements and ways because she is dying with the desire to penetrate them deeply . . . [T]he soul ardently wishes to be engulfed in these judgments and know them from further within. And, in exchange, it will be a singular comfort and happiness for her to enter all the afflictions and trials of the world, and everything that might be a means to this, however difficult and painful, even the anguish and agony of death, all in order to see

---

22. Thomas Merton, "Baptism in the Forest: "Wisdom and initiation in William Faulkner," *The Literary Essays of Thomas Merton,* ed. Brother Patrick Hart, OCSO (New York: New Directions, 1981) 100-101.

23. There were revisions of the Roman Calendars under both Pope John XXIII and Paul VI.

24. St. John of the Cross, "The Spiritual Canticle, Stanza 36," *The Collected Works of St. John of the Cross,* translated by Kieran Kavanaugh, OCD and Otilio Rodriquez, OCD (Washington, D.C.: ICS Publications, Institute of Carmelite Studies, 1973) 546.

herself further with her God.

(36-12) This thicket into which the soul thus wants to enter also signifies very appropriately the thicket and multitude of trials and tribulations, for suffering is very delightful and beneficial to her. Suffering is the means of her penetrating further, deep into the thicket of the delectable wisdom of God.

(36-13) Oh! If we could but now fully understand how a soul cannot reach the thicket and wisdom of the riches of God, which are of many kinds, without entering the thicket of many kinds of suffering, finding in this her delight and consolation; and how a soul with an authentic desire for divine wisdom, wants suffering first in order to enter this wisdom by the thicket of the cross![25]

It is a small point indeed, and tenuous at best, but if we are to hunt with Merton in the quest for a connection to the sufferings of the Native Peoples of North America, we have to be willing to see the tracks of the quarry before we see the animal itself. It was a comment tossed off at the moment, but a comment of deep passion all the same. Our understanding of others among the First Nations and especially regarding the Sun Dance rituals which I shall discuss below urges us to go beyond the parameters of our own culture and surmise new possibilities. And if we want to offer an opinion as to where Merton might have gone had he not died in Bangkok we need to know his ideas and methodology, indeed his theology. Let us now bring what we have learned from Merton into our dialogue with the Peoples, their history, and possible directions for the future.

LEGENDS AND STORIES AS ESSENTIAL ELEMENTS OF FIRST NATION EDUCATION

We need to open ourselves imaginatively to a time when people lived in larger communities during the winter and in smaller mobile hunting and gathering groups during the summer. At the end of the day, when campfires drew people together, a time of teaching occasioned the handing on to children of the next generation, the

---

25. St. John of the Cross, *The Collected Works of St. John of the Cross,* translated by Kieran Kavanaugh, OCD and Otilio Rodriguez, OCD with Introductions by Kieran Kavanaugh, OCD (Washington, D.C.: ICS Publications, 1973) 548-549.

precious stories that gave meaning to life.[26] The child learns when the child is old enough to ask questions and to hear the meaning of the story. For the Ojibway, the lessons must speak to the whole person. Information and imagination are integrated with humor and emotion to give flesh and bones to the values of the ancestors who gave them life. Some of the legends strike a tone of subtle humor and others are more ribald than would be allowed in our day. To fully appreciate the legends, we need to place ourselves among the wide-eyed children and allow ourselves to be entertained as well as instructed. We do not need to translate their ideas into our categories and concepts or rationalize their cultural patterns to our own. Such an action would be a refusal of acceptance and an artificial sociological distinction of their world view from our own. Like children everywhere, our listening requires an openness and the possibility of acceptance.

> Dr. Jacqueline Weitz NIB (National Indian Brotherhood) consultant, clearly stated the difficulties: "The opportunity to learn in his own way, a way with deep cultural roots and implications, must be provided in the school. We cannot teach Indian children using the educational psychology which dominates today's classrooms. Dependence on the teacher, time blocked activities, programmed learning, are a few practices which violate the learning psychology of the Indian child. Teaching methods, materials, subject matter and goals must conform to the teaching methods of Indian parents and to their goals for education.[27]

The many stories told by a *Mishomis* (Grandfather) and a *Nokomis* (Grandmother) were treasures that had been carried in their memories and shared with their own *Nooshenh* (Grandchild).[28] These stories are complex. Some are similar, one nation to another, but others are unique to a particular region. They are symbols shared rather than puzzles to be unraveled by a translation into our concepts and misconceptions. They are part of the world of wonder so necessary to our time in the technological wilderness. Perhaps a few selected examples will illustrate the matter at hand and indi-

---

26. Peter S. Schmalz, *The Ojibwa of Southern Ontario* (Toronto: University of Toronto Press, 1991) 257.

27. As quoted by Peter S. Schmalz, op. cit., 241.

28. These are An-ish-in-aub-ag (Ojibway) terms.

cate the subtleties needed to encounter a culture whose origins are wrapped in the mists of time itself.[29]

The Legend of Sky Woman and Her Children

> Among the "Wendat" (also called Hurons by the French and "Wyandot" by the English) the creation story begins with a woman because all life comes from the mother. Sky Woman fell from the sky into a world that was all water. Two loons[30] who were swimming on the water happened to look up and see her falling so they placed themselves under her to cushion her fall and save her from drowning. They called to the other animals for help. The calls of the loons can be heard for great distances. The Turtle offered to let her rest on his back for his back was more wide than the other animals. The animals held a council and it was decided that Sky Woman would need earth to live on. So, the animals took turns diving into the depth to see if they could bring up soil from the bottom. Otter, Beaver, and Muskrat, made attempts to bring up the soil, but the water was so deep and they were so short on breath that they failed. Then one of them noticed that there was some soil on Muskrat's paws and in his mouth. And that was enough to put on the Turtle's back. It became Turtle Island which is the name by which the First People refer to the land of North America.
>
> Eventually the Sky Woman gave birth to twins and they had very different dispositions. The one wanted to be born in the normal way but the other broke through the side of the mother and she died. She was buried in the earth and from her came new life to feed everyone. From her head came the pumpkin, from her breasts came the corn, and

---

29. It should be noted that wherever possible, we will include names in the original language as a reminder that their words take precedence over ours and that just as one needs to learn a language in order to grasp what others are actually saying, so too, these words will remind us that it is we who are invited to change and move in the direction of acceptance. In colonial times, the interplay of language was often misused by those who sought to displace the original people and obfuscate the processes of domination. With intent, we have turned the process around.

30. The loons of the northern lakes mate for life. They know life on the surface and life beneath.

from her limbs came the beans. Even today the pumpkin, beans, and corn are called the Three Sisters.

Now the brothers were not men but beings with super-natural powers and opposite dispositions. The evil brother whose name meant "like flint" created monstrous animals to terrify and destroy humanity: serpents, bears, cougars, and mosquitoes that were as large as turkeys, (There are still some of these around so it is said.) and a giant toad that drank up all the fresh water in the world.

The Good brother created the harmless animals such as the dog, the deer, the elk, and buffalo and many of the birds like the partridge. But the partridge flew off to the land of the Flint looking for fresh water. There was a great battle to protect the fresh water and it was only won when the Good Brother came and cut open the toad allowing fresh water to flow over the land. The flowing water made riv-ers. At first, the Good brother wanted the waters to flow both up and down so that the people would not have to work hard when traveling regardless of the direction taken. But the bad brother did not want this to be, so he made all the rivers flow down stream. He also made the rapids, the whirlpool, and the waterfalls.

In the end, the brothers engaged in combat as had been foretold in a dream. The Good brother said that he could only be destroyed if he was beaten with a bag of corn or beans. The evil brother admitted that he could only be destroyed if he was beaten with the antlers or horns of an animal. After the Good brother won, the bad brother went away to the west. The west is where the dead go after dy-ing. . ... At least that is where they went until the Christian missionaries changed the story.[31]

31. Cf. Ella Elizabeth Clark, *Indian Legends of Canada* (Toronto: McClel-land & Stewart, 1960) paraphrase 1-3. For a more complete rendition of this story we recommend further reading in a new book by Brian Rice, *The Rotinonshonni: A Traditional Iroquoian History Through The Eyes of Teharonhia:wako and Sawiskera* (Syracuse, NY: Syracuse University Press, 2013). A further reason for recommending this work is that, in its completion, it takes the story of the two brothers Teharonhia:wako and Sawiskera and develops the parable as a rational-ization behind the historical legend of Ayenwatha (Hiawatha), Atotarhoh and Tekana:witha (Two-currents-coming-down), also known as The Peacemaker. With these three, the Great Peace was established and proclaimed with the Wampum of peace. This legend stands as a traditional source for the writing of the Consti-

This foundational story of the creation demonstrates the use of metaphor in dealing with the issue of the goodness of creation and the problematic presence of evil as an observed reality in the world. It deals with the life force that sustains animals and humankind and sets the stage for many other applications; all of which are in a presentable form for teaching children. The moral choice is also presented as a choice between two who are as close as brothers, and there is a connection to light and darkness, life and death, struggle and peace. At the level of narrative, it is quite simple. At the level of metaphor, it becomes prophetic. In time, the people of the First Nations saw themselves as those related to the good brother and the newcomers with their bearded faces, their strange customs and instruments of destruction as being those related to the bad brother.

The Legend of the Tree and the Four Directions

The oral traditions and legends of the various First Nations are supported by more than implied metaphors. There is also a substructure of symbols which implies a catholicity of meaning behind certain ideas. They are free standing ideas and likely have roots even more ancient than the legends which are regionally typical. They may even predate the trans-Beringian migrations during the last ice-age. Though the origins of these symbols are not immediately evident, their consistent presence among the First Nation Peoples is more than coincidental.

All across Turtle Island, belief in the Sacred Tree appears to have a central position in the ongoing spiritual (philosophic) stability of the people. The roots reach deep into Mother Earth, and the branches are uplifted to the Sky Father. The virtuous life is protected by the Sacred Tree which is a central gathering place of those who are loving, compassionate, patient, wise, just, generous, courageous, respectful, and humble. Black Elk, a visionary mystic of the Oglala Lakota Sioux is reputed to have described his initial vision as follows:

> Then I was standing on the highest mountain of them all,
> and round about beneath me was the whole hoop of the
> world. And while I stood there I saw more than I can tell

---

tution of the American Democracy and also as one source for the Charter of the United Nations. Cf. also Megan McClard and George Ypsilantis, *Hiawatha and the Iroquois League* (Englewood Cliffs, NJ: Silver Burdett Press of Simon and Schuster, Inc., 1989) 119-121.

and I understood more than I saw: for I was seeing in a
sacred manner the shape of all things in the spirit, and the
shape of all shapes as they may live together like one being. And I saw that the sacred hoop of my people was one
of many hoops that made one circle, wide as daylight and
as starlight, and in the center, grew one mighty flowering
tree to shelter all the children of one mother and one father.
And I saw that it was holy.[32]

It is not possible to discuss the spirituality of North American Native
Peoples without discussing the Sacred Tree and the Hoop of the
World. These are common metaphoric images that speak instantly
to those who embrace the teaching. The ideas are presented in an
evidentiary manner rather than by syllogistical argument. Because
it is more art and poetry in form, each person has to find his or her
level of understanding and the means to apply that which they have
learned. No one judges another with a fundamentalist or naturalistic
orthodoxy because the message in visions like those of Black Elk is
in the realm of symbol, not scientific cause and effect. These ideas
challenge one to know and how to relate to the context of being a
people. They are more exhortation than proclamation and therefore,
without bias and judgment, while being open to each person's interpretation. It is not a legalism but a path of life; a cultural *gnosis*
and *praxis* with which Black Elk in his own life was able to retain
the idea of the Sacred Tree and accrete the Cross of Christ, even
as he embraced Catholicism without contradiction.

The ancient ones taught us that the life of the Tree is the
life of the people. If the people wander far away from the
protective shadow of the Tree, if they forget to seek the
nourishment of its fruit, or if they should turn against the
Tree and attempt to destroy it, great sorrow will fall upon
the people. Many will become sick at heart. The people
will lose their power. They will cease to dream dreams and
see visions. They will begin to quarrel among themselves
over worthless trifles. They will become unable to tell
the truth and to deal with each other honestly. They will
forget how to survive in their own land. Their lives will
become filled with anger and gloom. Little by little they

---

32. John G. Neihardt, *Black Elk Speaks* (Lincoln, NE: University of Nebraska
Press, 1961).

will poison themselves and all they touch.

It was foretold that these things would come to pass, but that the Tree would never die. And as long as the Tree lives, the people live. It was also foretold that the day would come when the people would awaken, as if from a long, drugged sleep; that they would begin, timidly at first but then with great urgency, to search again for the Sacred Tree.

The knowledge of its whereabouts, and of the fruit that adorns its branches have always been carefully guarded and preserved within the minds and hearts of our wise elders and leaders.[33]

THE MEDICINE WHEEL

Another basic symbol functions in Native communities in North and South America. The Medicine Wheel has its roots in the ancient system of the four directions of the world. The double bifurcation of a circular form is intuitive rather than logical. Once visualized, other phenomena seem to support it affirmatively. The wheel gives equal footing to the four directions, the four seasons, the four races: White, Red, Yellow, and Black. The wheel teaches that the basic elements of life: Fire, Earth, Air, and Water, must be protected to sustain life. A balance must be maintained in the four aspects of human life: Mental, Spiritual, Emotional, and Physical. These are the seeds planted within the heart that potentially can become an expression of the tree. All life requires wholeness, protection, nourishment, and growth. The wheel is mysterious and unexplainable for "The tree could be cut into a thousand pieces, and no new fruit will be found, yet when the conditions are right for its growth (warm sunshine, open space, rain, and nourishing soil), the tree will develop the fruit in all of its luscious beauty."[34]

The colors are placed within a circle, and the circle is alive. All life is based on the circle. The circle has no beginning and no end. It is complete and whole. When we sit in a circle, all are equal. Good feelings are shared with all who sit in the circle. The drum

---

33. Judie Bopp, Michael Bopp, Lee Brown, and Phil Lane, collaborators in the writing of *The Sacred Tree* (Alberta, Canada: Four Worlds Development Press, University of Lethbridge, 4401 University Drive, Alberta, Canada, T1K 3M4) 7. This work is perhaps the clearest presentation of these teachings ever done. It is used successfully in the Self-Help Communities of Western Canada.

34. Bopp et al., op. cit., 34.

is made in a circle. It was given to the Anishnaabe (Ojibway)[35] as
a means of communication with the Great Spirit. When the drum
is struck, the sound goes down into the earth and then rises to the
sky. It is the beat of life. The drum or circle is a visual symbol of
the spiritual strength of the people. The drum or circle carries with
it the message of hope and better understanding among peoples.[36]

The Medicine Wheel is the matrix of the moral life of all the
people of the First Nations, from the eldest to the youngest. It is
the basis of communication, understanding, and social stability for
many people. These concepts are not just a set of defining ideas.
They call for a deeply lived relationship, both individual and communal. Beyond the stories and the communal telling of these ideas,
there are the rituals which bring the legends, adventures, and tales
into the very life of the member of a community or nation.

THE NAMING CEREMONY

Giving a name to a newborn in most societies is simple enough.
A child is given the name of a member of the immediate family or
perhaps a second name to identify ethnicity. It is then understood
that there is a sense of belonging for the child and perhaps honor
for the persons after whom the child is named. The basis for this
sort of naming is sociological rather than spiritual. It is quite different among the Ojibway. The giving of a name is something of
great importance and in early times it would have followed many
days of meditation and nights of dreaming. The person who was
to be the giver of the name would fast and cleanse his spirit in the
Sweat Lodge. What was to be given to the child was more than
simply a label to distinguish them from others; it was the beginning
of an identity; something that would be with them for life and into

35. Anishnaabe is the word used by the Ojibway/Chippewa to describe
themselves. It means "original man." Similarly, they describe their culture as
Anishnaabec. We do the same when we use words like Scot and Scottish.

36. When the Anglican Anishnaabe artist Leland Bell was invited by the Roman Catholic community of M'Chigeeng, Ontario, to design a series of paintings
depicting the Stations of the Cross, he resisted the idea of painting the cross with
squared corners. Instead, each image of the cross has rounded corners in order
to conjoin the healing power of the cross to the circle of life and the medicine
wheel. These paintings now hang in the Church of the Immaculate Conception in
M'Chigeeng. The images are also featured in a book. Cf. George Leach and G.
J. Humbert, with illustrations by Leland Bell, *Beedahbun: First Light of Dawn*
(Espanola, Ontario: Tomiko Publications, Anishnaabe Spiritual Centre, PO Box
665, Espanola, Ontario, P0P 1C0, Canada).

which their personality would grow. Giving a name was a great responsibility and the one asked to give the name would be like a second father to the child.

On the day of the naming, when the feast had been prepared, and the lodge cleansed, and friends invited, the one giving the name would gather the people and explain the journey he had been on to discover the name of the child. In one sense, the person giving the name was initiating the legend of the person to be named. A good vision led to a good name. The person giving the name would stand in the midst of the community holding the child silently to his chest. In this gesture, he was giving the child part of his own life, something to be shared between them; something beyond words was being transmitted. The dream of the dreamer was seen to become the dream of the child. The power of the dream became the power of the child and for life. Once the name was given, the feast would be eaten and the child who had been named would have a recognized place in the larger community. His name was a personal call to live a continuation of the vision.[37]

THE VISION QUEST

When the boy was of the proper age and when his father had determined that the time was right, he would be invited to undertake a quest for a vision. Fourteen would be an appropriate age. Even though the father would have told him to prepare for his special day and to spend time preparing for the ensuing obligations, the suddenness of the Father's command would still come as a surprise.

The place of the quest would have been made known to the father according to his understanding. It could be a place deep in the forest or on a high mountain. In Northern Ontario, on the road to Manitoulin Island, there is a place called Dreamer's Rock. It is a high promontory of white rock. From the road below it seems almost insignificant, but after it has been approached in a round-about way, the greenery of the pine, maple and birch forest falls away, and the Rock stands out against the blue sky. A dreamer can see the Lacloche mountains of white quartz to the north; the inner

---

37. The language of the Anishnaabe is a very expressive language. A few ideas can be joined together in a way that might be compared to a play on words, or an intuition like a Zen koan, or an internalized expression of a larger legend. The child's totem might be blended with the intuition or the word play. Translation into a European Language sounds banal but in the original each person would understand greater implications and feel the power of the name.

bay of the Birch Island Reserve to the east; the limestone bluffs of Manitoulin Island to the south; and the Bay of Islands on the North Channel of Lake Huron in the west. There is a slight indentation on the top of the Rock, and it is said that this is the mark of the many dreamers who have come to this place in quest of their vision.

From the perch of the Rock, the land drops steeply to the forest floor far below. The quest begins with tobacco being offered in prayer to the four directions. Appreciating the freedom of the raven birds, as they dash back and forth below him, the seeker allows his inner vision to be set free. Off in the distance, he can hear the cry of the Blue Jays, the hammering of the Pileated Woodpeckers and the scolding of the ubiquitous gulls. With arms and legs blackened with ash to signify his purpose and intent for being in such a place, the initiate sits and waits for the vision to emerge. He has his sacred bundle beside him and a birch container of water and the rest is waiting. In the light of day, there is much to see. In the darkness of night, strange sounds scratch in the forest below or flutter by between the seeker and the stars above. What he sees and what he feels enlivens the legends on which he was raised, and a feeling of patience and hope stirs his inner spirit. It may take two or three days of solitude. His spirit may protest the loneliness or the emptiness he feels within, but eventually, acceptance comes and dread peels away. The bees, beetles, and ants go about their daily routine, and he has a chance to see them as he has never seen them before. In lazy circles, high flying eagles invite the dreamer to let his heart soar, or an osprey passing below with a fish in its claws on its way to feed its young reminds him of the fasting and the emptiness he feels in his stomach.

In time, the vision will become real, but he will have to wait until it is confirmed by his father and the Medicine Man of the village.[38] What they say tells him if the testing had been accomplished, the dream true, and its power evident. It is the beginning of the journey that takes a lifetime for the quest to be fulfilled by the manner in which he lives with other people.

Thomas Merton may not have gone on a vision quest in the traditional manner of a First Nations man, but he would certainly have understood the ritual. In one of his meditations, he seems to offer a parallel experience when he writes in a sardonic, almost

---

38. This process of confirmation is not unlike the Zen process of a Master accepting that his novice has attained Satori.

"Daliesque" tone toward modern twentieth-century living.[39]

> I admit that nothing has happened all afternoon and that it
> continues to happen. It is true; I have my feet in an anthill
> by mistake. (ah, now we are getting somewhere!!) I might
> as well confess it. There are ants on the paper as I write.
> They are determined to take over all the writing, but mean-
> while, the sun shines, and I am here under the pine trees.
> While there is still time, I confess that there are ants on the
> paper and a fly in my ear. I do not try to deny that there
> is a fly in my ear and another on my sleeve. Honestly, I
> don't care. I am sorry. I have no desire to get rid of them.
> If I had a grain of true patriotism, those flies would make
> a difference. I beg the forgiveness of the state.
>   The sun? Yes, it is shining. I see it shine; I am in full
> agreement with the sunshine. I confess that I have been
> in sympathy all along with the sun shining, and have not
> paused for two seconds to consider that it shines on account
> of the state. I am shattered by the realization that I have
> never attributed the sunshine to its true cause, namely the
> state. Pretty soon the ants will take over all the sunshine,
> but while there is still time I confess it: The sun is shining.
> Signed...
>   (*Deposition of a reliable witness:* He came to the wood
> with his shoes in his hand, and with a book. He has sat
> with papers and a book. He has done no work, but stood
> and sat in the sun over and around an anthill, at the sound
> of a bird. The ants are on his hands and feet while he is
> lying down, standing up, walking about, running, and even
> running very fast. Yes, there are ants all over the sunshine,
> running very fast.)[40]

Colonialism and Reserves after the End of Empire

Thomas Merton was obviously aware of larger processes of social
change happening in the nations of the world. At the time of his
writings, the seeming demise of colonialism and empire was casting
a shadow over what had once been the British Empire. What had

---

39. Cf. Salvador Dali's famous painting, *The Persistence of Memory,* 1931.
40. Thomas Merton, "A signed Confession of Crimes against the State," *The
Behavior of Titans* (New York: New Directions, 1961) 69-71.

begun with Gandhi was gradually becoming a global phenomenon. One by one, new states were declaring their freedom from the European ruling powers. Having supported the military efforts "for God and Crown" during the two great wars, those returning from service brought a new sense of who they might be on the global stage. During the American war of independence, the war of 1812 and in both world wars, the Natives of Reserves across Canada had joined their non-native compatriots in the ranks of the enlisted. In many cases, the percentage of enlisted Native men far exceeded the average of other towns and cities. With the end of the wars, and having enjoyed parity with others soldiers of their own country, the people of the reservations began to see themselves in a new light. This process changed their attitude from passive acceptance to a more proactive declaration of needs and rights.

> Changing attitudes among the Ojibwa and the mainstream population of Ontario in the mid-twentieth century must be viewed as a thread in the broader tapestry of decolonization that was unfolding throughout the world. European powers in Asia, Africa, and South America were being forced to give up their colonial domination over the indigenous people. In most cases, the success of native people in achieving self-determination rested on the fact that they had superior numbers and a central geographic focus in the power struggle with the Europeans. Independence among blacks in the Caribbean, for example, gave birth to demands for equality in the United States. The achievements of blacks south of the border stimulated native groups as well as the French in Canada. The postwar conditions of the southern Ontario Ojibwa must be viewed in this broader context of global change.[41]

Having been aware of the decolonization processes from his youth and certainly with the international milieu of his family, it is not surprising that Thomas Merton got around to raising the consciousness of his readers. The little volume on Ishi and the other indigenous peoples about whom Merton wrote indicate that he was ahead of the curve in these matters too. Many were surprised that Merton was aware of needs in this corner of humanity. Merton was probably surprised that he had waited so

---

41. Peter S. Schmalz, op. cit., 235-236.

long to initiate the conversation on these matters.

Thomas Merton's sensibilities were so deeply offended by the knowledge he had garnered in his readings concerning the Native Peoples of America that, in his article, *"The Shoshoneans,"* he adopted the mask of sarcasm in order to give voice blackly to the prejudice that proffers the lie of superiority and the exaggeration of subjugation. He makes the words difficult to read, for his intent seems to be one of pulling from the public throat all the lies that have been told for generations: treating the indigenous people as failures, as "minors" incapable of their own care and the care of their own; culpable of "depredations" and allowing themselves to be seen interminably as victims of those who victimized them. Merton's writing softened when he commented on the images photographed by Leroy Lucas: "The aboriginal owner has a face marked with suffering, irony, courage, sometimes desperation: always with a human beauty which sometimes defeats obvious degradation."[42] Then, suddenly, throwing aside the guise of romanticism and demanding that we see with the eyes of one accustomed to hearing and dancing to a different drum, Merton turned and shouted:

> The Indian has been forcibly confined within the limits of a mental definition that is at once arbitrary and unlivable. Of this, his existence on the reservation (principally), as a minor and ward of our government, as a being who is assumed to be unable to decide anything for himself, is only a symbolic, ritual expression. The real confinement, the real reduction and unmanning of the Indian is the reduction to a definition of him in terms of his relations with us. More exactly, a definition of him in terms of a relationship of absolute tutelage imposed on him by us.
>
> In defining and limiting the Indian as we have, we are also expressing a definition and limitation within ourselves. In putting the Indian under tutelage to our own supposedly superior generosity and intelligence, we are in fact defining our own inhumanity, our own insensitivity, our own blindness to human values.[43]

Thomas Merton marked the date and the demise of the First Na-

---

42. Thomas Merton, "The Shoshoneans," *Ishi Means Man* (Greensboro, NC: Unicorn Press, Inc.) 7.

43. Thomas Merton, "The Shoshoneans,"*Ishi Means Man"* op. cit., 9-10.

tions by recalling Big Bear's failure to achieve the "Ghost Dance" on December 29, 1890, because of the Massacre of Wounded Knee. But it was not the end. Those who survived, and those who remembered, understood that the time of Sawiskera was at hand, but truth does not die, and death is never the final victor. A young boy who witnessed the massacre prophesied that seven generations later, the days of darkness would yield to a new cultural rebirth. That boy, Black Elk, and those who gathered around to hear his teaching chose to bide their time by letting the generations pass, and then, with democratization, begin a new practice not just for themselves but for all; a reclaiming of the visions that would build the nations and invite them to dance.

LIVING VISIONS IN CLAY, IN BASKETRY, WEAPONRY, AND CLOTHING

Visions change the way we see the world. Life always comes as a gift. These visions change the ordinary into extraordinary. It is a way of treating life as a sacred presence. The everyday handmade articles of the First Nations artists give witness to their sacred view of life.

From time immemorial, their vision quests, their crafts, music, and dances became symbolic expressions of their communal life and the personal life of the practitioner. Totems were painted on the buffalo hide coverings of the Comanche tepees. The painted masks of *Kachina* dancers were hidden away when the dances were forbidden for fear they might be sold to museums by the custodians of the reservations. Today, these signs and symbols of a former life have begun to reappear in the design of bowls or of canteens by those who choose to dedicate their work to something far more important than its utilitarian function.[44] While tourists wander through markets looking for the decorative and the traditional arts of First Nation craftsmen, they go in search of souvenirs. What they buy are the living memories of artists celebrating their survival and a care for a life which is fragile enough to be lost. Among the Navaho, there are those who still remember the art of the black pot-

---

44. The author of this article has a canteen decorated with a Spirit Dancer hanging on his wall. It was made by Sadie Adams of Flagstaff, Arizona, and it won a red ribbon prize in the Coconino Fair, 20 August, 1971. Cf. also Alfred E. Dittert, Jr. and Fred Plog, *Generations in Clay; Pueblo Pottery of the American Southwest* (Flagstaff, AZ: Northland Publishing, in coöperation with the American Federation of Arts, 1980).

tery which only they can make. The double spouted pitchers made of hand-coiled clay and smoothed with stones; stones handed down from mother to daughter to remember and celebrate the marriage of the people to their land.

Women artisans who first heard legends and teachings as children now know that the heart of the people depends on the hands of the mothers. When weaving their basketry for practical purposes, such as harvesting the plenitude of creation, their deft hands weave patterns of life and legend. To the tourists who buy them, they appeared clever. To the artists and their children, images of the "trickster" or the "man in the maze" prompt the retelling of stories to accompany their work. Among the Ojibway, birch bark baskets trimmed with sweet-grass and covered in the dyed quills of porcupines have now become treasured collection pieces but also manifest a resurgence of cultural pride.

Materials used in weaving are a silent testament to the contemplative hands that crafted these articles. Split wood, bark, grasses, bird quill, cedar root, cedar bark and alder and many other items were woven into baskets that carry culture along with the gathered harvest. Some of the most astonishing masterpieces are those made by the Alaskan Eskimo who learned to weave whale baleen into lidded baskets adorned with knobs carved in ivory of whale's tails or walrus head breaching the surface of the sea.[45]

The classic image of the Indian bravely riding across the prairies astride an Appaloosa pony is certainly one of the iconic images of the First Nations people. We see the fringes on the shirt and leggings. We notice the number of feathers on the Coup stick or the length of the tail feathers falling behind the war bonnet. In earlier times, even the design of the toe puckering or flaps of the moccasin identified the owner by nation and by clan. They wore their identity as a celebration of who they had become by vision and by social structure. Nothing was simply functional. The men wore decoration, perhaps more than the women, as a testimony of who they were and what they were about.[46]

Among the Sioux, four men were designated to wear shirts that named them leaders of a special sort; the Shirt Wearers. Quite

---

45. Cf. Sarah Peabody Trunbaugh and William A. Turnbaugh, *Indian Baskets* (Atglen, PA: Schiffer Publishing Ltd. 1987, 1997, and 2004).

46. Theodore Brasser, *Native American Clothing: An Illustrated History* (Richmond Hill, Ontario) Firefly Books Ltd., 2009).

literally, these few wore their people on their backs; a "chasuble," if you will, of their religious significance in the life of the people.

One of the most important responsibilities delegated to the *Wicasa Itacans* (of the Oglala Sioux) in all divisions was the appointment of the Shirt Wearers. Shirt Wearers were the official executives of the tribe. As such, they were the voice of the *Wicasa Itacans*. At their investiture, they were presented with either a blue-and-yellow or a red-and-green painted shirt fringed with hair locks. It is said that some men might instead be given a solid yellow shirt or one decorated with vertical black stripes; however, the usual shirt had a blue upper half and a yellow lower half, or a red upper half and a green lower half. The colors are said to have symbolized the potency of the supernatural Controllers – blue the Sky, yellow the Rock, red the Sun, and green the Earth. The fringe of hair locks represented the people of the tribe for whom the Shirt Wearers were responsible, for they were the owners of the Tribe.

The welfare of the people was their primary obligation, and upon them fell the final responsibility for providing bountiful hunting and good campgrounds. Not only were the Shirt Wearers delegated executive authority, but they were supreme counselors . . .. Such was the famous Crazy Horse, son of a shaman."[47]

In his essay, "War and Vision," Thomas Merton was aware of the power of vision in the life of the Native communities. He is also very much aware that these "visions," these "dreams" are not mere transliterations or parallels to what he would call mystical experiences. The formalized rituals that supported these experiences could not be denied and neither could the consequent practices affecting the life of the people.

There is a certain fascination even in dry anthropological studies of Indian culture but there also exist living records of personal experience: the stories told by men who had fasted for vision and who had tried to follow the instruc-

---

47. Royal B. Hassrick, in collaboration with Dorothy Maxwell and Cile M. Bach, *The Sioux: Life and Customs of a Warrior Society* (Norman, OK: University of Oklahoma Press, volume 72 in the Civilization of the American Indian Series, 1964) 26-27.

tions of their vision person. When we read these stories, we realize that there was really a deep psychological validity to this way of life. It was by no means a mere concoction of superstitious fantasies and mythic explanations of realities that only science could eventually clarify. However, one may choose to explain the fact; these stone age people had inherited an archaic wisdom which did somehow protect them against the dangers of a merely superficial, willful and cerebral existence. It did somehow integrate their personality in such a way that the conscious mind was responsive to deep unconscious sources of awareness. Those who were most in contact with a powerful vision person tended to have an almost phenomenal luck and dexterity in war or the hunt. "Vision" was perhaps more often a deepening of the common imagination than a real breakthrough of personal insight.[48]

Merton was also aware that the practice bore a residual level of expectation and that some could, for purposes of their own, seek a less than true kind of experience. One can almost hear Merton in his role as the Master of Novices voicing his concerns for one who thought his vocation was valid but who was going at it in all the wrong directions. How many times did Father Louis (the monastic name of Thomas Merton) have to break through the ideation of a novice to set them on the path of real contemplative prayer? We don't know, but his critique of a man called Two Leggings shows how "he (Two Leggings) tried to make his mysticism serve his career." In the end, Two Leggings came to an insight and stunning defeat when he went to the store and saw all the things he could buy with a five-dollar gold piece. He realized then that it was:

> . . . a new kind of medicine, and it was associated with a new kind of war: indeed, with a whole new kind of world, and with a different notion or vision of life, and of what made a human being important. In this world, there was no longer any place for an obsolete bison hunter and stone age warrior, nor was there any point in fasting for vision. In a very real sense, he was deprived of his full identity. Contact with his spirit world was broken because for him this contact depended entirely on a certain cultural context

48. Thomas Merton, "War and Vision," *Ishi Means Man*, op. cit., 21.

in which spirit-guidance gave meaning to his personal ambition.[49]

By contrast, Ishi and the other members of the Yahi did not suffer this disconnection in their life. They withdrew into a social solitude until Ishi was the last to remain. Merton acknowledged that Theodora Kroeber was correct in her assessment of Ishi and the Yahi:

> The Yahi found strength in the incontrovertible fact that they were in the right. *Of very great importance to their psychic health was the circumstance that their suffering and curtailments arose from wrongs done to them by others.* They were not guilt ridden.[50]

When Norval Morrisseau began to draw pictures according to the traditional visions among the Anishinabeg peoples, he received accolades from the Art World and warnings from those who wished their wisdom to be kept secret by the people. Norval was tortured by his desire to live in the two worlds. Being a ``two-spirited`` man, he was accustomed to difficulties but he was also driven to the brink of insanity in trying to achieve it. Those who followed in his footsteps appreciated his effort to put the visions of his people before the eyes of the world.

> How needful it is to enter into the darkness and to admit the coincidence of opposites to seek the truth where impossibility meets us. – Nicholas of Cusa[51]

Norval got caught up in the pursuit of the mystical. For a while he even discarded his Roman Catholic spirituality and embraced the cultic movement of Eckankar. During this time, he focused on past lives and astral travel. He was in company with some earlier artists of the non-native community who found themselves enmeshed in the extrapolated concepts of Darwinism and Theosophy. In time, these cultic expressions

49. Thomas Merton, op. cit., 24.

50. Thomas Merton. "Ishi: A Meditation," *Ishi Means Man*, op. cit., 30

51. Ad Reinhardt was a classmate of Thomas Merton when they studied at Columbia University. Thomas Merton went on to become a monk. Ad Reinhardt became a famous artist/painter of the Minimalist school. He was most especially known for his "Black Paintings." Ad Reinhardt quotes Nicholas of Cusa in his unpublished notes of 1965. Can there be any doubt that this connection is based on his friendship with Merton? Cf. *Art as Art: The Selected Writings of Ad Reinhhardt,* ed. Barbara Rose (Berkely: University of California Press, 1991) 10.

also fell away, and the original vision was restored.[52]

The cultural identity that had been suppressed by residential schools was slowly coming to the surface. Artists such as Daphne Odjig, Blake Debassige, Shirley Cheechoo, Leland Bell, Francis Kagige, Roy Thomas, and Jay Simon Mishibinijima, inspired others to follow the path of prideful integrity and a new day dawned.

Why had this begun to happen? It happened because there is something in the vision of the Native culture that enables them to see through the systems of legality, consistency, and power to a creative world of compassion, poetry, and the mystery. They have seen the destructive side of pragmatism, merciless resocialization and economic determinism and rejected it for the godlessness that it is. Their art, their poetry, their dance, regalia, and style of life gently offer to those who have open hearts, a possibility to see that which could be redemptive even for the oppressors. Merton wrote: "Law is consistent. Grace is 'inconsistent.'"[53] He continued the thought:

> [This is] the ultimate temptation of Christianity! To say that Christ has locked all the doors, has given one answer, settled everything and departed, leaving all life enclosed in the frightful consistency of a system outside of which there is *seriousness and damnation,* inside of which there is the intolerable flippancy of the saved – while nowhere is there any place left for the mystery of the freedom of divine mercy which alone is truly serious, and worthy of being taken seriously.[54]

For Merton, his primary goal was not to align an absolute connection between all faiths and religious cultures by resolving the theological and sociological issues into one system of thought. Merton is not trying to grapple with the issues of inclusion for Native Peoples in the great melting pot of American thinking. Rather, he was trying to get the dominant culture to stand "with," rather than over-and-above those who were of a different faith or culture. Like Thich Nhat Hanh once said, "If you want the tree to grow, it won't help to water the leaves. You have to water the

---

52. Armand Garnet Ruffo, *Norval Morrisseau: Man Changing into Thunderbird* (Madeira Park, British Columbia: Douglas and McIntyre Ltd. 2014) 195-199.

53. Thomas Merton, "To Each His Darkness," notes on a novel of Julien Green, *The Literary Essays of Thomas Merton,* ed. Brother Patrick Hart (New York: New Directions, 1981) 127.

54. Thomas Merton, *ibid.,* 127.

roots. Many of the roots of the war are here, in your country."[55]

Merton's hope left openings for respect, attentiveness to heart-felt dialogue, and understanding that what all peoples are seeking is a level ground of sapiential thinking which is

> . . . the capacity to bridge the cognitive gap between our minds and the realm of the transcendent and the unknown, so that without "understanding" what lies beyond the limit of human vision, we nevertheless enter into an intuitive affinity with it, or seem to experience some such affinity. At any rate, religious wisdoms often claim not only to teach us truths that are beyond rational knowledge but also to *initiate* us into higher states of awareness. Such forms of wisdom are called mystical beyond the aesthetic, moral, and liturgical levels and penetrate so far as to give the initiate a direct, though perhaps incommunicable, intuition of the ultimate values of life, of the Absolute Ground of life, or even of the invisible Godhead. Christian wisdom is essentially theological, Christological, and mystical.[56]

Speaking from one culture to another always involves translation. The customary forms of one language/culture may appear similar to the other, but the assumption of full parity or equality is not always guaranteed. The best that can be done is for the conversation to begin. Intentions will determine the pace to be set for the journey toward each other and the struggle for honesty will promise a future where the compromises will be less. Theresa S. Smith, in her insightful examination of the parish church at M'Chigeeng (formerly West Bay) on Manitoulin Island, reminds us of what Pope Saint John Paul II spoke to a Native American gathering in Phoenix, Arizona in 1987. He opened the door for reconciliation and dialogue when he said:

> The early encounter between your traditional cultures and the European way of life was a harsh and painful reality for your peoples. The cultural oppression, the injustices, and disruption of your life and your traditional societies

---

55. James Forest, "Nhat Hanh: Seeing with the Eyes of Compassion," in Thich Nhat Hanh, *The Miracle of Mindfulness! A Manual on Meditation* (Boston: Beacon Press, 1975) 103.

56. Thomas Merton, "Baptism in the Forest: Wisdom and Initiation in William Falkner" op. cit., 100-101.

must be acknowledged . . .. From the very beginning, the Creator bestowed his gifts on each people. I encourage you, as Native people, belonging to different tribes and nations in the East, South, West, and North, to preserve and keep alive your cultures, your languages, the values and customs which have served you well in the past and which provide a solid foundation for the future. These things benefit not only yourselves but the entire human family. This sharing of cultural riches must also include the Church that native cultures are called to participate in and enhance.[57]

Theresa Smith goes on to point out that the process today is much different from that presented to the Native Peoples during the past five centuries. In olden days, the doctrinaire might of the missionary Church of the Counter Reformation challenged and intimidated new believers by denying any validity to their prior forms of belief. Upon further reflection in our own time, we hear a new tone sounded. "It is an evangelism that is no longer so concerned with the Christianization of Indians as with the Indianization of Christianity."[58] There is a rejection of mere syncretism for the sake of uniformity.

In the rebuilding of the Church of the Immaculate Conception in M'Chigeeng, an effort was made to design the building in a form thought to reflect Native culture. As it exists today, the new church is a collection of Native and Post Vatican II elements. Instead of a long nave, the structure has some aspects shaped like the Kiva of the Navaho in that the parishioners sit on benches that surround the altar which is below ground level. The roof is a flattened tipi structure with the "smoke hole" as the only natural light source for the interior. Neither the Kiva nor the Tipi are typical structural forms of the Anishnaabe, the Potawatomis, or the Odawa. Inside the smoke hole window, we see a Thunderbird which suggests that the Thunderbird and the Holy Spirit of the Trinity are the same. They are not. The use of sweet grass at the beginning of the liturgy suggests an equation with the rite of incense. They are not the same. Smith suggests that rather than bringing the people together,

---

57. Cf. Theresa S. Smith, "The Church of the Immaculate Conception: Inculturation and Identity among the Anishnaabeg of Manitoulin Island" in Irwin, Lee, *Native American Spirituality: A Critical Reader* (Lincoln, NE: University of Nebraska Press, 2000) 146.

58. Theresa S. Smith, op. cit., 146.

the juxtaposition of artistic elements divides the congregation into several groups: those who are non-Native seem to accept the rite as a form of Native incense. Those who stand between the two traditions struggle to accept the compromise. Those who practice the traditional faith of the Native communities are offended and will depart. But the effort to begin the dialogue has begun.

Even more, the Stations of the Cross which hang in the Church in M'Chigeeng were designed by the artist Leland Bell. Both he and his wife are members of the Midewewin Society. These are not the traditional Stations as depicted in most Roman Catholic parishes. Bell insisted on painting them with a fifteenth Station of the Resurrection. He said that it was impossible for the Native community to celebrate death. He chose to strike a balance by celebrating "love." When Leland painted a draft of the first Station: the picture of Jesus standing before Pilate, he included the Roman arch because he thought it was important to the story.[59] Then he found out that this was the arch in the chapel of the Sisters of Zion in Jerusalem, the traditional site of the first Station. Over time, the arch had been included in so many versions of the Stations that it had become an essential detail of the preferred European design. The final presentation of the first Station by Bell does not include the arch because it was not essential to the story nor is it part of the building tradition of Native culture.

> In creating this series, he struggled with two challenges: first, the depiction of violence – a subject that he has intentionally avoided in his art – and second, the need to create Christian iconography while using an artistic style that, in its use of color and form, is founded on *mide* teachings. Bell has said: "I wanted to try to say something from my point of view, but I also wanted to respect the other tradition . . .. I found the balance in Love. With the Stations (of the Cross) it was a great time of healing, a great time of purification. That's my cultural perspective." Bell is not merely inserting Mide-wiwin vocabulary into a Christian context, but translating a story, not so much communicating the Stations to *Anishnaabe* people or *handing Anishnaabe teachings to*

59. This draft copy of the First station is now in the possession of the author of this paper.

Christians. For Bell, this is an important difference.[60]

Theresa Smith concludes her study by saying:

> Inculturation, syncretism, Christianization, and the Indian-ization of Christianity are issues that appear to be of more interest at present to scholars and theologians than to the *Anishnaabe* parishioners or traditionalists of Manitoulin. For both Christian and non-Christian *Anishnaabeg*, the symbolism of the church may be not about identification with one religious system or another, but about identity itself.[61]

Identity is central to the spirituality of Native culture, and it has always been. It is more than mere tribalism or linguistic uniformity. For visionaries like Black Elk, identity is the pivot of the relation-ship between the created world of nature and all that can only be seen by vision. In his book, *The Sacred Pipe,* the book which gives an account of the seven rites of Oglala Sioux (a book which was in the possession of Thomas Merton as early as 1963),[62] we find an account of how the Sun Dance came to be.

The Sun Dance began with a man by the name of Kablaya[63]

60. Theresa Smith, op. cit., 151.
61. Theresa Smith, op. cit., 155.
62. Cf. footnote 6.
63. Kablaya, according to Clyde Holler, in his book *Black Elk's Religion,* is dismissed as a non-historical person, a mere story telling device, and he bases his idea on the translation of his name which means to "make level by beating"; e.g. a holy place, or to open, as the eyes of a young dog for its first sight. I would suggest that the name is meaningful to anyone who knows of the Grass-Dancers who do exactly that. At modern Powwows, the Grass-Dancers open the ceremony. The Grass-Dancers have a distinctive regalia to set them apart from other dancers. In the opening moments of the Powwow, the Grass-Dancers move around the Sun Dance Lodge in a clockwise direction like the Sun and with their distinctive footsteps flatten the grasses so that others may dance with no obstructions. The matter of the young dog opening its eyes for first sight might have a larger mean-ing than Holler chooses to ignore, that of the mystic's awakening to the secret knowledge of God. Holler also chooses to equate the seven rites recorded in *The Sacred Pipe* as some kind of parallel with the seven sacraments of the Catholic Church. I see no connection at all except the number seven. There are four direc-tions and in the Sun Dance Lodge there are seven times four trees surrounding the outer perimeter of the Lodge. In both, Holler has reduced the rites to the function of an antique cultural ritual and missed the meaning at the level of mysticism. If he were to approach the mystical tradition of the Roman Catholic Church, his understanding would be broadened. According to Kieran Kavanaugh OCD, in

who said, "Long ago *Wakan-Tanka* told us how to pray with the sacred pipe, but we have now become lax in our prayers, and our people are losing their strength. But I have just been shown, in a vision, a new way of prayer; in this manner *Wakan-Tanka* has sent aid to us."[64]

With these words, Kablaya began to instruct the people on the meaning and the practice of the new rite. He explains the elements needed for the people to celebrate the rite correctly, the kind of drum to direct the dancing, the colors of paint to be used, and the level of participation for all the people during the days when the rite was to be celebrated. But he also explains the totality of relationship everyone is to have to all of these elements, not just for themselves, but to set right all that was currently out of place in their practice of prayer. Notice what he says concerning the tree to be used at the center of the rite and around which all will be enacted.

In this new rite, which I have just received, one of the standing peoples has been chosen to be at our center; he is the *wagachun* (the rustling tree, or cottonwood); he will be our center and also the people, for the tree represents the way of the people. Does it not stretch from earth here to heaven there? This new way of sending our voices to *Wakan-Tanka* will be very powerful; its use will spread, and, at this time of year, every year, many people will pray to the Great Spirit. Before I teach you the holy songs, let us first offer the pipe to our Father and Grandfather, *Wakan-Tanka*.[65]

We cannot here relate all the aspects of the search for the tree which is to stand in a position of centrality, but it is important to note that the tree is to be hunted by the men of the community and ceremonially carried to the place where the Sun Dance is to be celebrated. At one point, Black Elk explains why this particular tree was chosen. He says,

I think it would be good to explain to you here why we

his introduction to the Spiritual Canticle of John of the Cross, we are told that, "This mystical understanding, wisdom, or theology is also what spiritual persons call contemplation . . . . Some spiritual persons call this contemplation knowing by unknowing."

64. Black Elk, op. cit., 68.
65. Black Elk, op. cit., 69-70.

consider the cottonwood tree to be so very sacred. I might mention first, that long ago it was the cottonwood who taught us how to make our tipis, for the leaf of the tree is an exact pattern of the tipi, and this we learned when some of our old men were watching little children making play houses from these leaves. This too is a good example of how much grown men may learn from very little children, for the hearts of little children are pure, and, therefore, the Great Spirit may show to them many things which older people miss. Another reason why we choose the cotton-wood tree to be at the center of our lodge is that the Great Spirit has shown to us that, if you cut an upper limb of this tree crosswise, there you will see in the grain a perfect five pointed star, which, to us, represents the presence of the Great Spirit.[66]

Black Elk's explanation opens up when he describes the other twenty-eight forked sticks that surround the cottonwood tree and support the other branches which reach inward and touch the holy tree to complete the roof of the Sun Dance Lodge. He says:

I should explain to you here that in setting up the sun dance lodge, we are really making the universe in a likeness; for, you see, each of the posts around the lodge represents some particular object of creation, so that the whole circle is the entire creation, and the one tree at the center, upon which the twenty-eight poles rest, is *Wakan-Tanka,* who is the center of everything. Everything comes from Him, and sooner or later everything returns to Him. And I should also tell you why it is that we use twenty-eight poles....

And he does, including the twenty-eight days in their lunar month (7x4), the twenty-eight eagle feathers in a war bonnet, and twenty-eight ribs in a buffalo. Black Elk also explains that the pattern of the dance inside the lodge traces the pattern of a cross.[67] But it is the set of instructions that Black Elk remembered coming from Kablaya for those entering the Sun Dance Lodge that defines what most people know about this rite and also what most repulsed the non-Natives who witnessed it.

---

66. Black Elk, op. cit., 74-75.
67. Black Elk, op. cit., 80-81.

When we go to the center of the hoop we shall all cry, for
we should know that anything born into this world which
you see about you must suffer and bear difficulties. We
are now going to suffer at the center of the sacred hoop,
and by doing this, may we take upon ourselves much of
the suffering of our people.[68]

Each of them then declared which of the sacrifices he would undergo, and Kablaya made his vow first: "I will attach my body to
the thongs of the Great Spirit which comes down to earth – this
shall be my offering.

(I think I should explain to you here, that the flesh represents ignorance, and, thus, as we dance and break the
thong loose, it is as if we were being freed from the bonds
of the flesh.)[69]

In the end, all the dancers were successful in achieving their goal
of being pierced for the sake of the people, even the eighth person
who was a woman. And then Kablaya spoke again.

My relatives, I wish to say something. Listen closely! This
day you have done a sacred thing, for you have given your
bodies to the Great Spirit. When you return to your people
always remember that through this act you have been made
holy. In the future, you will be the leaders of your people,
and you should be worthy of this sacred duty. Be merci-
ful to your people, be good to them and love them! But
always remember this, that your closest relative is your
Grandfather and your Father, *Wakan-Tanka* and next to
Him is your Grandmother and your Mother the Earth.[70]

We can choose to see more than an intuitive regard for Great Spirit,
perhaps even a mystical orientation operative in the traditional stories and rituals of the First Nations. The 36th Stanza of the Spiritual
Canticle states,

Let us rejoice, Beloved,
And let us go forth to behold ourselves in Your beauty,
To the mountain and to the hill,

68. Black Elk, op. cit., 85.
69. Black Elk, op. cit., 85.
70. Black Elk, op. cit., 99.

To where the pure water flows,
And further, deep into the thicket.

St. John speaks: *"Let us rejoice, Beloved,"*

Kablaya, the man who had the vision which began the celebration of the Sun Dance ritual, was sitting with other elders who were silently considering their situation and all the tragedy they had faced since their lands had been invaded.

Suddenly, Kablaya rose up with wisdom and insight from his contemplation and began to dance with such joy that the others thought he had gone mad. When they too rose to see that which he was doing, they found him to be so deeply happy and in love, they joined the dance.

St. John speaks again: *"Let us go forth to behold ourselves in Your Beauty."*

Ike McCaslin, the main character in Faulkner's "The Bear" had been going forth for years. Now his moment of truth had arrived. At the very moment of the encounter between man and bear, there is silence, a mutual regard and viewing of the other. It is singular as an event, but so expansively filled with meaning that silence brackets the mutual regard of man and bear. This seems to suggest that, to be loved by the Great Spirit is to be loved by all and in a new way. St. John of the Cross comments, and at some length:

(36-5) That I be so transformed in Your beauty that we may be alike in beauty, and both behold ourselves in Your beauty, possessing now Your very beauty; this, in such a way that each looking at the other may see in the other his own beauty, since both are Your beauty alone, I being absorbed in Your beauty; hence, I shall see You in Your beauty, and You shall see me in Your beauty, and I shall see myself in You in Your beauty, and You will see Yourself in me in Your beauty; that I may resemble you in Your beauty, and You resemble me in Your beauty, and my beauty be Your beauty and your beauty my beauty; wherefore I shall be You in Your beauty, and You will be me in Your beauty, because Your very beauty will be my beauty; and therefore we shall behold each other in Your beauty.

St. John speaks again: *"To the mountain and to the hill."*

This suggests the words of Black Elk when he says, "Then I

was standing on the highest mountain of them all, and round about beneath me was the whole hoop of the world. And when I stood there I saw more than I can tell and I understood more than I saw."

St. John speaks, *"To where the pure water flows."*

This reminds me of that taped moment in his talk to the novices, when Merton mentioned the paw prints slowly beginning to fill with water, there is a moment of breathless silence, and then all the novices burst into a joyful knowing laughter. Where words fail, delight overtakes the hearers. They are like Native children listening to a tale which they have heard many times before, but never with as much nervous knowing glee.

St. John speaks, *"And further, deep into the thicket."*

(36-10) "This thicket of God's wisdom and knowledge is so deep and immense that no matter how much the soul knows she can always enter it further."

(36-11) "And, in exchange, it will be a singular comfort and happiness for her to enter all the afflictions and trials of the world, and every thing that might be a means to this, however difficult and painful, even the anguish and agony of death, all in order to see herself further within her God."

(36-12) "The purest suffering brings with it the purest and most intimate knowing, and consequently the purest and highest joy because it is a knowing from further within. Not being content with just any kind of suffering, she insists: And further, deep into the thicket, that is, even to the agony of death to see God."

(36-13) "Oh! If we could but now fully understand how a soul cannot reach the thicket and the riches of God, which are of many kinds, without entering the thicket of many kinds of suffering, finding in this her delight and consolation; and how a soul with an authentic desire for divine wisdom, wants suffering first in order to enter this wisdom by *the thicket of the cross* [my italics]."[71]

We cannot make a link, item to item, incident to incident, nor can we fully anticipate the work Merton might have written, but if we accept the propinquity of these images for what they are, then, suddenly the Sun Dance (even in what strikes us as gruesome)

---

71. All the quotes of St. John of the Cross are taken from Kieran Kavanaugh OCD, op. cit., 546-549.

makes sense of the joyful love expressed in personal sacrifice for a community which is led by wise and compassionate, even contemplative, elders. The Sun Dance Lodge can be seen as a cultural externalization of everything experienced in loving their nation in the face of great suffering and deprivation, of cultural genocide and colonial aggression. In the pain of the practitioners, we see a willingness to suffer compassionately for all, (even for those who do not understand) and to wear the signs of brutal degradation. To be the people their Creator has called them to be, they gladly and awesomely enter deeper into the Sun Dance Lodge as to *the thicket of the cross*, even into that which St. John of the Cross found himself at pains to describe when he had experienced a higher reality in mystical prayer.

In our day, much needs to be changed. But, the changes required are not in the world of economics and social structures or realms political. The changes needed are in the manner of our seeing; a seeing Merton saw was before his time, and timely never finished. He has left his task to us.

BIBLIOGRAPHY

Benn, Carl. *The Iroquois in the War of 1812*. Toronto: University of Toronto Press, 1998.

Benton-Banai, Edward. *The Mishomis Book: The Voice of the Ojibway* Minneapolis: University of Minnesota Press, 1988.

Black Elk. *The Sacred Pipe: Black Elk's Account of the Seven Rites of the Oglala Sioux,* recorded and edited by Joseph Epes Brown. Norman, OK: University of Oklahoma Press, 1953.

Brasser, Theodore. *Native American Clothing: An Illustrated History.* Richmond Hill, Ontario: Firefly Books, 2009.

Bopp, Judie, and Michael Bopp, Lee Brown, Phil Brown. *The Sacred Tree*. Lethbridge, Alberta: Four Worlds Development Press, The University of Lethbridge, 1985.

Clark, Ella Elizabeth. *Indian Legends of Canada*. Toronto: McClelland and Stewart, 1960.

Dickason, Olive Patricia. *Canada's First Nations, A History of Founding Peoples from Earliest Times*. Toronto: McClelland and Stewart, 1994.

Dittert, Alfred E. Jr. *Generations in Clay: Pueblo Pottery of the*

American Southwest. Flagstaff, AZ: The Heard Museum and the American Federation of Arts, Northland Publishing, 1980.

Edmunds, R. David. *The Potawatomis: Keepers of the Fire*, vol. 145 in the Civilization of the American Indian Series. Norman, OK: University of Oklahoma Press, 1978.

Gwynne, S. C. *Empire of the Summer Moon: Quanah Parker and the Rise of the Comanches, the Most Powerful Indian Tribe in American History.* Toronto: Scribner, 2011.

Hassrick, Royal B. *The Sioux: Life and Customs of a Warrior Society*, vol. 72 in The Civilization of American Indian Series. Norman, OK: University of Oklahoma Press, 1964.

Holler, Clyde. *Black Elk's Religion: The Sun Dance and Lakota Catholicism.* Syracuse: Syracuse University Press, 1995.

Irwin, Lee. *Native American Spirituality: a Critical Reader.* Lincoln, NE: University of Nebraska Press, 2000.

Johnston, Basil. *Ojibway Ceremonies.* Toronto: McClelland and Stewart, 1982.

Kavanaugh, Kieran OCD. "Introduction to the Spiritual Canticle," in *The Collected Works of St. John of the Cross.* Kieran Kavanaugh OCD and Otilio Rodriguez OCD, translators, with an introduction by Kieran Kavanaugh OCD. Washington, DC: ICS Publications, 1973.

Leach, George P. and Greg J. Humbert, with paintings by Leland Bell. *Beedahbun: First Light of Dawn.* North Bay, Ontario: Tomiko Publications, 1984.

Meaford Heritage Association. *St. Vincent: A Beautiful Land.* Thornbury, Ontario: Conestoga Press, 2004.

McClard, Megan and George Ypsilantis. *Hiawatha and the Iroquois League.* Englewood Cliffs, NJ: Simon and Shuster, Inc., 1989.

Merton, Thomas. *A Thomas Merton Reader*, ed. Thomas P. McDonnell. New York: Harcourt, Brace & World, 1962.

————. *Entering the Silence: Becoming a Monk & Writer: The Journals of Thomas Merton: vol. 2. 1942-1952,* ed. Johathan Montaldo. San Francisco: HarperSanFrancisco, 1996.

————. *Ishi Means Man: Essays on Native Americans*, Greensboro, North Carolina, Unicorn Press, Inc. 1976.

————. "Baptism in the Forest": Wisdom and Initiation in William Faulkner, *The Literary Essays of Thomas Merton.* Ed. Brother Patrick Hart. New York: New Directions, 1981.

————. "A Signed Confession of Crimes against the State," *The Behavior of Titans.* New York: New Directions, 1961.

————. *The Letters of Thomas Merton and Victor and Carolyn Hammer*, ed. F. Douglas Scutchfield and Paul Evans Holbrook, Jr. Lexington, KY: The University Press of Kentucky, 2014.

Neihardt, John G. *Black Elk Speaks: Being the Life Story of a Holy Man of the Oglala Sioux.* New York: Pocket Books, 1975.

Trunbaugh, Sarah Peabody and William A. Trunbaugh. *Indian Baskets.* Atglen, PA: Schiffer Publishing Ltd., 2004.

Reinhardt, Ad. *Art as Art: The Selected writings of Ad Reinhardt*, ed. Barbara Rose. Berkeley: University of California Press, 1975.

Rice, Brian. *The Rotinonshonni: A Traditional Iroquoian History Through the Eyes of Teharonhia:wako and Sawiskera.* Syracuse, NY: Syracuse University Press, 2013.

Robinson, Michael. *Touching the Serpent's Tail.* Keene, Ontario: Martin House Publishing, 1991.

Ruffo, Armand Garnet. *Norval Morrisseau: Man Changing into Thunderbird.* Madeira Park, British Columbia: Douglas & McIntyre Ltd., 2013.

Schmalz, Peter S. *The Ojibwa of Southern Ontario.* Toronto: University of Toronto Press, 1991.

Steltenkamp, Michael F. *Black Elk: Holy Man of the Oglala.* Norman, OK: University of Oklahoma Press, 1993.

Steltenkamp, Michael F. *The Sacred Vision: Native American Religion and Its Practice Today.* New York: Paulist Press, 1982.

Nhat Hanh, Thich. *The Miracle of Mindfulness! A Manual on Meditation.* Boston: Beacon Press, 1975.

Tomkins, William. *Indian Sign Language.* New York: Dover Publications Inc., 1969.

Warren, William W. *History of the Ojibway People,* 1st ed. 1885. St. Paul, MN: Minnesota Historical Society Press, 1984.

Wright, Ronald. *Stolen Continents: Conquest and Resistance in the Americas*. Toronto: Penguin Canada, 2003.

AUDIO RECORDINGS

Thomas Merton. No. 6. Classical Values in Faulkner (1/1967), *Thomas Merton on William Faulkner and Classical Literature*. Gethsemani Classroom Series, 5 discs with an introduction by Dr. Michael W. Higgins, Ph.D.

————. No. 7. Faulkner's "The Bear": Spiritual Formation and Mystical Union," (1/1967), *Thomas Merton on William Faulkner and Classical Literature*. Gethsemani Classroom Series, 5 discs with an introduction by Dr. Michael W. Higgins, Ph.D.

SUGGESTED READING LIST OF BOOKS
USED IN WRITING *ISHI MEANS MAN*

Dorn, Edward and Leroy Lucas. *The Shoshoneans: The People of the Basin-Plateau*. New York: William Morrow & Company, Inc., 1966.

Kroeber, Theodora. *Ishi in Two Worlds: A Biography of the Last Wild Indian in North America*, deluxe illustrated ed. Berkeley: University of California Press, 1961.

Morley, Sylvanus G. *The Ancient Maya,* 3rd ed., revised by George W. Brainerd. Stanford, CA: Stanford University Press, 1966.

Navokov, Peter. *Two Leggings, the Making of a Crow Warrior*. New York: Thomas Y. Crowell Company, 1967.

Paddock, John, ed. *Ancient Oaxaca, Discoveries in Mexican Archeology and History*. Stanford, CA: Stanford University Press, 1966.

Reed, Nelson. *The Caste War of Yucatan*, foreword by Howard F. Cline. Stanford, CA: Stanford University Press, 1964.

WITH MALINOWSKI IN THE POSTMODERN DESERT: MERTON, ANTHROPOLOGY, AND THE ETHNOPOETICS OF *THE GEOGRAPHY OF LOGRAIRE**

Małgorzata Poks

INTRODUCTION: *THE GEOGRAPHY OF LOGRAIRE*

Published posthumously in 1969, and organized into four cantos named after the four cardinal points of the compass (South, North, East, and West), Thomas Merton's long poem *The Geography of Lograire* was an attempt "to build or to dream the world in which he live[d]."[1] Intended as a "wide-angle mosaic of poems and dreams" in which Merton "without scruple mixed what is [his] own experience with what is almost everybody else's" (*GL* 1), *Lograire* juxtaposes the poet's personal memories with the dreams, myths, and nightmares of the world's diverse traditional and modern cultures, including the consumer culture of America. Composed largely as a collage of quotations, "found" poems, and heavily edited versions of such narratives as the Amerindian Ghost Dance Movement, the Melanesian "Cargo" cults, the persecution of the English Ranters (a religious sect of the seventeenth century), Ibn Battuta's travels in the East, etc., the text allows divergent points of view to clash, even contradict one another. Dominant cultures and marginalized voices are placed side by side to construct their radically different cultural narratives. Within the poem the other is given a hearing; minority perspectives supplement official histories, exposing the ideological provenance of the latter. In a letter

---

* Originally published in *The Merton Annual 25* (Louisville: Fons Vitae, 2012) 49-73.

1. Thomas Merton, "Author's Note," *The Geography of Lograire* (New York: New Directions, 1969) 1; subsequent references will be cited as "*GL*" parenthetically in the text.

to a friend Merton called his new poem a "summa of offbeat anthropology."[2]

INTRODUCTION: ANTHROPOLOGY

Modern anthropology was born in the wake of geographical discoveries and its initial aim was to satisfy the Western world's insatiable curiosity about its "primitive" others – their ways of life, cultures, and societal organizations. Assuming a common human essence but more often than not assigning non-white peoples an inferior rung on the evolutionary ladder – even if not openly weighing their "animal" characteristics against their purely "human" traits – anthropology became a natural ally of colonial domination and was expected to provide justification of the imperialist project – the "white man's burden" and the corollary colonial exploitation of the "savage." Any discussion of the anthropological dimension of Merton's *The Geography of Lograire* is bound to revisit questions of colonialism, ideology, and representation.

MERTON AND ANTHROPOLOGY

Anthropology started to engage Merton's imagination most intensely in the last decade of his life. It seems that his interest in modern anthropology in general and archeology in particular can be traced back to his intense engagement with Latin America. As early as 1958, impressed by Ernesto Cardenal's poetic recreation of the Mayan world and by the literary achievements of the Nicaraguan indigenist movement, Merton steeped himself in pre-conquest history and studied the art of ancient Mesoamerica. Archeologist Sylvanus Griswold Morley with his highly influential *The Ancient Maya* (1946)[3] was soon to emerge as Merton's most trusted guide through the maze of ancient Mesoamerican cultures.[4]

In the late 1960s, however, it was the structural anthropology of Claude Lévi-Strauss that held sway over Merton's imagination.

---

2. Thomas Merton, *The Hidden Ground of Love: Letters on Religious Experience and Social Concerns*, ed. William H. Shannon (New York: Farrar, Straus and Giroux, 1985) 235 [9/24/1967 letter to W. H. Ferry].

3. Sylvanus Griswold Morley, *The Ancient Maya*, 3rd ed. (Stanford, CA: Stanford University Press, 1956).

4. See Małgorzata Poks, *Thomas Merton and Latin America: A Consonance of Voices* (2007; Saarbrücken, Germany: Lambert Academic Publishing, 2011) c. 6: "The Early Legend that Returns."

In October 1967 the Frenchman emerged as "someone who has extraordinary views and is ahead of everyone (even though he may be 'wrong')."[5] At that time Merton was trying to plough through Lévi-Strauss's *Le Cru et le Cuit* (1964; translated as *The Raw and the Cooked* in 1969[6]), but got "snowed under the sheer mass of material." He was soon to revel, however, in the earlier monograph, *La Pensée Savage* (1962; *The Savage Mind*, 1966[7]), which he appreciated especially for its revaluation of neolithic thought – "more sophisticated and complex than some modern 'scientific' common-sense categorizing" (*LL* 299), as he put it.

Within his more immediate cultural context, Merton was discovering a spate of revisionist histories of the First Nations of North America, such as anthropologist Theodora Kroeber's story of the last of the Yana tribe, *Ishi in Two Worlds* (1961);[8] Peter Nabokov's *Two Leggings*, the story of a Crow Indian (1967);[9] *Black Elk Speaks*, a story, recorded by John Neihardt in 1932, of an Oglala Sioux medicine man;[10] and Cora Du Bois' account of the Ghost Dance movement (*The 1870 Ghost Dance*, 1939[11]). Moreover, his deep sympathy with African Americans struggling for basic human rights, his readings in Afro-American literature and culture, or his opposition to the American intervention in Vietnam allowed Merton to formulate the currently well-established connection between colonial and imperialist subjugation of the "exotic" other and the internal colonization of Afro-Americans and Native Americans in the USA.

---

5. Thomas Merton, *Learning to Love: Exploring Solitude and Freedom. Journals, vol. 6: 1966-1967*, ed. Christine M. Bochen (San Francisco: HarperCollins, 1997) 299; subsequent references will be cited as "*LL*" parenthetically in the text.

6. Claude Lévi-Strauss, *Le Cru et le Cuit* (Paris: Plon, 1964); *The Raw and the Cooked*, trans. John and Doreen Weightman (New York: Harper & Row, 1969).

7. Claude Lévi-Strauss, *La Pensée Sauvage* (Paris: Plon, 1962); *The Savage Mind* (Chicago: University of Chicago Press, 1966).

8. Theodora Kroeber, *Ishi in Two Worlds: A Biography of the Last Wild Indian in North America* (Berkeley: University of California Press, 1961); see "Ishi: A Meditation," in Thomas Merton, *Ishi Means Man: Essays on Native Americans* (Greensboro, NC: Unicorn Press, 1976) 25-32; subsequent references will be cited as "*IMM*" parenthetically in the text.

9. Peter Nabokov, *Two Leggings: The Making of a Crow Warrior* (New York: Crowell, 1967); see "War and Vision" (*IMM* 17-29).

10. *Black Elk Speaks: Being the Life Story of a Holy Man of the Ogalala Sioux*, as told to John G. Neihardt (New York: Crowell, 1932).

11. Cora Du Bois, *The 1870 Ghost Dance* (Berkeley: University of California Press, 1939).

In October 1967 Merton was getting excited about the suddenly glimpsed convergences between such diverse events as the Caste War in the Yucatan (1847-1901),[12] the American Black Power Movement, and the Melanesian cargo cults[13] he was intensely studying at that time. "I want to write about this!"[14] he enthused. Four months later he wrote in his journal, "I am really turned on by social anthropology and cargo cults" (*OSM* 55). His reading in I. C. Jarvie's *The Revolution in Anthropology* (1964)[15] gave Merton insight into the crisis brought about by cargo in the professional world of anthropology and alerted him to the irony of the anthropologists' own cargo-like response to that phenomenon. Their "ritual methodological celebration," Merton concluded, helped disguise the professional world's helplessness in the face of a phenomenon far beyond the anthropologists' coping capabilities (*OSM* 55-56).

Following in the footsteps of Robert Daggy's famous description of the "French Cable" (#35)[16] as embedded at the very heart of Merton's antipoem *Cables to the Ace*,[17] I am tempted to forward an equally bold, though decidedly more problematic proposition concerning *The Geography of Lograire*. I want to argue that the "East with Malinowski" section (*GL* 89-90) – placed in the volume's "East" Canto between the narrative of the fourteenth-century

12. See "The Cross-Fighters" (*IMM* 35-52).

13. The "cargo" label is often contested as an essentially Western creation. Lamont Lindstrom of the University of Tulsa lists such alternative, nonstigmatizing names as: "nativistic movements, revitalization movements, messianic movements, millenarian movements, crisis cults, Holy Spirit movements, protonationalist movements, culture-contact movements, and the like" ("Cargo Cults" available at: http://www.berkshirepublishing.com/rvw/022/022smpl1.htm: accessed 4/27/2011); see also Lamont Lindstrom, *Cargo Cult: Strange Stories of Desire from Melanesia and Beyond* (Honolulu: University of Hawaii Press, 1993). For the purpose of this essay I will, however, preserve Merton's usage of the term "cargo," since it has gained widespread currency among Merton scholars.

14. Thomas Merton, *The Other Side of the Mountain: The End of the Journey. Journals, vol. 7: 1967-1968*, ed. Brother Patrick Hart, OCSO (San Francisco: HarperCollins, 1998) 6; subsequent references will be cited as "*OSM*" parenthetically in the text. See "Cargo Cults of the South Pacific," Thomas Merton, *Love and Living*, eds. Naomi Burton Stone and Brother Patrick Hart, OCSO (New York: Farrar, Straus and Giroux, 1979) 80-94.

15. Ian C. Jarvie, *The Revolution in Anthropology* (New York: Humanities Press, 1964).

16. Thomas Merton, *Cables to the Ace* (New York: New Directions, 1968) 24-27.

17. Robert Daggy, "Hurly-Burly Secrets: A Reflection on Thomas Merton's French Poems," *The Merton Seasonal* 21.2 (Summer 1996) 23.

Muslim traveler Ibn Battuta and the "Cargo" section, the latter itself richly interspersed with references to early colonial presence in Papua New Guinea – provides an important key to unlock some of *Lograire*'s many secrets.[18] Credited with starting the postmodern revolution in anthropology,[19] Bronislaw Malinowski's *Diary*[20] suffuses Merton's poem with an unmistakably poststructural and postcolonial sensibility and provides the necessary background for the discussion of cargo.

MERTON THE ETHNOGRAPHER

Before the late nineteenth century, the anthropologist was mostly an ethnologist – a scientist constructing general theories about humanity – and so was distinct from the ethnographer – a field-worker, collector of data and report writer. Cultural historian James Clifford believes Malinowski to have been one of the first "new" anthropologists, in whom those two functions merged. "Squatting by the campfire; looking, listening, and questioning; recording and interpreting Trobriand life,"[21] Malinowski sanctions a new mode of anthropological authority – one based on participant observation – while his groundbreaking ethnographic narrative, *Argonauts of the Western Pacific*,[22] establishes a powerful new genre, at once

---

18. "East with Malinowski" is the title of Section II of *Lograire's* "East" Canto and depicts Bronislaw Malinowski's boat trip to the Melanesian village of Tupuseleia on Wednesday February 10, 1915 and back to Port Moresby on the following day. Another segment excerpted from Malinowski's diary is to be found in the "East" Canto's section III, entitled "Cargo Songs," where it parasitically disrupts passages culled from Peter Worsley, *The Trumpet Shall Sound: A Study of "Cargo" Cults in Melanesia* (London: MacGibbon & Kee, 1957); subsequent references will be cited as "Worsley" parenthetically in the text.

19. See Grazyna Kubica, Wstep [Introduction] to Bronislaw Malinowski, *Dziennik w ścislym tego slowa znaczeniu* [*Diary in the Strict Sense of the Term*] (Kraków: Wydawnictwo Literackie, 2001) 26.

20. Bronislaw Malinowski, *Diary in the Strict Sense of the Term*, trans. Norbert Guterman (New York: Harcourt, Brace & World, 1967); Bronislaw Malinowski, *Diary in the Strict Sense of the Term* with a New Introduction by Raymond Firth (Stanford, CA: Stanford University Press, 1989); subsequent references to the latter edition will be cited as "Malinowski, *Diary*" parenthetically in the text.

21. James Clifford, *The Predicament of Culture: Twentieth-Century Ethnography, Literature, and Art* (Cambridge, MA: Harvard University Press, 1988) 28; subsequent references will be cited as "Clifford, *Predicament*" parenthetically in the text.

22. Bronislaw Malinowski, *Argonauts of the Western Pacific: An Account of Native Enterprise and Adventure in the Archipelagoes of Melanesian New Guinea*

"scientific and literary" (Clifford, *Predicament* 30). Ethnology was a powerful scientific project, but its successor, modern ethnography is, as Clifford explains, "from beginning to end, enmeshed in writing. This writing includes," as he clarifies, "minimally, a translation of experience into textual form. The process is complicated by the action of multiple subjectivities and political constraints beyond the control of the writer. In response to these forces, ethnographic writing enacts a specific strategy of authority. This strategy has classically involved an unquestioned claim to appear as purveyor of truth in the text" (Clifford, *Predicament* 25). As a result, ethnography is for Clifford a "compromised" science: allied with textuality, open to charges of inventing rather than describing its objects, sensitive to questions of representation and power.

Inspired by Clifford's definition of ethnographic practice as "diverse ways of thinking and writing about culture from a standpoint of participant observation" (Clifford, *Predicament* 9), I believe that a poet like Merton is an ethnographer.[23] In some parts of *The Geography of Lograire* he is more of an actual participant (e.g. "Queens Tunnel"), in others more of an observer, but whether writing from first-hand experience or participating only imaginatively in the lives and cultures he studies, the author invariably "finds himself off center among scattered traditions," attempting to make sense of "the condition of rootlessness and mobility" (Clifford, *Predicament* 3) characteristic of the postmodern era. Written from positions of cultural undecidability, *Lograire* dramatizes the historical and cultural hybridity of the (post)colonial world, in which all identities are "inauthentic." It can, therefore, be read in terms of an ethnography of conjunctures, which Clifford opposes to the totalizing project of classical (Western) anthropology. "Constantly moving between cultures," the Cliffordian ethnography of conjunctures is "perpetually displaced, both regionally focused and broadly comparative, a form both of dwelling and of travel in a world where the two experiences are less and less distinct" (Clifford, *Predicament* 9).

(New York: E. P. Dutton, 1922).

23. Clifford makes this claim about the William Carlos Williams of "To Elsie," a poem focusing on a racially mixed girl from New Jersey and the new America where everything is "out of place. A doctor-poet-fieldworker, Williams watches and listens to New Jersey's immigrants, workers, women giving birth, pimply-faced teenagers, mental cases. In their lives and words, encountered through a privileged participant observation both poetic and scientific, he finds material for his writing" (Clifford, *Predicament* 6).

THE SCANDAL OF MALINOWSKI'S *DIARY* AND
A REVOLUTION IN ANTHROPOLOGY

Bronislaw Malinowski (1884-1942) is widely acclaimed as one of the founding fathers of modern anthropology. Between 1914-1918, during his pioneering fieldwork in Melanesia, he transformed the ethnographic practice by pitching a tent in the middle of a native village, rather than staying in a mission house and meeting his native informants on its verandah, as was the custom of the day. No longer in a position of privilege (a white man's house in a native settlement; an elevated verandah suggesting Western culture's superiority), Malinowski became part of the society he studied, trying to understand it from "the native's point of view" – with scientific objectivity and without prejudice.

This myth of an unbiased fieldworker crumbled with the posthumous publication of that anthropologist's field diary. Written in Polish mixed with a considerable heteroglot input, the diary was not intended for publication.[24] In 1967, however, at the height of the Malinowski cult, his literary executor decided to have the diary published in English and in a much abbreviated form: the English version consisted of only two notebooks covering the period crucial to the evolution of the discipline: the Mailu and the Trobriand Islands notebooks.

Reviews of *Diary in the Strict Sense of the Term* varied from, at best, judging it a mere "footnote to anthropological history"[25] to, at worst, proclaiming Malinowski "a crabbed self-preoccupied, hypochondriacal narcissist."[26] Accusations of racism abounded. More perceptive reviews were rare. An isolated voice would point to the cathartic function of diary-writing for an individual stranded in an alien culture and left "alone with his instincts." Having worked through conflicting emotions by writing about them, continued the reviewer, Malinowski was thus much more capable of empathizing with the cultural "other" (quoted in Firth xxiv). Another sympathetic chord was struck by Anthony Forge, a practicing fieldworker

24. The original diary consisted of seven separate notebooks spanning a ten-year period between 1908, when Malinowski took his doctoral degree at the University of Krakow, through to his brief recuperative stay in the Canary Islands, his studies in Leipzig, Germany and at the London School of Economics, and his extended fieldwork in Melanesia between 1914-18.

25. Raymond Firth, Introduction to Malinowski, *Diary* xviii; subsequent references will be cited as "Firth" parenthetically in the text.

26. Clifford Geertz, quoted in Firth xxvi.

himself, who recognized his own conflicting emotional states in Malinowski's notes (quoted in Firth xxvi). But the majority of the anthropological world was up in arms, mostly because the *Diary* repeatedly dismantles Malinowski's mythical status by portraying him as a fully embodied and largely imperfect human being: sickly, grumpy, demotivated, imperialistically-minded, obsessed by sexual fantasies, drugged by escapist fiction. To better understand the ambiguities of Malinowski's field experience, however, it should be noted that that Polish-born citizen of the Austro-Hungarian Empire, surprised by the outbreak of World War I while on an ethnographic expedition in the Britain-controlled region of Papua New Guinea, was considered an "enemy alien" and could neither return to Europe nor remain in Australia outside an internment camp. His only remaining option was a protracted ethnographical expedition. In consequence of unfavorable historical circumstances, this cosmopolitan European, affiliated professionally with the London School of Economics, spent three consecutive years on the colonial frontier, in a situation of cultural liminality, grappling with incompatible cultures and languages, and struggling against personal and cultural disintegration.

Two decades after the publication of Malinowski's *Diary*, Clifford, writing from a transformed historical and theoretical awareness, was to introduce the term "ethnographic self-fashioning" as a way of approaching the apparent aporias of ethnographic fieldwork.[27] Championing ethnography as the practice of writing (*gráphō*) about a particular people (*ethnos*) at a particular place and time, Clifford claims that anthropologists, like other writers, invent rather than represent the objects of their study.[28] He finds it natural that within this textual framework Malinowski should have assumed – ironically, as he perceptibly notices – diverse colonial masks, including that of "Kurtz-like excess" (Clifford, *Predicament* 105).

But by the end of the 1980s, Malinowski's *Diary* had already become a focal point for a fascinating theoretical debate. Far from being a mere footnote to anthropological history, it emerged as a

27. The chapter from Clifford's *Predicament of Culture* is entitled "On Ethnographic Self-Fashioning: Conrad and Malinowski," and draws intriguing parallels between those two famous Poles stranded between languages and cultures.

28. James Clifford and George E. Marcus, eds., *Writing Culture: The Poetics and Politics of Ethnography* (Berkeley: University of California Press, 1986) 2; subsequent references will be cited as "Clifford & Marcus" parenthetically in the text.

canonical text articulating a new ethnographic subjectivity – one situated within and circumscribed by the ethnographer's own culture, no matter how hard s/he should try to see things "from the native's point of view." In *The Predicament of Culture*, a work that momentarily assumed a canonical status in cultural anthropology, Clifford helpfully attributes the importance of Malinowski's *Diary* for the postmodern and poststructural discourse to its being written at "the moment [the 1910s] when the ethnographic (relativist and plural) idea [of culture] began to attain its modern currency" (Clifford, *Predicament* 10). Revealing the constructedness of cultural identity and thus corroborating post-structuralist theories of the de-centeredness of cultures and subjectivities, it was bound to deal a blow to traditional anthropological assumptions. In short, in 1967, the year of its publication, the professional milieu's opposition to Malinowski's *Diary in the Strict Sense of the Term* was almost unanimous because the text ruthlessly dismantled two myths most cherished by the discipline: that of cross-cultural understanding and that of a self-possessed, coherent subjectivity. Both proved to be rhetorical constructs enmeshed in situations of ambivalence and power (Clifford, *Predicament* 112).

Anthropology's "Experimental Moment"

By the mid-sixties the crisis of representation was beginning to register in many related disciplines as the traditional means of describing social realities were being challenged by the eclipse of "grand narratives" and as sensitivity to difference and close attention to detail, contextuality, irregularities and indeterminants demonstrated the inadequacy of accepted theories. As argued by Marcus and Fischer in their informative *Anthropology as Cultural Critique*, anthropology's "experimental moment," i.e. the discipline's involvement with experimental ethnographic writing, is reflective of the overall crisis of representation and therefore revealing of "the current conditions of knowledge."[29] Predictably, the publication of Malinowski's *Diary* yielded a crop of essays reflecting on the anthropologist as author. In a work thus subtitled cultural anthropologist Clifford Geertz analyzes in retrospect the "strategy of anthropological text-building" that Malinowski's *Di-*

---

29. George E. Marcus and Michael M. J. Fischer, *Anthropology as Cultural Critique* (Chicago: University of Chicago Press, 1986) 5.

ary made manifest in the 1960s. Contrary to the myth of scientific objectivity, as Geertz argues, the ethnographer had to construct his or her story of native life within and out of complex situational and cultural contexts. Factors naturally registering on ethnographic representations of native lives include, according to Geertz, the combined effects of: landscape, the sense of isolation, the presence of a local European population, one's memories of home and what one has left behind, the sense of vocation and future life, the unpredictability of human emotions, the fragility of one's physical and spiritual condition, the vagaries of one's thoughts.[30] This realization helped the author formulate a new paradigm of interpretive anthropology. Since "man is an animal suspended in webs of significance he himself has spun," he declares: "I take culture to be those webs, and the analysis of it to be therefore not an experimental science in search of law but an interpretative in search of meaning."[31] As a result, Geertz considers ethnographies to be "interpretations, or misinterpretations . . . as inherently inconclusive as any others" (Geertz, *Interpretation* 23).

ANTHROPOLOGY AND THE HISTORICAL MOMENT

By the mid-1960s, the Western world was not completely unprepared for the shock delivered to the anthropologist profession by Malinowski's *Diary*. World War II had contributed to the dismantling of the colonial system, while political independence had empowered the newly emergent nations to question Western constructions of native cultures and identities. As a result, important insights into the complex relations between culture, class, and race were being offered by "Third World" intellectuals. It is worth remembering, though, that African Americans had been involved in shaping cultural and racial politics at least since the Harlem Renaissance in the 1920s, and that 1961 saw the publication of the founding text for the emerging postcolonial studies: Franz Fanon's *The Wretched of the Earth*.[32] By the mid-1960s the universality of

30. Clifford Geertz, *Works and Lives: Anthropologist as Author* (Stanford, CA: Stanford University Press, 1988); subsequent references will be cited as "Geertz, *Works*" paenthetically in the text.

31. Clifford Geertz, *The Interpretation of Cultures* (New York: Basic Books, 1973) 5; subsequent references will be cited as "Geertz, *Interpretation*" parenthetically in the text.

32. Franz Fanon, *The Wretched of the Earth* (New York: Grove Press, 1963). Merton read Fanon and even used a chapter from *The Wretched of the Earth*,

the term "culture" – in the singular and limited to the Western world only – was being hotly debated. In 1966 another important opening was made. A year before the publication of Malinowski's *Diary*, French philosopher Jacques Derrida proclaimed the "event" of rupture in Western philosophy.[33] His three important books followed in 1967: *Speech and Phenomena*, *Of Grammatology* and *Writing and Difference*.[34] With Derrida's announcement of "The end of the Book and the beginning of Writing,"[35] the theory of textuality was rapidly spreading beyond its Parisian nursery.[36]

MALINOWSKI AND THE HISTORICAL MOMENT

It is against those developments that one should situate the "rupture" and "scandal" of Malinowski's *Diary*. There is little doubt nowadays that the author's morbidly honest presentation of his ever renewed and never fully successful attempts to articulate a coherent subjectivity and a coherent vision of a society thorough the multiple, often conflicting sites of "language, desire, and cultural affiliations" (Clifford, *Predicament* 102) began to transform anthropology from the older model of an exact, verifiable science to the humanistic discipline it is today – a discipline engaged in a continual effort of "ethnographical self-fashioning." In a chapter from *The Predicament of Culture* entitled "On Ethnographic Self-Fashioning," Clifford observes that Malinowski's *Argonauts of*

---

entitled "Colonial War and Mental Disorders," in his interpretation of Albert Camus' *The Stranger* (see Thomas Merton, *The Literary Essays of Thomas Merton*, ed. Brother Patrick Hart, OCSO [New York: New Directions, 1981] 299-301; subsequent references will be cited as "*LE*" parenthetically in the text).

33. Jacques Derrida, "Structure, Sign and Play in the Discourse of the Human Sciences," a talk delivered at the Johns Hopkins Symposium of 1966, in Jacques Derrida, *Writing and Difference*, trans. Alan Bass (Chicago: University of Chicago Press, 1978) 278-95; rept. in *Modern Criticism and Theory: A Reader*, ed. David Lodge (London and New York: Longman, 1991) 108-23; subsequent references to the latter source will be cited as "Derrida, 'Structure'" parenthetically in the text.

34. Jacques Derrida, *La Voix et le Phénomène: Introduction au Problème du Signe dans la Phénoménologie du Husserl* (Paris: Presses Universitaires de France, 1967); Jacques Derrida, *De la Grammatologie* (Paris: Éditions de Minuit, 1967); Jacques Derrida, *L'Écriture et la Différence* (Paris, Éditions du Seuil, 1967).

35. Title of the opening section of Derrida's *Of Grammatology*.

36. Merton was not ignorant of the new developments: in 1967 he was reviewing Roland Barthes' *Zero Degree of Writing* (see "Roland Barthes – Writing as Temperature" [*LE* 140-46]) and, as I shall argue elsewhere, drifting close to the premises of textuality.

234 • Małgorzata Poks

the Western Pacific, the anthropological fruit of his fieldwork in Melanesia, "giv[es] wholeness to a culture (Trobriand) and to the self (the scientific ethnographer)" (Clifford, *Predicament* 112) at the cost of a lie. That lie was the exclusion of the diary material from his ethnographic work on the Trobriand society. With this exclusion all the disrupting contradictions and incoherencies of the complex cultural-anthropological picture presented in *Argonauts* became conveniently suppressed. Thus, concludes Clifford,

> the discipline of fieldwork anthropology, in constituting its authority, constructs and reconstructs coherent cultural others and interpreting selves. If this ethnographic self-fashioning presupposes lies of omission and rhetoric, it also makes possible the telling of powerful truths. . . . The best ethnographic fictions are, like Malinowski's, inherently truthful; but their facts, like all facts in the human sciences, are classified, contextualized, narrated, intensified. (Clifford, *Predicament* 112-13)

Ethnographic fictions, those inescapable half-truths, are recorded by embodied, positioned subjects both affected by and affecting the lives they study.

In 1986, almost twenty years after the shock caused by *Diary in the Strict Sense of the Term*, Clifford looks at a photograph depicting Malinowski poised at his writing table inside his celebrated tent to observe, in a passage strikingly resembling Derrida, that "[w]e begin, not with participant-observation or with cultural texts (suitable for interpretation), but with writing, the making of texts" (Clifford & Marcus 2). Clifford's conclusion is irresistible: with the crumbling of the ideology of transparency of representation and cultural codes, "writing has emerged as central to what anthropologists do both in the field and thereafter." Like any other writers, anthropologists invent rather than represent (Clifford & Marcus 2).

ETHNOCENTRISM, METAPHYSICS AND THE POST-STRUCTURALIST MOMENT

When Merton was composing *Lograire*, the social sciences lay in the overwhelming shadow of structuralism and the anthropology of Claude Lévi-Strauss, the author of *Tristes Tropiques* (1955),[37]

---

37. Claude Lévi-Strauss, *Tristes Tropiques* (Paris: Plon, 1955).

Anthropologie Structurale (1958)[38] and *La Pensée Sauvage* (1962), with his impressive four-volume *Mythologiques* starting to come out in 1964 (*Le Cru et le Cuit*). Merton's attempt to deploy an "urbane structuralist" tactic in his new poetry was hugely influenced by the Frenchman's structuralist anthropology, as attested by Merton's fascinating struggle with Lévi-Strauss recorded in the pages of his working notebook. Known as the "Cargo" Notebook #30, it attests to Merton's attempt to reconcile Lévi-Strauss' "totemic thinking" with his interest in a-historical structures and relations (which Merton calls syntax), and the hermeneutic of Paul Ricoeur with his "historic event thinking" rich in content (semantics). On October 12 Merton wonders: "If the analogy of language gives key to understanding of parental systems, will it also give key to art, religion and all cultural phenomena?"[39] A few days earlier in the pages of his journal he had just eulogized the founder of structural anthropology for having "extraordinary views" and being "ahead of everyone" (*LL* 299).

Decidedly, by the late 1960s Lévi-Strauss was very much *the* anthropologist within the Western world, and Merton's uneasy *agon* with his model of anthropology was in itself a sign of the contemplative monk's keen attunement to the spirit of the time. It is not without significance for the exegesis of *Lograire* that Jacques Derrida used the anthropology of Lévi-Strauss to support his thesis of the decentering of Western culture. In his talk "Structure, Sign and Play in the Discourses of the Human Sciences," he located a significant post-structuralist moment in Lévi-Strauss' writings. According to the philosopher, the "scandal" that destabilizes the project of structural anthropology is, as Lévi-Strauss himself admitted, the incest prohibition, a concept that escapes the nature/culture opposition fundamental to Western philosophy. Lévi-Strauss believed that the incest prohibition belongs to the realm of culture in so far as it is a system of rules and norms (a prohibition), but he also realized that by virtue of its universality – the fact that incest is prohibited in all known societies – it seems to have been instituted by nature itself. To Derrida's regret, however, rather than follow suit and plunge "outside philosophy" to, consequently, begin to dismantle the system of binaries on which Western philosophy is founded,

---

38. Claude Lévi-Strauss, *Anthropologie Structurale* (Paris: Plon, 1958).
39. Thomas Merton, "Cargo" Notebook 30 (September-November 1967) (Thomas Merton Center [TMC] archives, Bellarmine University, Louisville, KY).

Lévi-Strauss preserved the opposition as a useful methodological tool while denying it any truth value. This double bind launches Derrida's inquiry into other inconsistencies in the anthropologist's discourse, which results in the deconstructionist philosopher's conviction that Lévi-Strauss ultimately abandoned "all reference to a center, to a subject, to a privileged reference, to an origin, or to an absolute archia" (Derrida, "Structure" 115-16). It is in this context that Derrida links the twentieth-century revolution in anthropology with the end of metaphysics, proclaiming: "there is nothing fortuitous about the fact that critique of enthocentrism – the very condition of ethnology – should be systematically and historically contemporaneous with the destruction of the history of metaphysics (Derrida, "Structure" 112). For Derrida, the question that needs to be addressed is the future of anthropology when "the name of man . . . [is] the name of that being who, throughout the history of metaphysics or of ontotheology – in other words, throughout his entire history – has dreamed of full presence, the reassuring foundation, the origin and end of play" (Derrida, "Structure" 122).

What can *Lograire* – written at that critical moment of history, that swelling juncture of multiple concerns that made themselves manifest at the emergence of "the as yet unnameable which is proclaiming itself" (Derrida, "Structure" 122) – offer its readers? What wisdom, what vision, what "saving fiction" can it offer to the world in crisis?

MERTON AND MALINOWSKI

"There are good observations in Malinowski's diary," notes Merton on February 26, 1968. "I laugh at him, but he was really working things through in his own life and this [fragments from the *Diary* copied in Merton's journal] shows it" (*OSM* 59). The ethnographer's heroic efforts to control his ailing body and flagging spirits in an alien environment by imposing an almost monastic self-discipline must have won Merton's grudging admiration. The following observation that Merton culled from Malinowski sounds eerily close to Zen or some wisdom of the desert: "To get up, to walk around, to look for what is hidden around the corner – all this is merely to run away from oneself, to exchange one person for another." "Good!" notes the monk with appreciation (*OSM* 59-60). But his overall attitude to the anthropologist is marked by ambivalence. What the monk and contemplative appreciates – the honesty, the struggle, the hard-won disappointing truth[40] – the artist must "use" in a way that suits his poetic vision. Even though Merton has "[n]othing against" Malinowski, he admits: "I use him nevertheless, perhaps a little ruthlessly, in *Lograire*." He further explains that his objective is to use the anthropologist as an epitome of "a certain kind of mentality, pre-war European, etc. in confrontation with Cargo" (*OSM* 59).[41] That this mentality was essentially that of a quintessential English gentleman adds a personal note to Merton's experiment. In the pages of the "East" Canto of *Lograire* Merton is, in effect, reconstructing a mentality he himself shared as a one-time aspiring member of the English intellectual elite who was being groomed for diplomatic service. Although he would later laugh at the Oakham chaplain's exegesis of 1 Corinthians 13, which substituted "gentlemanliness" for charity,[42] and would see in the "gentlemanly" England of his adolescence a "moral fungus" that bore the fruit of war (*SSM* 126-27), he used to be fascinated, e. g., by the worldliness and cultural refinement of his English guardian, Tom Izod Bennett, who was very much *the* gentleman and Merton's role model in those days. Bennett, and to some extent the young Merton himself, would thus emerge as other correlates of that pre-war European mentality that *Lograire* attempts to deconstruct by drawing on the intimate diary of Bronislaw Malinowski, another cosmopolitan European and a member of the elitist academic establishment.[43]

PRE-WAR EUROPEAN MENTALITY RECONSTRUCTED

"East with Malinowski" echoes the title of the poem's previ-

40. *Diary in the Strict Sense of the Term* ends with Malinowski's recognition of defeat: "Truly I lack real character" (Malinowski, *Diary* 657).

41. Merton repeatedly applies this procedure in his "antipoetry." Already in the early *Original Child Bomb* (New York: New Directions, 1962), he "used" the US Fleet Admiral William D. Leahy in a similar fashion. Within that poem, the admiral's professed lack of belief in the atomic bomb serves as an incentive to the Manhattan Project team to work even harder towards success. Merton never even alludes to Admiral Leahy's strong opposition to the use of the bomb on Japan.

42. Thomas Merton, *The Seven Storey Mountain* (New York: Harcourt Brace, 1948) 73-74; subsequent references will be cited as "*SSM*" parenthetically in the text.

43. In an unpublished November 4, 1962 letter to the Dutch psychoanalyst Joost Meerloo, Merton writes: "You speak very much for the world in which I grew up and to which I still belong: pre-war Europe with its particular heritage and traditional outlook" (TMC archives).

ous section, "East with Ibn Battuta" (*GL* 82-88). But while the
fourteenth-century travel narrative richly fulfills its promise and
introduces the reader to vivid images and – yes – a participant-
observer's experience of cultures and places, of politics, religious
beliefs, customs, legends, cuisine, and daily life of almost half the
hemisphere (there are vignettes of Cairo, Syria, Mecca, Isfahan,
Delhi and Calicut), the other narrative, six centuries into the future,
fails to deliver. "We tack into the lagoon" (*GL* 89) – the story begins in a classic ethnographic fashion. The rest, however, thwarts
the expectations created by the opening. Instead of following with
details of the unfamiliar new world he has just entered, the narrator
turns within, to his inner landscape: "Shipping water I am ready/
To throw up" (*GL* 89).

Unlike Ibn Battuta's, Malinowski's narrative is dominated by
the physiological functions of a body transplanted into an alien and
incomprehensible environment. In between vomiting, urinating, and
emptying his bowels, he claims to be "Having/The time of [his]
life" (*GL* 89). This claim seems rather absurd unless one attends
to images suggesting the European narrator's dominance over the
exotic environment, such as urinating "from a height of 13 feet"
or emptying the bowels "From a privy above the water" (*GL* 90).
The elevated position of his body suggests authority, including the
ethnographic authority to represent the cultural other. There is no
doubt who is in control, who has taken metaphorical possession of
the place – "no man shall sit higher in Trobriand than I," sarcastically comments Merton in Malinowski's voice (*GL* 95).[44]

It soon becomes clear that by analyzing acts of language and
drawing radical conclusions from the diarist's rhetoric, Merton
uses Malinowski to reveal the abiding colonialist mentality of the
supposedly unbiased Europeans (whether anthropologists, colonial
agents or missionaries), their irredeemable cultural situatedness,
and hidden assumptions concerning the "primitive" societies they
study/invent. In the canto's section III Malinowski becomes simply
"the anthropologist" (*GL* 91, 92, 93, 95). Divested of his proper
name, his function is limited to merely spelling out the characteristics of the colonialist-patriarchal mentality characteristic of
pre-war Europe. Despite his obsessive self-preoccupation, the narrator of the Tupuseleia section has an artist's eye for details, is not

44. Merton parodies here Governor William MacGregor's famous claim
"Nobody shall sit higher in New Guinea than I," quoted in Worsley 51.

unappreciative of natural beauty, and sporadically articulates this appreciation in poetic language – like the observation that at high tide the Kurukuru-covered houses "Dip their long thatch beards/ In the water" (*GL* 90). But this beauty deserves no more appreciation (and no more space in the travel notes) than the novelty of urinating from the raised platform when the tide is low. Nor does the visionary landscape with "gentle hills" and "Sprawling spidery trees" at high tide the next morning prevent him from emptying his bowels "straight into the sea" (*GL* 90) – which he evidently does with a touch of excitement. The familiar reality has remained behind, in the metropolis; what confronts the anthropologist on the cultural frontier is the exotic and the bizarre, which dictates a different code of behavior than that of the high Georgian society of his adopted England.

The historical Malinowski, like Mr. Kurtz – that iconic colonial character from Joseph Conrad's *Heart of Darkness* – was keenly aware of the seductive pull of desire on the colonial frontier. His rigorous, though not always successfully maintained, self-discipline was meant to be an antidote to the Conradian realm of "the horror," whose presentiment haunts the pages of *Diary in the Strict Sense of the Term*. Merton's anthropologist figure, however, lacks Malinowski's nuance and real-life drama. Thus, for instance, when Merton's Malinowski, outraged at the Melanesian natives' lack of cooperation, confesses: "My feeling towards them: exterminate the brutes" (*GL* 95), Merton both misquotes Malinowski's actual words,[45] and leaves out the despair and dark irony of his original confession to make the desired generic profile more convincing. Yes, Merton uses Malinowski rather ruthlessly,[46] but he does so with an eye to exposing the dark lining of the "civilized" Western mind. By selecting, condensing and rephrasing snatches from Malinowski's diary and arranging them in meaningful configurations,

45. "My feelings towards the natives are [on the whole] decidedly tending to 'exterminate the brutes'" (Malinowski, *Diary* 69).

46. Academic honesty requires that a corrective be added to this one-sided picture of the "early" Malinowski. Archeologists Nancy Scheper-Hughes and Philippe Bourgois reclaim the broader picture by stressing that in his later years "Malinowski sided with the anticolonialist revolutions of the mid-twentieth century. He argued passionately against the archeologist as a neutral and objective observer and 'bystander' to the history of colonial violence and the suffering that is visited upon the people and cultures with whom anthropology had cast its lots" (Introduction to *Violence in War and Peace: An Anthology* [Malden, MA: Blackwell, 2004] 7).

the author of *Lograire* allows some "intricately truthful" fiction to emerge, as James Clifford would put it (Clifford, *Predicament* 112).

This truthful fiction is the result of Merton's skillful editorial work. Not without significance is the fact that Merton's selection and arrangement of the *Diary* material encodes Malinowski's desire for absolute control over "his" territory – an ambition he shares in the poem with other European travelers (see especially "Place Names" [*GL* 96-97]) – in his body language. It is body language that qualifies him as a dominant male who urinates to mark his territory and parades his alpha status by towering over the submissive herd (in one vignette from Tupuseleia he shares a canoe with a native policeman "And another savage" [*GL* 89]). But the instinctive adoption of an animal male's boundary-staking strategy undermines the anthropologist's claim to refinement and high culture. The latter are expected to belong in the realm of "civilization" as opposed to the primitive realm of desires, bodily drives, and naked instincts, and yet, has Malinowski not just demonstrated that he belongs with the same naked natives that his "civilized" mind dismisses as cultureless "savages"? Even if he has, this recognition does not haunt his conscious mind. The self-styled arbiter of culture feels an abysmal distance between himself and the naked "Bronze bodies" (*GL* 90) glimpsed inside the kurukuru-covered huts. Anonymous and dehumanized in his vision, the natives almost blend into a homogenous mass, safe for the occasional and rather unsavory sight of "firm breasts stick[ing] out" (*GL* 90).[47] But postcolonial theory would see his instinctive shrinking from this state of "savagery" as a recoil from the shadow, a disgust caused by the vague recognition of a "distant kinship"[48] with the civilized world's uncanny double. In his anticolonial reading of Conrad's masterpiece, Nigerian critic Chinua Achebe makes an observation bearing directly on this point. "The meaning of *Heart of Darkness* and the fascination it holds over the Western mind," specifies the critic, "lies in the following comment made by the novel's narrator: 'What thrilled you was just the thought of their [the Africans'] humanity – like yours . . .

---

47. Malinowski suffered from a "Fear of pointed objects" (*GL* 90).

48. This is how Chinua Achebe diagnoses Conrad's Marlow's troubled description of natives lining the shores of the Congo: see Chinua Achebe, "An Image of Africa: Racism in Conrad's *Heart of Darkness*," *Massachusetts Review* 18 (1977) (rpt. in *The Norton Anthology of Theory and Criticism*, ed. Vincent Leitch [New York: W. W. Norton, 2001] 1789]); subsequent references will be cited as "Achebe" parenthetically in the text.

Ugly'" (Achebe 1786). The West's negative projection of itself is what cosmopolitan Europeans of Conrad's and Malinowski's generation find on the colonial frontier and what they recoil from.

Ambiguity, ambivalence, and postmodern ontological irony saturate the whole section of Merton's poem. Upon entering the village of Tupuseleia, Merton's anthropologist reports: "Dark inside/ Bronze bodies appear/At the doors" (*GL* 90). This sight apparently activates his worst racialist self: "Do not shoot," we hear him comment in a parenthetical aside, "Til you see the whites of their eyes" (*GL* 90). This Kurtz-like excess, an evocation of the central character of Conrad's *Heart of Darkness*, is Merton's skillful contribution to the presentation of a composite Western mentality, whose strengths and weaknesses Kurtz, to a large degree, epitomizes. "All Europe contributed to the making of Kurtz,"[49] confides Marlow, the Conradian narrator, when referring to the mixed background of the novel's protagonist. In a very real sense, the diabolically intelligent Kurtz is an epitome of the colonialist, pre-war mentality. His drive to absolute control over the natives, culminating in his demand that they worship him as a god, fits in with the anthropologist's sense of royal superiority expressed in the slogan: "No man shall sit in Trobriand higher than I." Additionally, Conrad's character seems to embody the colonialist myth of "white man's burden" gone sour better than anyone else.

On a different note, one would be hard pressed to find those exact words, "Do not shoot,/Til you see the whites of their eyes," in Malinowski's diary – not the sentiment, though. This statement is historically attributed to General William Prescott at the time of the Battle of Bunker Hill. Re-contextualizing this phrase, so closely associated with the American Revolutionary War and the poorly armed colonists' determination to prevail against the superior military potential of the British forces, Merton invests Malinowski's colonial encounter with some fearful symmetry: oppressor and oppressed collapse in this double-edged act of semantic violence. The suggestion is, once again, that any identity is constructed in opposition to the demonized Other. Moreover, Merton's use of this famous phrase interestingly illustrates the textual provenance of the poem: *Lograire* is a narrative of "language that speaks man" (Heidegger) and a nar-

---

49. Joseph Conrad, *Heart of Darkness*, *The Norton Anthology of English Literature*, 8th ed., vol. 2, ed. Stephen Greenblatt (New York: W. W. Norton, 2006) 1926.

rative of man as an "être parlant" (Lacan, Bachelard)[50] – a speaking subject, always already constituted by the codes of culture. In a larger sense, Merton's entire poem is a labyrinth of "signifyin" practices (Henry Louis Gates, Jr.): of (mis)quotations, parodies and imitations of other voices and other narratives in the differential repetition of which the strategies of the original discourses are reversed and the repressed traces of alterity reclaimed.

Back in Port Moresby, the town removed from the dangerous "savagery" of the frontier, the anthropologist is self-composed and self-possessed again. With other refined European males he converses about "sun and moon/And the causes of things" (*GL* 90) while enjoying cold drinks and other desirable "cargo" in the luxury setting of McCann's Hotel – a hotel, no doubt, for whites only. Even in this decently regulated, "civilized" environment, however, some other prejudices, equally foundational for the fiction of the West's cultural integrity, come to light. "That woman/ Vulgar beyond endurance" (*GL* 90) – this is how the anthropologist summarily dismisses an unidentified female. Tellingly, this is the only flesh-and-blood European woman in the entire East Canto. There are evocations of other white women in the canto's section III, but they function as either nostalgic correlatives of boyhood safety (Malinowski's mother) or male fantasies of ideal womanhood (as epitomized by Miss Nussbaum in her "glacier blue outfit" [*GL* 93]). There is more than a hint of misogyny in the patriarchal mentality of the empire.

In between the view of Tupuseleia at high tide and the image of its bronze-bodied inhabitants comes this cryptic passage: "*Stimmung* – desertion/(Death in Venice)" (*GL* 89) to contribute a touch of decadence to the composite portrait of the Western traveler. Fin-de-siècle moods characterize cultures in crisis – decadent, dying cultures, morbidly drawn to death. Decadence was fashionable in the artistic circles of the high modernist society in which the historical Malinowski moved, whether in his native Poland or in his adopted England. Merton's explicit allusion (not to be found verbatim in Malinowski's *Diary*) to Thomas Mann's novella *Death in Venice* – no doubt inspired by the lagoon-like landscape

---

50. In September 1967 Merton comments on Bachelard's *La Poetique de l'Espace*: "Trivializing of contemplative life when it either gets lost in words or loses the sense of man as *être parlant* and of the truly human as logos" ("Cargo" Notebook #30 [Sept.-Oct. 1967] [TMC archives]).

of the coast – grounds the anthropologist's high modernist status while undermining his society's claim to superiority, especially in its confrontation with the vibrant, vital cultures, uninfected by the Stimmung. The combined effect of such words as "desertion" and "death" would be enough to highlight the morbid condition of the West and its representative – the hypochondriac anthropologist. But adding this allusion to the Mann novella, the erudite Merton is reinforcing this impression by enmeshing Malinowski in a significant cultural intertext. The leitmotif of *Death in Venice* is an aging intellectual's obsession with a beautiful adolescent boy[51] and the ongoing association between Aschenbach's corrupted love for the boy and an outbreak of cholera in the Italian city of art and romance. Impressed by Nietzsche's views on decadence and decay, Mann was notable for his insights into the soul of the European artist and intellectual and was a closeted homosexual himself. Thus, with the evocation of *Death in Venice*, Merton broadens the range of objective correlatives for the turn-of-the-century European mentality, while simultaneously hinting at Malinowski's troubled sexuality and homosexual inclinations vis-à-vis native informants, especially his favorite informant/masseur Igua.[52]

INTRICATELY TRUTHFUL FICTION

The above is a shorthand portrait of the Western anthropologist's world of privilege. On the one hand, this is an exclusive white man's club, a highly selective fraternity – whose lingering influence could still be felt in the several boarding schools attended by Thomas Merton, at the Cambridge of 1933/34, and perhaps most pervasively in the household of Tom Izod Bennett, Merton's godfather, guardian, and role model after Owen Merton's death. On the other, it is a world of surfaces, hypocrisy, and corruption of values officially cherished as "civilized." Reconstructing this mentality, the Malinowski section of Merton's *Lograire* lays bare some of

51. The stunningly beautiful boy, whose name is Tadzio, is a young Pole staying in Venice with his parents. This is an interesting coincidence, although totally unrelated to Merton's interest in that other Pole, Bronislaw Malinowski. Being a Pole myself, I feel excited to be finding the (rather implicit) Polish allusions in so limited a fragment as "East with Malinowski."

52. Polish cultural anthropologist Joanna Tokarska-Bakir traces Malinowski's coded autoeroticism and hints of homosexual practices in her article "Malinowski, czyli paradox kłamcy" ["Malinowski, or the Liar's Paradox"], *ResPublica Nowa* 11 (October 2002) (Warszawa: "Polityka" Spoldzielnia Pracy) 60-67.

the underlying causes of professional anthropology's failure in its confrontation with Cargo. It is no coincidence that at the very moment when, according to Peter Lawrence, the Cargo movement was entering the phase of the "third belief" in the nearby Madang province,[53] the professional ethnographer of Merton's meditation, authorized to understand and describe the cultural other, "lay low,/ Shivered under the hot compress/Read Bronte and pissed black/... thinking of French chophouses in Soho/Of anything in fact/But Trobriand Islanders and coral gardens" (*GL* 91).

Yet, even when criticizing and distancing himself from it, Merton is conscious of having been shaped by that very mentality as a culturally situated subject. If he devotes so much effort to (re)inventing it in the pages of the Malinowski section, it is because the imperialist figure of the anthropologist is the "other" within himself, whose trace is only partially erased within the agonistic and open-ended process of his subjectivity construction.[54] The jingoist, hypochondriac, and disintegrating anthropologist, at least in Merton's "intricately truthful" fiction of Malinowski, is therefore the monk-poet's and his culture's disavowed "other." In the psychoanalytic process of identification "the subject of desire is never simply a Myself," postcolonial critic Homi Bhabha reminds us; and vice versa, "the Other is never simply an It-self, a front of identity, truth or misrecognition."[55] Identification is a process of "negotiation at the borders," famously claims Bhabha; it takes place "in-between disavowal and designation" (Bhabha 72). Bhabha's post-Lacanian theory helps us to navigate the complex process of Merton's psychological identification as reflected in *Lograire* and to identify "Malinowski" as that part of his cultural makeup that the poem's implied author rejects.

MERTON, MALINOWSKI, AND BATTUTA: NEGOTIATION AT THE BORDERS

The similarities between both cosmopolitan Westerners stranded between various cultures and languages are notable. Born in the

---

53. Peter Lawrence, *Road Belong Cargo: A Study of the Cargo Movement in the Southern Madang District, New Guinea* (Manchester: Manchester University Press, 1964) 63-86.

54. French intellectual Julia Kristeva first introduced the concept of *sujet-en-procès* (in the double meaning of subject "in process" and "on trial") in *Polylogues* in 1977.

55. Homi Bhabha, The *Location of Culture* (1994; London and New York: Rutledge, 2010); subsequent references will be cited as "Bhabha" parenthetically in the text.

French Pyrenees to an American mother and a New Zealand father with Welsh ancestry, Tom straddled cultures and languages from his earliest childhood. He was brought up in America, educated at prestigious schools in France, England and the USA, and groomed for the diplomatic service. He travelled widely in Europe before withdrawing from the world of activism to the monastic margin. The sickly Malinowski, born in the part of Poland that belonged to the Austro-Hungarian empire, shuttled constantly between the metropolitan city of Kraków, the nearby Tatra mountains with their distinct culture and pronounced dialect, and the health resorts of Italy, Africa, and the Canary Islands; he studied at Leipzig and London before leaving on an anthropological expedition to Australasia where he was to receive the status of enemy alien. Malinowski's and Merton's early exile from the bourgeois values of the West conferred on both a degree of cultural difference, which facilitated their assumption of the ethnographic position – the position of distance vis-à-vis the cultures and societies they visited and lived in.

Although shaped by many cultures, both identified most profoundly with the Anglophone world. In addition, both received thorough, elitist education, belonged to avant-garde intellectual and artistic circles, kept in touch with the newest intellectual trends and developments, at various points of their lives maintained rigorous monastic (Merton) or quasi-monastic (Malinowski) discipline, and helped redefine their respective professional fields: monasticism and anthropology. On top of that, both kept private diaries, which have since been published to become acclaimed classics. The diaries of both articulate, albeit in different idioms, insights into the spiritual turmoil of the postmodern age, as their authors are seen struggling with the decentering, disintegrating forces within modern subjectivity caught in an ongoing movement of ambivalence and contradiction. How, under those circumstances, could Malinowski's *Diary* not be the repressed trace, the displaced, disavowed other of Merton's literary and literal self?

On the other hand, it is imperative to note that "East with Malinowski" is placed in a dialectical relationship with the section symmetrically entitled "East with Ibn Battuta." Both sections constitute complementary narratives of traveling east.[56] Importantly, though,

---

56. James Clifford sees Ibn Battuta's "traveling East" as a "trajectory of a different cosmopolitanism": non-western, non-white male, non-middle-class. Additionally, Battuta's travel notes appear to elude the fraught polarizations into

246 • Małgorzata Poks

if both are subject to close scrutiny, the fourteenth-century Muslim from Morocco might emerge as no less ethnocentric and no less biased than the modern anthropologist, and his style will probably be deemed just as infected by cultural projection as Malinowski's. Like the anthropologist, although decidedly in a subtler fashion, Ibn Battuta cannot help seeing the other through the prism of cultural expectations and prejudices. Thus, for instance, his narrative elevates Islam over other religions when the hazardous lifestyle of cosmopolitan Calicut forces him to escape to the Maldives "Where all the inhabitants/Are Muslims" (*GL* 87) and where life is predictable and livable again. Moreover, he distinguishes between "true believers" and "heretics," and misrepresents the Shi'ite minority, repulsive to his mainstream Sunni sensitivity, as "abominable"[57] (*GL* 83).

Yet, Ibn Battuta's big advantage over Malinowski is that he traveled through a predominantly Islamic world, which spoke the same sacred language and whose "exoticism" was thus seriously delimited. Consequently, Battuta's cultural identity was not seriously undermined in the course of his journey. This both saved him from Malinowski's extreme self-consciousness and conferred on his narrative a greater degree of objectivity. In contrast, the author of *Diary in the Strict Sense of the Term* was, during his prolonged stay among the Trobriand, immersed in cultures and languages vastly different from his own and almost totally unknown to most Westerners of his generation. This is why the effect of cultural difference is incomparably stronger in his section of Merton's ethnopoetic meditation. Yet, if Merton implies that "the anthropologist" never manages to leave the West behind and that he keeps "traveling West," in the sense of projecting his distinctly "Western" worldview on the "exotic" other, the travel narrative of the fourteenth-century African Muslim is, *mutatis mutandis*, not quite free from similar

---

West and East, empire and colony, oppressor and oppressed that so heavily inform Malinowski's notes (*Travel and Translation in the Late Twentieth Century* [Cambridge, MA: Harvard University Press, 1997] 5; subsequent references will be cited as "Clifford, *Travel*" parenthetically in the text).

57. This word carries a warped echo of what English Puritans saw as "ABOMINABLE PRACTISES" (*GL* 65) of the Ranters, a millenarian sect persecuted in 1650s. Merton seems to be relativizing historical experience by his play on perspective: the sympathetic cosmopolitan Ibn Battuta and the cruel persecutors of Ranters stigmatize the incomprehensible other with the same harmful word. In both instances semantic violence opens the way to actual violence.

defects of perspective. It is interesting that Merton never seems to notice it. What is more, the juxtaposition of the two travelers and their narratives clearly favors the medieval Muslim to the discredit of the modern ethnographer from Europe. Merton, who in 1968, when the poem was being composed, was a seasoned traveler East, albeit more in spirit than in flesh, quite obviously sympathizes with what he considers to be the more open-minded and affirmative attitude of Battuta. But it is precisely at this point that Homi Bhabha's assertion about identification taking place "in-between disavowal and designation" (Bhabha 72) can become helpful in understanding Merton's *sui generis* interstitial identity. "Malinowski," as a correlate of the turn-of-the-twentieth century racialist mentality of the West that has shaped Merton, continues to persist within the author's identity in the form of a displaced, disavowed trace; "Ibn Battuta," whose travel narrative complements and critiques Malinowski's, articulates a sort of "discrepant cosmopolitanism" (Clifford, *Travel* 36) which is much closer to Merton's sensitivity. One feels that the poet's sympathy gravitates toward the Moroccan and the East while his cultural affiliation with the West is fraught with ambivalence. This agonistic process of "negotiation at the borders" is a form of Merton's personal self-fashioning, as well as a reminder that "identity is conjunctural, not essential"[58] (Clifford, *Predicament* 11).

ETHNO-POESIS OF *LOGRAIRE*

In his introduction to *The Predicament of Culture*, Clifford revisits one of the key notions of ethnography, namely, the notion of orientation. Derivable from "Orient," it is "a term left over from a time when Europe traveled and invented itself with respect to a fantastically unified 'East'" (Clifford, *Predicament* 13). In the twentieth century an orientation so defined was to be seriously challenged by the new practices of dwelling and traveling that had brought the Oriental (along with other "exotic" peoples) into the very heart of the West. In effect, as Clifford notices, nowadays "difference is encountered in the adjoining neighborhood, the familiar turns up at the ends of the earth" (Clifford, *Predicament* 14). Ethnographic modernity is thus de-centered and dis-oriented; it can no longer

---

58. The process of self-fashioning is also central for the elected Welshness of the speaker in the "Prologue" to *Lograire* (*GL* 3-6).

claim any privileged Archimedean point for its cultural analysis. When Malinowski was researching Kiriwinian culture, the "West" as represented by missionaries, colonial agents and anthropologists had already struck deep roots within the "East," transforming, translating and hybridizing its culture(s). In *Lograire*'s "East" Canto this idea is effectively dramatized by the cargo movement, which was well under way in Melanesia in the 1910s, just when "The anthropologist lay low" (*GL* 91), too self-preoccupied to notice. Given the spatial dis-orientation of modernity as theorized by Clifford, it is symptomatic that the East invented in the pages of Merton's poem makes no claim to totality. Far from yielding a complete picture of that geopolitical entity, Merton's canto evokes an outrageously fragmentary and radically imbalanced view of that region, privileging Papua-New Guinea to the exclusion of cultures generally considered more "typically" Oriental, for instance India, China or even Japan. To illustrate the point, let it suffice to say that out of the canto's ten sections, only one offers a panorama of snapshots – in themselves highly selective and discontinuous – of a broader Islamic world of the East, while its remaining sections focus exclusively on Melanesia. The list of absentees would be too long to compose also with respect to religious traditions. Indeed, the "East" fashioned in Merton's meditation seems to exclude more than it includes, as important traditions as Hinduism, Buddhism, or Shinto have been disregarded altogether. If Merton chose not to use the large geopolitical canvas for his *Lograire* and to attend to highly localized, not to say idiosyncratic, hi/stories instead, this strategy may rightly strike one as avant-garde, even prophetic in the late 1960s, when the postmodern paradigm shift in anthropology was still in progress. More than three decades after Merton's death, in an essay aptly entitled "The World in Pieces," Clifford Geertz insists that such ethnocentric formulas as the East or the West are in fact vastly complex and often contradictory realities and "conglomerate[s] of differences . . . resistant to summary."[59] Within a world in which neat systems broke down to yield an endless play of difference, Geertz pleads for ways of thinking and doing anthropology that would be "responsive to particularities, to

---

59. Clifford Geertz, "The World in Pieces: Culture and Politics at the End of the Century," *Available Light: Anthropological Reflections on Philosophical Topics* (Princeton: Princeton University Press, 2000) 224; subsequent references will be cited as "Geertz, 'World'" parenthetically in the text.

individualities, oddities, discontinuities, contrasts, and singularities" (Geertz, "World" 224). The intimacies of local knowledge,
Geertz believes, will contribute to our better understanding of
cultures and societies.

It is well worth remembering that Geertz was one of the first
anthropologists to mine the textual potential of ethnography, and,
equally importantly, that his research sealed the death of structural
anthropology by helping shift the discipline's attention from the
structures to the interpretation of cultures, from ethnography as
science to ethnography as a form of writing. In 1973, only four
years after the publication of *Lograire*, he famously launched the
interpretive paradigm in anthropology by declaring the discipline
to be "not an experimental science in search of law but an interpretative in search of meaning" (Geertz, *Interpretation* 5). Given
the general concurrence on the significance of Malinowski's *Diary*
to the emergence of the new interpretive anthropology, Merton's
appropriation of Malinowski as much as his poetic ventures in
ethnographic modernity deserve an in-depth research which would
open up an exciting – postmodern, poststructural and postcolonial
– reading of his late poetry.

More than exciting, such a reading might well prove to be both
urgently needed and somehow belated – which conviction was in-
sightfully articulated in 1995 by Georg de Nicolò in the following
words: "The fact that Merton utilizes unusual anthropological insights for *The Geography of Lograire* is a hint as to which direction
the project was taking. Merton was not merely looking to the past
for solutions as so many poets have done before him. . . . He focused
rather on recent anthropological studies for a way out of the crisis of
modern society and culture."[60] This is also my conviction and with
its irresistible logic it returns me to that haunting question, which
like a refrain should recur now, at the conclusion of my preliminary
venture into Merton's ethnopoetics: what wisdom, what vision,
what "saving fiction" can *Lograire* offer to the (Western) world
in crisis? The bold claim with which I started this essay – about
the centrality of the "Malinowski" section for Merton's *Lograire*,
a section seemingly insignificant and frequently overlooked by
scholars – rests on this conviction, especially in view of the fact

---

60. Georg de Nicolò, "Thomas Merton's Anti-Poetry: Genetic and Functional
Aspects of *Cables to the Ace* and *The Geography of Lograire*," unpublished master's thesis (Regensburg-Harting, Germany: Universitat Regensburg, 1995) 198.

that, unlike the other three cantos, the "East" Canto relies almost exclusively on a collage of anthropological materials.

Concluding, I merely wish to emphasize that what has been written with reference to the "East" Canto is true of Merton's entire "work in progress" (*GL* 1), in which drastically incomplete and selective portrayals of the four geopolitical regions are made up of sections radically fragmented in themselves, each section being divided into discrete units of information disconnected from others, which juxtapose disparate narratives and incompatible points of view. As a consequence, *Lograire* is a discontinuous collage of fragments, which fact mimics "the world in pieces" and the mosaic character of postmodern/postcolonial perception with its localized knowledges of reality.[61]

---

61. The splintered world of late modernity and the fragmentation of history and syntax enacted in *Lograire* have fascinating theological-spiritual potential. David Tracy believes that fragments depict "the spiritual situation of our times" and as such contain "a sign of hope, perhaps . . . the only signs of hope for redemption" (David Tracy, "Fragments: The Spiritual Situation of Our Times," *God, the Gift, and Postmodernism*, eds. John D. Caputo and Michael J. Scanlon [Bloomington: Indiana University Press, 1999] 173). I plan to develop the theological-spiritual dimension of *Lograire* in another essay.

INTRODUCTION
TO THE PREFACE
FOR LATIN AMERICAN READERS
IN MERTON'S *OBRAS COMPLETAS*
(COMPLETE WORKS)

Marcela Raggio

In 1958, Thomas Merton wrote the Preface to his *Obras Completas*[1] ("Complete Works") to be published by Editorial Sudamericana, one of the main Latin American publishers based in Buenos Aires, Argentina. The first volume (the only one eventually published) provided Merton an opportunity to reach the continent he so much loved even if he had seen only a small bit of it during his 1940 visit to Cuba. While publishing with Sudamericana presented Merton with the chance to widen his public, it allowed the opening of his horizons as well.

On March 30, 1958, Merton noted in his journal, "Wrote several things this week and I think they were good (the new Sacred Art article and the preface to the Sudamericana volume). . . . So much evasion in this dream of South America! If it were really love, how strong I would be!"[2]

If one reads Merton's writings of 1957-1958, it is possible to detect references to Latin America as if the region were being unveiled for him, little by little. Upon Ernesto Cardenal's arrival at Gethsemani, Merton breaks the news to James Laughlin in a letter that seems to be the starting point of his interest in the South of the continent: "One of our novices is a Nicaraguan poet, Ernesto Cardenal. . . . I think an awful lot about South America these days, and I want to read everything I can lay hands on, especially about the Bolivar countries up in the top left-hand corner – Venezuela,

---

1. Thomas Merton, "Prefacio para el lector iberoamericano," *Obras Completas,* vol. 1. (Buenos Aires: Sudamericana, 1963).

2. Thomas Merton, *A Search for Solitude: Pursuing the Monk's True Life 1915-1968*, ed. Lawrence Cunningham (San Francisco: HarperSanFrancisco, 1996) 187.

Colombia, Ecuador."[3] This letter is dated August 30, 1957. What did Merton know about South America back then? Why was he so interested in it? Critics seem to agree that his turn toward Latin America (or, for that matter, his turn "toward the world") is signaled by the 4th and Walnut experience. Mark Meade notes that the event of March 18, 1958, "is commonly seen as a shift for Merton away from an insular view of the monastic life, a view that saw the goal of monasticism and the spiritual life as denying the world outside the cloister wall in favor of an idealized life of prayer and asceticism. . . . This change forced him to reconsider his monastic vocation and to now include in it a concern for problems of the world."[4] Less than two weeks after the 4th and Walnut moment, Merton wrote the Preface to *Obras Completas*.

Ernesto Cardenal's arrival (together with other postulants from Latin America) had already awakened Merton's intellectual interest; the mystical experience in downtown Louisville expanded that interest into a spiritual and social concern (however paradoxical these two terms may seem). The Preface already shows strong proof that Merton is reaching out to South America, even if the style is more idealistic, and not quite *"engaged"* as is his writing from the 60s. In fact, the journal entry quoted above speaks of an "evasion in this dream of South America." His "dream" would become "really love," as he had wished in the journal, by the time volume I of the *Obras Completas* was published two years later. In the December 13, 1960 entry of his journal Merton wrote, "Yesterday, F[east]. of Our Lady of Guadalupe, Vol. I of the *Obras Completas* arrived from Buenos Aires, with the preface I had written (in 1958). I mean that preface. The day emphasized my meaning of it."[5] Merton is suddenly aware of the important and existential meaning of his Preface, a meaning only underlined by his realization's proximity to the Latin American feast of Our Lady. What are the implications of Merton's awareness of his Preface's "meaning"? A philological consideration of his Preface will deepen its importance to him.

---

3. Thomas Merton and James Laughlin, *Thomas Merton and James Laughlin: Selected Letters,* ed. David D. Cooper (New York: Norton & Co., 1997) 125.

4. Mark Meade, "From Downtown Louisville to Buenos Aires: Victoria Ocampo as Thomas Merton's Overlooked Bridge to Latin America and the World," *The Merton Annual 26* (Louisville, KY: Fons Vitae, 2013) 172-173.

5. Thomas Merton, *Turning Toward the World: The Pivotal Years 1960-1963,* ed. Victor Kramer (San Francisco: HarperSanFrancisco, 1996) 74.

I Am One of Those Millions

Throughout the Preface, our attention is drawn to Merton's use of the first-person plural and other grammatical devices that make him a part of the whole (which means, in this context, a part of his Latin American readership: significantly, the title of the text is "Prefacio *para* el lector iberoamericano," a preface *for* Spanish American readers). The preposition is not a small detail; on the contrary, from the title itself Merton makes it clear that he is addressing Latin Americans and, in fact, that this Preface is not for just any reader of his works: it is specifically written, *ad hoc*, for those in the South of the continent who speak Spanish.

The text is an attempt to become one with them, and the first step he takes to achieve this is to point out that he, like his readers, is "one of those millions whose destiny brought them from the European coasts to become . . . people of the New World." This is the first of a series of binary elements on which Merton builds his argument, bridging the gaps to show that in a synthesis there is unity among all, even if he acknowledges, respects, and salutes difference and diversity. Merton's words discard binary pairs that would imply prejudice and discrimination, as he approaches the others of South America in formerly unrealized ways. David Cooper has noted that the Merton proposes a new type of humanism, whose "radical character resulted from Merton linking his religious humanism to social criticism."[6] Merton's horizons expand beyond the intellectual and affective enclosures of his monastery to grasp a reality which not only includes the wisdom of the past but also calls for action to answer the needs of the present.

Throughout the Preface, the word "partial" appears four times. In all cases, partiality means considering only one element in the pair of opposites, which goes against Merton's thinking. The first time he uses the word, Merton says that he cannot "satisfy the requirements of [his] vocation with anything partial or provincial," and he goes on to remind us that he "cannot be a 'North American.'" The notion would be very clear for his Spanish American readers. To us living in South America, the word "America" (América) includes the whole continent, North, Central, and South America. We consider ourselves "American" (americanos), and we use the

---

6. David D. Cooper, *Thomas Merton's Art of Denial: The Evolution of a Radical Humanist* (Athens, GA: University of Georgia Press, 1989) 244.

term "North American" to refer to U.S. citizens. All this was very clear to Merton. He knew that in defining himself as an "American" all inhabitants of the continent were included. In so much of his writing, he uses "North America" to refer to the United States, and he keeps the word "America" for the continent at large. In this way, he was taking a step towards unity, respect, and inclusion of the richness and diversity of "América" (and I keep the Spanish accent to differentiate it in the way Merton was using the word).

The second and third times he uses the term "partial," it is to stress that he is neither "a partial American" nor a "partial Catholic." Just as he wants to be a "complete" American, he wants to be a complete "Catholic." Just as in other writings he reflects upon the etymology of the word, in the Preface "Catholicism" is not just *universal* in the usual sense of the term; Merton goes beyond that. Catholicism is not only the traditional, obvious reference to the Irish, the French, or the Spanish American baroque heritage. To Merton, its universality extends across place, culture, and time, so that it encompasses all humanity: "Catholicism embraces the whole world and all times. It was there at the beginning of the world." So, if it was there at the beginning of the world, it must have been there even before Europeans came spreading their religion to the "New" World. The *wisdom* of ancient America contained already Christ's image, just as the fallen man Adam's did.

The fourth appearance of the word reads, "Without contemplation, we remain small, limited, divided, partial." Both action and contemplation, then, are necessary elements of Catholicism in its truest, universal meaning. The binary elements are not mutually exclusive, but on the contrary, can and must coexist. For Merton, action and contemplation are dimensions of a unified reality. They must fertilize one another so that neither dimension betrays the universal vocation of the Christ. Catholicism is universal not only in its embrace of all humanity, but also in its wide scope that includes different, complementary vocations.

Another significance of Merton's meaning in his Preface attaches to his use of words that would normally appear in the singular but which Merton chooses to present in the plural. I consider two cases in particular: the first one is early in the Preface, where Merton argues that the Contemplative Life can be found everywhere, "wherever there are hopes . . .." One would usually say that we have "hope for the future," that humanity shares the "hope for a better life"; but Merton sees beyond the surface and acknowledges that there may be as many *hopes* as people and cultures, individuals and lifestyles. Some pages later, near the conclusion, we read, "It is in this love of Christ in Himself, and of Christ in our neighbor, that New Worlds are built on everlasting foundations." The reflection upon the universality of Catholicism has brought Merton to consider that the newness of the world cannot refer only to a geographical location (the sense in which the term is used in the second paragraph when he speaks of himself as a citizen of the New World). If we see Christ in each of our brothers and sisters, then we must be aware of their uniqueness; and then New *Worlds* in the plural will arise. Imposing one ideology, one culture, one way of thinking upon all would destroy the richness, variety, and beauty that come with diversity: that is why, if we see Christ in each of our neighbors, new *worlds* will be possible, based on respect, tolerance, and understanding. "Above all this, there is the problem of understanding and love, the problem of unity, the problem of man." Merton's humanistic thought proceeds along the lines of the biggest paradox of humanity: our uniqueness and at the same time, our equality. Only in God, through God, can that paradox be solved.

THE DEEP ROOTS OF ANCIENT AMERICA

At some point, one may argue that this is Merton's Preface not only to his Complete Works in Spanish but to his writings of the 1960s. The notions that he sketches on these pages prefigure what he would develop in the next decade in letters, essays, poetry, and journals. One of the central texts regarding Merton's views on Latin America is his *Letter to Pablo Antonio Cuadra Concerning Giants*. The letter, which significantly was published first in its Spanish translation in several Latin American journals, and only later in English, says, "If only North Americans had realized, after a hundred and fifty years, that Latin Americans really existed. That they were really people. That they spoke a different language. That they had a culture. That they had more than something to sell!"[7] These ideas, written in 1961, can already be found in the Preface composed three years earlier when Merton had already manifested his admiration for the wisdom of Latin America.

---

7. Thomas Merton, *Emblems of a Season of Fury* (New York: New Directions, 1960) 85.

In the Preface, there are two aspects he appreciates in the south of the continent: the first one has to do with its natural variety and beauty. Merton marvels at "the vast and lonely pampas, the frosty brilliance of the Bolivian highland, the fine air of the Incas' terraced valleys, Quito's splendor and softness, the cold Bogotá savannah, and the extreme mystery of the Amazonas jungle." Such natural splendor speaks with God's voice, and in these South American climates, Merton hears the call of his vocation to be a contemplative, and a *complete* American. The richness of the South is so great that disregarding it would mean only incompleteness, both as an American and as a Catholic.

Yet, Merton also admires South American culture. He claims this culture might be older and wiser than those studied by historians so far. The ancient Mexican civilizations that he evokes and the pregnant silences of the Peruvian wisdom/culture display for Merton the echoes of proto-Christianity when he states that both civilizations kept "an image of Truth which no person has yet recognized as Jesus' hidden image, wrapped in symbol and prophecy." Those are the deep roots that Merton finds still alive in Latin America, and this is why he feels that there is a wisdom to be learned from the South. Following his method of pairs of opposites explained earlier, here too Merton sees a difference between North America, "where there are no longer any Indians, where the land was colonized and cultivated by Puritans," and the South, where the Indian heritage is a living part of "the America of Mexico and of the Andes."

If Merton could grasp the splendor of Latin America, the power of its Indian heritage, and the vivifying role of its Church, it is because he knew Latin America can contribute to the renovation of Catholicism. Interestingly, the Preface was written four years before the beginning of the Second Vatican Council, yet Merton prefigures many of the changes Vatican II would instigate in the relation between the Church and its people. In his appreciation of what Latin American Catholics contribute to the Church, Merton considers the need to see the Virgin Mary as a Mother, and he recalls how *La Morena* is usually represented holding the baby Jesus in her arms. To his Spanish American readers, this would be the normal image of the Virgin: we see Mary portrayed as a mother with her Infant in chapels, cathedrals, stamps, and reliquaries, just as throughout the continent ordinary mothers, regardless of class or racial differences, carry their children in their arms. In his appreciation of the wisdom of a people who see Mary as a Mother, Merton draws a contrast between *La Morena* and the pale, childless representation of the Virgin Mary in North America. Not only that, but he also points out how *La Morena* led the Independence armies throughout Latin America. Our "founding fathers," *Los padres de la Patria*, were also wise in their regard of Mary the Mother and Protector, and the tradition has been kept alive to our day. Our Lady of Aparecida in Brazil, Our Lady of Guadalupe in Mexico, Our Lady of Angels "La Negrita" in Costa Rica, Our Lady of Caridad del Cobre in Cuba, Our Lady of Quinche in Ecuador, Our Lady of Suyapa in Honduras, Our Lady of Carmen in Chile and Argentina, and the Patron Saint of my country (Argentina), Our Lady of Lujan, are some of the representations of *La Morena* Merton writes about. These images of the Holy Mother were present at the first steps of our independent Latin American nations, have been venerated throughout our histories, and are still part of our contemporary cultures.

When Merton receives his copy of *Obras Completas* in the mail from Buenos Aires, he finds new and deeper meaning in his own words precisely because it is the Feast of Our Lady of Guadalupe. In his religious imagination, the Virgin, as she appeared to the Indian Juan Diego, the *Morena* Mother of Latin America, had brought back the book with a message to himself in the words he had written for Spanish American readers.

A Responsibility for the Future

Merton saw that the New World called for a renewed Church that was not a relic from the past but was "the Mother of the future." Throughout the Preface, Merton stresses the need for the Contemplative Life. He even writes that, through contemplation in the solitude of Gethsemani, he has heard the voice of the New World. This "voice" is different from those that tourists hear as they travel from place to place, as they wander and misunderstand the indigenous wisdom of "so many Indians" who are named after Jesus.[8]

What is more, the voices of South America that he heard in the solitude of contemplation called for action. "Contemplation alone

8. Thomas Merton, *Emblems of a Season of Fury* (New York: New Directions, 1960) 86.

does not feed the hungry, does not clothe the naked, does not educate the ignorant, nor does it guide the unfortunate sinner towards peace, truth, and union with his God." Merton was aware of a reality that unfortunately has not changed in the sixty years since he wrote the Preface that the voices he heard were those of cities "with generous opulence and terrible indigence, side by side." Contemplation alone will not solve inequality. Action alone, on the other hand, will also mislead us, by turning our action into a factious response. Once again, Merton calls for completeness, for nothing "partial or provincial." And in so doing, the voice of the Contemplative, far from being isolated from the world, becomes truly committed: "it is in this love of Christ in Himself, and of Christ in our neighbor, that New Worlds are built on everlasting foundations." Solutions and ideologies that come from abroad, such as "the dollar diplomacy," "imperialist technology," and "the Russian deformation" of Marxism or fascism cannot bring about the New World(s) for which Merton had hoped.

A sense of our humanity in Christ, an awareness of the unity of all people, of the *completeness* that he repeatedly mentions throughout the Preface is what will create New Worlds. In the last paragraph, Merton speaks of himself and his readers as *builders*. It is in this sense that he refers to a responsibility of the future: what is being built is yet unfinished, and Merton proposes that we should all strive towards unity between the North and the South of America, between contemplative and active vocations, between the various heritages from the past and the need of a New World. Without Latin America, America is incomplete. Without contemplation, action is incomplete. This is the wisdom that Merton seems to find contained in the deep roots of the South of the continent, latent with a "destiny which is still hidden in the mystery of Providence."

In Conclusion

I am writing these pages from Argentina, which according to Merton's Preface is characterized by "strength, refinement, and prodigality . . ., with all the lyricism of its tormented and generous soul." Sixty years have passed since Merton wrote this, and the words are still accurate and deeply connected to Latin American roots. The strength of our countries has allowed us to survive civil wars, dictatorships, and foreign intervention. The refinement learned from

Europe and the prodigality of local cultures "rooted in a past that has never yet been surpassed in this continent" (*Emblems* 1963:86) have produced a rich, multicultural society in which the melting pot metaphor seems more appropriate than the North American mosaic. These generous lands that still welcome migrants and the displaced speak with a myriad of accents that show the *completeness* of its language Merton so much loved. Yet, the "generous opulence and terrible indigence" still coexist side by side. Many look away as if ignoring poverty would make it disappear. And still in many of our countries eyes are set upon distant shores, as if foreign answers could fulfill our local needs.

Writing from Latin America, then, this is where I find the contemporary value of Merton's word. If there is indigenous wisdom in South America, one we have not yet fully acknowledged but which was here from the very beginning, and which may provide an answer to "the human problem" in the rich multicultural, *complete* vein of Latin America, why look elsewhere? South America is not only an heir to European customs but an emerging indigenous offspring of more ancient cultures. South America can continue to realize its destiny in the mystery of our ways inherited from pre-Columbian times. Only then will Latin America be wholly able to "enter the world" and contribute its rich heritage to the future (a notion that goes against what many propose, that by imitation of foreign ways we may find the way out of poverty and isolation). The love of truth, passion for freedom, and adoration of God that Merton foresaw in his message to Spanish American readers will make us all, North and South American readers, *complete*. Our wholeness as Americans depends on our mutual understanding of our deep identities, both in our singularities, and in our affinities, rooted in our histories, cultures, and indigenous wisdom still raising its voices for our attention in our twenty-first century.

CITED WORKS

Cooper, David D. *Thomas Merton's Art of Denial: The Evolution of a Radical Humanist.* Athens, GA: University of Georgia Press, 1989.

Meade, Mark. "From Downtown Louisville to Buenos Aires: Victoria Ocampo as Thomas Merton's Overlooked Bridge to Latin America and the World," *The Merton Annual 26:* 168-

180. Louisville, KY: Fons Vitae, 2013.

Merton, Thomas. *Emblems of a Season of Fury*. New York: New Directions, 1960.

————. "Prefacio para el lector iberoamericano." *Obras Completas,* vol. 1. Buenos Aires: Sudamericana, 1963.

————. *A Search for Solitude: Pursuing the Monk's True Life 1915-1968*, ed. Lawrence Cunningham. San Francisco: HarperSanFrancisco, 1996.

————. *Turning Toward the World: The Pivotal Years 1960-1963,* ed. Victor Kramer. San Francisco: HarperSanFrancisco, 1996.

Merton, Thomas and James Laughlin. *Thomas Merton and James Laughlin: Selected Letters.* ed. David D. Cooper. New York: Norton & Co., 1997.

PREFACE
FOR LATIN AMERICAN READERS
IN MERTON'S *OBRAS COMPLETAS*
(COMPLETE WORKS)[1]

Thomas Merton

A New Translation of Merton's Original Spanish
Preface by Marcela Raggio[2]

It is an honor that my *Complete Works* will be first published in South America before anywhere else. I think this is quite significant. I believe it deserves very special recognition from me.

In the first pages of this volume, readers will realize I am one of those millions whose destiny brought them from the European coasts to become citizens of the western hemisphere, people of the New World. I belonged already to the New World because my mother's family had lived in it for several generations. I came to it looking for an answer to the inscrutable problems of life, and in it, I found an answer at once eternally old and new – an answer which does not belong to any particular time, continent, country, or culture. I found, in this New World, the word of Salvation. I also found in it a paradoxical vocation for the Contemplative Life, a vocation which some have not been able to understand as if the Contemplative Life belonged only to the Old World which is dying rather than to the New World that is being born.

I believe the main message on these pages is that the Contemplative Life exists wherever there is life. Where human beings and their society exist, wherever there are hopes, ideals, aspirations for a better future; where love exists – where there is pain alongside with happiness – there also the Contemplative Life finds its place. Because life, happiness, pain, ideals, hopes, work, art, and every-

---

1. Thomas Merton, *Obras Completas (Complete Works)* (Buenos Aires: Editorial Sudamericana, 1960). The Preface in Spanish appears in the Appendix.

2. Translated by Marcela Raggio, Cuyo National University (UNCuyo) and National Council for Scientific and Technological Research (CONICET), Argentina.

thing else are significant. If they do not have any significance, why then waste time on them? But if they do have significance, then the individual significance of each one of them must converge around a central and universal significance that illuminates it from the interior of its most intimate essences. This central reality must be a "catholic" reality, a "divine" reality. This central significance of life is Life itself, Life in God. This is the Contemplative's objective.

In my case, the word of salvation, Jesus' Gospel, has led me to solitude and silence. Maybe mine is a rare vocation. But contemplation flourishes not only within the cloister. Each person called to live a life full of meaning is called, for that reason only, to know the inner significance of life and to find that intimate significance in his inscrutable existence, above himself, above the world of appearances, in the Living God. All people born on this earth are called to find themselves and become full in Christ and thus, to understand their unity in Christ with all other human beings, so that he loves them as he loves himself, to be one with them almost as he is one with himself: because Christ's spirit is One in those who love Him.

Among the silence of the fields and the woods, in the cloistered solitude of my monastery, I have come to discover the whole Western hemisphere. Here, by God's grace, I have been able to explore the New World; not traveling from city to city, not flying over the Andes or the Amazonas, stopping for a day or two here, then there, then going on. Perhaps, had I traveled this way through the hemisphere, I might not have seen anything: because in general, those who travel the most, see the least.

On the contrary, I think in the silence of my monastery I have heard the voice of the whole hemisphere speaking from the depths of my soul with a clarity at once magnificent and terrible: as if I had in the depths of my heart the vast and lonely pampas, the frost brilliance of the Bolivian highland, the fine air of the Incas' terraced valleys, Quito's splendor and softness, the cold Bogotá savannah, and the extreme mystery of the Amazonas jungle. I think whole cities live inside of me, with generous opulence and terrible indigence, side by side. As if the southern Chilean rains fell on my soul, and the sun of Ecuador fell perpendicularly on the summit of my being. As if all the ancient Mexican civilizations, older than Egypt, accumulated their inscrutable silences in my heart, and as if in them and the even deeper silences of Peru I could hear forgotten syllables murmuring ancient wisdoms which never died and which kept in their secret an image of Truth which no person has yet recognized as Jesus' hidden image, wrapped in symbol and prophecy. I feel as if the inexhaustible beauty of all the New World, and its almost infinite possibilities, were moving inside me as a sleeping giant, in whose presence I cannot remain indifferent. In fact, sometimes I feel this presence inside me speaks with God's own voice: and I struggle in vain to grasp and understand any word, any syllable about the great destiny of the New World, that destiny which is still hidden in the mystery of Providence.

One thing I know: that in my destiny of being at once a contemplative, a Christian, and an American, I cannot satisfy the requirements of my vocation with anything partial or provincial. I cannot be a "North American," who knows only the rivers, the plains, the mountains, and the cities of the North, where there are no longer any Indians, where the land was colonized and cultivated by Puritans; where among the bold and sarcastic splendor of skyscrapers only seldom a Cross is spotted; and where, if represented at all, the Holy Virgin is pale and melancholic, and never carries the Child in her arms. This Northern part is great, powerful, rich, and intelligent; it also has its own warmth, a surprising humility, goodness and inner purity unknown to the stranger. But it is incomplete. It is not even the largest or richest part of the hemisphere. It might probably be the most important part of the world nowadays; however, it is not self-sufficient, and it lacks deep roots. It lacks the deep roots of Ancient America, the America of Mexico and of the Andes, where silent and contemplative Asia came ages ago to build its hieratic cities. It lacks the fervor and intense fecundity of Brazil, which is also Africa, which beats with the music and simplicity of Africa, beams with the smile of Congo, and laughs with the childish innocence of Portugal. The northern half of this New World lacks the strength, refinement, and prodigality of Argentina, with all the lyricism of its tormented and generous soul.

I cannot be a partial American, and I cannot be a partial Catholic, which would be even sadder. To me, Catholicism is not confined within the boundaries of a culture, a nation, a period of time, a race. My faith is not merely the Catholicism of the Irish in the United States or the splendid and vital Catholicism, reborn during the last war, of my native France. Even if I admire the great cathedrals and the glorious past of Catholicism in Latin America, my Catholicism goes beyond this Hispanic heritage. I find it impossible to believe that Catholicism is so strongly connected to a group's destiny that it becomes just the expression of economic illusions of any given social class. My Catholicism is not the religion of the bourgeoisie, and it shall never be. Catholicism embraces the whole world and all times. It was there at the beginning of the world. The first man was Christ's image, and he already contained in his entrails Christ the Savior, even if he was fallen. The first man was destined to be his Redeemer's ancestor, and the first woman was the Mother of all Life, the image of an immaculate daughter who would be full of grace and Mother of all Mercy, Mother of the Saved.

That Holy Mother is the Mother of America – She is everywhere in America, the *Morena!* Her banner led the vanguard of the first Independence armies in Latin America. She is everywhere in America, particularly in Spanish America, and there she also shelters in the mystery, the Body of Christ.

To many, in our New World, the Church is just a respectable institution whose destiny is linked to the past. That is a grave and terrible mistake – which especially we, priests and religious men, must learn to dissipate not only with our teaching, but with our lives as well. We love our old traditions, but we are people of the future. Ours is a responsibility for the future, not for the past. The past does not depend on us. But the future does. It is true that, following our Teacher, we must say "our kingdom is not of this world," but as Him, we must understand that, whatever we do unto the humblest of those He loves, we do unto Him; and it is part of our job for people's salvation to help build a world in which people can get ready for the vision of God through a free life on earth.

The Church in the New World is more than just a relic from the past; she is the Mother of the future. Its members must open their eyes to that future and be aware of the signs that point at the path of that future. God Himself speaks through those signs in the mystery of history and in the living and particular evolution of the world around these signs. This is what the modern Popes have told us, calling us to the Catholic Action movement, calling for new priestly vocations as a new sign in the New World.

This new orientation is based on the ancient wisdom which the world has forgotten and only recently has started to remember again: the priority of spirituality and contemplation.

Contemplation alone will not build a new world. Contemplation alone does not feed the hungry, does not clothe the naked, does not educate the ignorant, nor does it guide the unfortunate sinner towards peace, truth, and union with his God. But without contemplation, we lack the perspective necessary to see what we are doing in our apostolate. Without contemplation, we cannot understand the intimate meaning of the world in which we must act. Without contemplation, we remain small, limited, divided, partial: we hold fast to insufficiency, we remain united to our limited group and its interests, we lose sight of the wider universal justice and charity, we let ourselves be carried away by the passions of factions and, finally, we betray Christ. For it is true: without contemplation, without the intimate, silent, secret search of truth through love, our action loses itself in the world and becomes dangerous.

What is more, if our contemplation is fanatical and false, our action will be even more dangerous. No, we must lose ourselves in order to find the world; we must submerge ourselves into the depths of our humility in order to find Christ everywhere and love Him in all creatures: otherwise, we will betray Him, if we do not see Him in those we harm unconsciously, while praying to Him in our "innocence."

The essence of my monastic rule is contained in these few words: "to prefer absolutely nothing whatever to the love of Christ." It is in this love of Christ in Himself, and of Christ in our neighbor, that New Worlds are built on everlasting foundations. A New World among us cannot be built on the Russian deformation of Marxist dialectics. The New World cannot be built through the destructive passions of fascist militarism. No New World at all will be built through the false magic of imperialist technology. And there is little hope that the dollar diplomacy will create anything but disappointment and confusion for all. The western hemisphere is immensely rich, probably richer than the rest of the world, and its riches belong to those who inhabit it; yet, the mere exploitation of such riches and their just distribution will not be enough to solve our problem. Above all this, there is the problem of understanding and love, the problem of unity, the problem of man. This is the most important of all, because man is the image of God, and when he is fully united, inside himself with his brothers and sisters, and with his God, then God's Kingdom has come and is manifested on earth so that everyone sees It. However, this cannot ever be achieved, except in Christ, and through the power of His Cross, and the victory of His Resurrection.

So this is what I find so important regarding "America," and the great role of my vocation in it: to know America *in its full extent* [italics in the original], to be a complete American, a human being of the whole hemisphere, of the whole New World; and from this starting point, to be also a complete contemplative, and thus help to bring Christ in the plenitude of maturity, in all the Universe, "until we all meet in the unity of faith and in the knowledge of the Son of God, as a perfect man, in the measure of the age of the fullness of Christ. So may we then no longer be little children, disturbed and carried about by every wind of doctrine, by the wickedness of men, and by the craftiness which deceives unto error. Instead, acting according to truth in charity, we should increase in everything, in him who is the head, Christ himself." (Ephesians 4, 13-15)

May all who read this book and I who have written it remain united in this ideal and this struggle! We work together as Americans and Christians, as brothers and sisters, and as builders. I with my prayers and my books, you with your work and your prayers. Separate, we are incomplete. Together, we are strong with God's strength. Oh, brothers and sisters from the South! I am glad that this book has united us in Christ, but the book was not necessary: we are already one in our love of truth, our passion for freedom, and our adoration of the Living God.

Thomas Merton
Abbey of Gethsemani
Easter, 1958

CONTRIBUTORS

Vine Deloria, Jr. (1933 – 2005). Named by *Time* magazine one of the greatest religious thinkers of the twentieth century, Deloria was a leading Native American scholar, whose research, writings, and teaching have encompassed history, law, religious studies, and political science. He is the author of many acclaimed books, including *Evolution, Creationism, and Other Modern Myths; Red Earth, White Lies; Spirit & Reason; and Custer Died for Your Sins*. From 1964 to 1967, he served as executive director of the National Congress of American Indians, increasing tribal membership from 19 to 156. Beginning in 1977, he was a board member of the National Museum of the American Indians, which now has buildings in both New York City and Washington, DC. He was influential in the development of what scientific critics called "American Indian Creationism," but which American Indians referred to as defenses against "scientific racism." Deloria became Professor of Political Science at the University of Arizona (1978-1990), where he established the first master's degree program in American Indian Studies in the United States.

Barbara Mainguy, M.S., is a creative arts psychotherapist, and is the Education Director with the Coyote Institute, Orono, Maine. She is affiliated with the School of Social Work at the University of Maine at Orono, and also works with Wabanaki Health and Wellness in Bangor. She is a graduate of the University of Toronto, and Concordia University, Montreal. Her most recent book is *Remapping Your Mind: the Neuroscience of Self-Transformation through Story* (with Lewis Mehl-Madrona). Her research interests lie in the applications of dialogical self-therapy and theory within indigenous contexts and in outcomes of pain management therapies.

Allan M. McMillan is a retired priest of the Roman Catholic Diocese of Sault Ste. Marie now living in Brantford, Ontario. Having studied sociology at St. John Fisher College, Rochester N. Y. and Boston College, he completed his studies at St. Peter's Seminary in London, Ontario. During his more than forty years in the priesthood he has been a pastor to parishes across the top of Lake Huron and Lake Nipissing where he ministered to English, French, and First Nation communities. It was during this time that he encountered the rich cultural works and life of the First Nation Artists of Manitoulin Island. He has collected the works of these artists and happily counts some of these artists as long-time personal friends.

Lewis Mehl-Madrona, M.D., Ph.D., is Associate Professor of Family Medicine at the University of New England College of Osteopathic Medicine, and is a Faculty Physician at the Family Medicine Residency of Eastern Maine Medical Center in Bangor. He is also Clinical Assistant Professor of Psychiatry at the University of Vermont College of Medicine. He graduated from Stanford University School of Medicine and completed his residencies in family medicine and in psychiatry at the University of Vermont. His research interests lie in narrative medicine and the role of nutrition in mental health. He is the author of *Healing Your Mind Through the Power of Story: The Promise of Narrative Psychiatry.*

Małgorzata Poks, Ph.D., is assistant professor in the Institute of English Cultures and Literatures, University of Silesia, Poland. Her main interests concern spirituality, civil disobedience, Christian anarchism, contemporary U.S. literature, Thomas Merton's poetry, U.S.-Mexican border writing, and Animal and Environmental Studies. She is a recipient of several international fellowships. Her monograph *Thomas Merton and Latin America: A Consonance of Voices* was awarded "The Louie" by the International Thomas Merton Society.

Donald P. St. John, Ph.D., is Professor Emeritus of Religion at Moravian College, Bethlehem, PA. He "joyously" earned his Doctorate under Thomas Berry at Fordham University. There he became deeply engaged in the study and appreciation of Native American Religions (and Eastern traditions), wrote essays for *The Encyclopedia of Religion* on both the broader cultural traditions and their impact on the growth of the individual Amerindian visionaries. He has offered courses since 1981 at Moravian College, shaped by a Euro-American tradition heavily involved with Native Americans (especially the Iroquois and their "prophet" Handsome Lake). His increasing influence by Thomas Merton's wisdom writings on the contemplative life deepened his own understanding of Native American traditions, especially as they influenced the male or female's ability to open their minds and hearts to new dimensions through ritual symbolism as when engaged in vision-quests, rites of passage, and gender-specific experiences of enlightenment. All were stages on the path of spiritual growth.

Marcela Raggio, Ph.D., is a tenured professor at the School of Philosophy and Letters at Cuyo National University, Mendoza, Argentina. She is a researcher in the social sciences and humanities at Argentina's National Council for Scientific and Technical Research (CONICET). Her main field of interests are American and British literature, Latin American culture and literature, translation studies, poetry, and film studies. Her most recent book is *Thomas Merton, el monje traductor.*

Peter Savastano holds a B.A. in Religious Studies and Philosophy from Montclair State University and a M. Phil. and Ph.D. in Religion and Society from Drew University. His areas of expertise are: the Anthropology of Religion with a focus on Christian (Catholic and Orthodox) mysticism, vernacular devotional practices, and issues of sexuality and gender in relation to Anglicanism, Catholicism, and Eastern Orthodoxy; Islamic Mysticism (Sufism) and Western Esotericism; the Anthropology of Consciousness with a focus on trance, and other psi phenomena such as spontaneous healing, visionary experiences, NDEs and premonitional dreams; world indigenous sacred ritual and healing traditions, most especially American Indian traditions and African Diasporic traditions. He has been studying the works of Thomas Merton since early adolescence and teaches a course entitled "Thomas Merton, Religion, and Culture." Peter Savastano is Associate Professor of Anthropology and Religious Studies at Seton Hall University in South Orange, New Jersey.

Kathleen Witkowska Tarr is the author of *We Are All Poets Here* (VP&D House, 2018) a blend of memoir and biography involving Thomas Merton and his 1968 journey to Alaska. She is a William Shannon Fellow of the International Thomas Merton Society and a Mullin Scholar at USC's Institute for Advanced Catholic Studies (2013-2015). She worked as the founding Program Coordinator of University of Alaska Anchorage's Low-Residency M.F.A. Program in Creative Writing. She holds a M.F.A. in nonfiction from the University of Pittsburgh. She lives and writes in Anchorage under the Chugach Mountains.

Robert G. Toth served as Executive Director the Merton Institute for Contemplative Living from 1998 to 2010. With Jonathan Montaldo he co-edited *Bridges to Contemplative Living with Thomas Merton*, a popular series designed for small group dialogue. He is a founding member of The Contemplative Alliance, an initiative of the Global Peace Initiative of Women, which organizes dialogues and programs to advance the contemplative movement. He currently serves on the Board of the Lake Erie Institute which works to recover the balance between human culture and civilization and the Earth.

William Torres first read Thomas Merton in his 16th year of Catholic education while studying anthropology at Seton Hall University. He crossed literary paths with Merton during a time of great spiritual turmoil in his life. William sought to understand what Catholicism had meant to him in his childhood and what it could mean to him as an adult. Now at the latter end of his twenties, his relationship with Merton has gone through many peaks and valleys but has always been built on a foundation of love, contemplation, and seeking. A former Daggy Scholar (2015) and current masters-level social worker, William practices as a school social worker in northern New Jersey, where he also resides with his two cats, Pippa and Christine.

ACKNOWLEDGMENTS

This volume has taken a long time to finally come to fruition. There are so many people to thank, too many to list here. However, there are some whom I wish to acknowledge and thank, for without them *Merton & Indigenous Wisdom* would still be just an idea. First and foremost, I wish to thank Eleanor Bingham Miller for her generous support and encouragement and for her great kindness. I would also like to thank the wonderful people at Fons Vitae, most especially Gray Henry, Neville Blakemore, and Anne Ogden. Even editors need an Editor. In this regard, I would have been lost without the masterful assistance of Jonathan Montaldo, General Editor of the *Merton &* series. I also thank my colleagues at Seton Hall University, most especially in the Department of Sociology, Anthropology & Social Work and in the Department of Religious Studies for supporting my sabbatical in the Spring of 2014 so that I could do the necessary reading and background research for this project. I am especially indebted to now retired Provost Dr. Larry Robinson and to the evaluation committee for the Provost's Course Release grant, which I was awarded for two semesters in the Fall of 2017 and Spring of 2018 in order to read and edit the essays submitted by the contributors to this volume. Finally, I wish to thank all of my friends and spiritual companions on the journey who supported and encouraged me to keep at it when I felt I was too exhausted to see it through to completion. Any errors or inaccuracies are my fault only.

Peter Savastano, Editor

The General Editors acknowledge with gratitude:

- All those contributors who offered their scholarship for this volume.
- The copyediting by Anne Ogden, the typesetting by Neville Blakemore, and the cover design by Steven Stivers. Our thanks to also Joan Rapp and Jill Cooper for additional proofreading assistance.
- The support of Paul Pearson and Mark Meade, archivists of the Thomas Merton Center at Bellarmine University,

Louisville, Kentucky.
- The Thomas Merton Legacy Trustees, Anne McCormick, Mary R. Sommerville, and Peggy L. Fox for their continuing coöperation in the production of the Fons Vitae Thomas Merton Series.
- Eleanor Bingham Miller, our volume's benefactor, for her unfailingly good guidance and generosity during the production of *Merton & Indigenous Wisdom*.

Additional Credits:

- "Preface for Latin American Readers in Merton's *Obras Completas (Complete Works)*," originally published from HONORABLE READER: REFLECTIONS ON MY WORK, copyright ©1988 by the Merton Legacy Trust. Reprinted by permission of New Directions Publishing Corp.
- "With Malinowski in the Postmodern Desert: Merton, Anthropology, and the Ethnographics of The Geography of Lograire," originally published in *The Merton Annual* 25 (Louisville: Fons Vitae, 2012). Reprinted by permission of the author, Dr. Małgorzata Poks.
- "The Indians of the American Imagination" by Vine Deloria, Jr., published in *God Is Red: A Native View of Religion* (30th Anniversary Edition). Copyright © 2003. Reprinted by permission of Fulcrum Publishing.

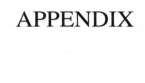

APPENDIX

THOMAS MERTON
(fr. M. Louis, O.C.S.O.)

OBRAS
COMPLETAS

I

LA MONTAÑA DE LOS SIETE CÍRCULOS
SEMILLAS DE CONTEMPLACIÓN
LAS AGUAS DE SILOÉ
EL EXILIO Y LA GLORIA
¿QUÉ LLAGAS SON ESAS?
LA SENDA DE LA CONTEMPLACIÓN
PAN EN EL DESIERTO

EDITORIAL SUDAMERICANA
BUENOS AIRES

PREFACIO PARA EL LECTOR IBEROAMERICANO

Es un honor para mí ver que la publicación de mis Obras Completas se efectúa, antes que en ninguna otra parte, en América del Sur. Y eso me parece muy significativo. Creo que requiere, de parte mía, un reconocimiento muy especial.

El lector de las primeras páginas de este volumen se dará cuenta de que yo soy uno de esos millones cuyo destino los ha hecho venir desde las costas de Europa para convertirse en ciudadanos del Hemisferio Occidental, en hombres del Nuevo Mundo. Yo pertenecía ya al Nuevo Mundo, porque la familia de mi madre había vivido en él durante varias generaciones. Vine a él buscando una respuesta a los inescrutables problemas de la vida y hallé en él una respuesta que es a la vez eternamente vieja y nueva – una respuesta que no pertenece a ningún tiempo, país, continente o cultura en particular. Hallé, en este Nuevo Mundo, la palabra de Salvación. También hallé en él una paradójica vocación para la Vida Contemplativa . . . una vocación que algunos no han sabido comprender, como si la Vida Contemplativa perteneciese al Viejo Mundo que se muere, no al Nuevo Mundo que está naciendo.

Creo que el principal mensaje contenido en estas páginas es que la Vida Contemplativa pertenece a donde haya vida. Donde esté el hombre, y su sociedad; donde haya esperanzas, ideales, aspiraciones de un futuro mejor; donde haya amor – donde haya dolor a la vez que alegría – también allí tiene su lugar la Vida Contemplativa. Porque la vida, la alegría, el dolor, los ideales, las aspiraciones, el trabajo, el arte y todo lo demás tienen un significado. Si no tienen significado, entonces ¿por qué perder tiempo en ellos? Pero si lo tienen, entonces el significado independiente de cada cosa tiene que converger de algún modo en un significado central y universal que la ilumine desde el interior de sus más íntimas esencias. Esta realidad central tiene que ser una realidad "católica," una realidad "divina." Este significado central de la vida es la Vida misma, la Vida en Dios. Y este es el objeto del contemplativo.

En mi caso, la palabra de salvación, el Evangelio de Jesucristo, me ha llevado a la soledad y al silencio. Mi vocación es rara, quizás. Pero la contemplación no solo florece dentro de los muros del claustro. Todo hombre llamado a vivir una vida plena de significado es llamado, sólo por eso, a conocer el significado interior de la vida y a hallar ese íntimo significado en su propia existencia inescrutable, por encima de sí mismo, por encima del mundo de las apariencias, en el Dios Vivo. Todo hombre nacido en esta tierra está llamado a hallarse y a realizarse en Cristo y, por ello, a comprender su unidad en Cristo con todos los demás hombres, de modo que los ame como se ama a sí mismo, y sea uno con ellos casi como es uno consigo mismo: pues el Espíritu de Cristo es Uno en los que le aman.

En el silencio de los campos y de los bosques, en la enclaustrada soledad de mi monasterio, he venido a descubrir el Hemisferio Occidental entero. Aquí es donde he podido, por la gracia de Dios, explorar el Nuevo Mundo; no viajando de ciudad en ciudad, no volando sobre los Andes y el Amazonas para detenerse un día aquí, dos allí, y luego seguir adelante. Quizás si hubiera viajado de esta manera por el hemisferio, no habría visto nada: pues generalmente los que viajan más, ven menos.

Pero me parece, por el contrario, que en el silencio de mi monasterio he oído la voz de todo el hemisferio que habla desde las profundidades de mi ser con una claridad a la vez magnífica y terrible: como si tuviera en las profundidades de mi corazón las pampas vastas y solitarias, la helada brillantez del altiplano boliviano, el aire fino de los terraplenados valles de los Incas, el esplendor y la suavidad de Quito, la fría sabana de Bogotá, y el intolerable misterio de la selva del Amazonas. Me parece que dentro de mí viven ciudades enteras, con generosa opulencia y terrible indigencia, lado a lado. Como si las lluvias del sur de Chile cayesen sobre mi alma y el sol del Ecuador cayese perpendicularmente sobre la cumbre de mi ser. Como si todas las antiguas civilizaciones de México, más viejas que Egipto, acumulasen en mi corazón sus inescrutables silencios, y como si en ellos y en los silencios aun más profundos del Perú oyese murmurar las sílabas olvidadas de sabidurías muy antiguas que nunca han muerto y que han contenido en su secreto una imagen de Verdad que ningún hombre ha reconocido aún como la imagen encubierta de Jesucristo, envuelta en el símbolo y la profecía. Me parece como si la inagotable belleza de todo el Nuevo Mundo, y sus casi infinitas posibilidades, se movieran dentro de mí como un gigante dormido, ante cuya presencia no puedo quedarme indiferente. En realidad casi me parece a veces que esta presencia que hay dentro de mí habla con la voz del mismo Dios: y yo lucho en vano para captar y entender alguna palabra, alguna sílaba del gran destino del Nuevo Mundo . . . ese destino que está aún oculto en el misterio de la Providencia.

Una cosa sé: que en mi destino de ser al mismo tiempo un contemplativo, un cristiano y un americano, no puedo satisfacer las exigencias de mi vocación con nada parcial y provinciano. No puedo ser un "norteamericano," que sólo conoce los ríos, las llanuras, las montañas y las ciudades del norte, donde ya no hay indios, donde la tierra fue colonizada y cultivada por puritanos, donde, entre el esplendor audaz y sarcástico de los rascacielos, se ve raramente la Cruz, y donde la Santa Virgen, cuando se la representa, es pálida y melancólica y no lleva al Niño en los brazos. Esta parte norte es grande, poderosa, rica, inteligente; también tiene su calor propio, una humildad sorprendente, una bondad, una pureza interior que el extraño no conoce. Pero es incompleta. No es siquiera la parte mayor y más rica del hemisferio. Es quizás, en este momento, la región más importante del mundo, pero, sin embargo, no puede bastarse a sí misma y carece de raíces profundas. Carece de las profundas raíces de la antigua América, de la América de México y de los Andes, donde el Asia silenciosa y contemplativa vino, hace milenios, para construir sus ciudades hieráticas. Carece del fervor y la fecundidad intensa del Brasil, que es también África, que palpita con la música y la simplicidad de África, sonríe con la sonrisa del Congo y ríe con la inocencia infantil de Portugal. La mitad norte de este Nuevo Mundo carece de la fuerza, el refinamiento y el prodigio de la Argentina, con todo el lirismo de su alma atormentada y generosa.

No puedo ser un americano parcial y no puedo ser, lo que es aun más triste, un católico parcial. Para mí, el catolicismo no está confinado dentro de los límites de una cultura, una nación, una época, una raza. Mi fe no es meramente el catolicismo de los irlandeses de Estados Unidos, o el catolicismo espléndido y vital, renacido durante la guerra pasada, de mi Francia natal. Aunque admiro mucho las grandes catedrales y el glorioso pasado del catolicismo en la América Latina, mi catolicismo es algo que va más allá de la hispanidad. Para mí es imposible creer que el catolicismo pueda estar tan ligado a los destinos de un grupo que resulte meramente la expresión de las ilusiones económicas de tal o cual clase social. Mi catolicismo no es la religión de la burguesía, ni lo será nunca.

El catolicismo abraza todo el mundo y todas las épocas. Data del comienzo del mundo. El primer hombre era la imagen de Cristo, y ya contenía a Cristo el Salvador en sus entrañas, aun cuando estuviera caído. El primer hombre estaba destinado a ser el antepasado de su Redentor, y la primera mujer era la Madre de toda la Vida, imagen de una Hija Inmaculada que iba a ser llena de gracia y la Madre de toda Misericordia, la Madre de los Salvados.

Esa Santísima Madre es la Madre de América – ¡está en todas partes de América, la Morena! –; su estandarte iba en las vanguardias de los primeros ejércitos de la independencia americana. Está en todas partes de América, particularmente en Iberoamérica, y allí también abriga, en el misterio, el Cuerpo de Cristo.

Para muchos, en nuestro Nuevo Mundo, la Iglesia es sólo una respetable institución cuyo destino está unido con una sociedad pasada. Eso es una grave equivocación y un error desastroso – un error que especialmente los que somos sacerdotes y religiosos tenemos que aprender a disipar no solo con nuestras enseñanzas, sino con nuestras vidas –. Amamos nuestras viejas tradiciones, pero somos hombres del futuro. Nuestra responsabilidad es del futuro, no del pasado. El pasado no depende de nosotros. Pero el futuro sí depende de nosotros. Es cierto que, como nuestro Maestro, debemos decir que "nuestro reino no es de este mundo," pero como Él tenemos que comprender que lo que hagamos al más humilde de Sus bienamados, se lo hacemos a Él; y parte de nuestro trabajo por la salvación del hombre es ayudar a construir un mundo en el cual el hombre se pueda preparar para la visión de Dios mediante una vida libre en esta tierra.

La Iglesia en el Nuevo Mundo es más que un símbolo decorativo del pasado, es la madre del futuro. Sus miembros tienen que abrir los ojos a ese futuro, tienen que darse cuenta de los signos que indican el camino de ese futuro: signos por los cuales el mismo Dios les habla en el misterio de la historia y en la evolución concreta y viva del mundo que les rodea. Esto es lo que nos han dicho los Papas modernos, llamándonos a la Acción Católica, pidiendo nuevas vocaciones para un sacerdocio de nueva orientación en el Nuevo Mundo.

Esta nueva orientación depende de la antiquísima porfía que el mundo moderno ha olvidado, y sólo recientemente ha comenzado a recordar: la prioridad de lo espiritual, la primacía de la contemplación.

No, la contemplación sola no construye un nuevo mundo. La contemplación sola no da de comer al hambriento, no viste al desnudo, no educa al ignorante, ni devuelve al desdichado pecador a la paz, la verdad y la unión con su Dios. Pero sin contemplación no tenemos la perspectiva para ver lo que hacemos en nuestro apostolado. Sin contemplación no podemos comprender el íntimo significado del mundo en el cual tenemos que actuar. Sin contemplación, permanecemos pequeños, limitados, divididos, parciales: nos aferramos a lo insuficiente, permanecemos unidos a nuestro limitado grupo y a sus intereses, perdemos de vista la justicia y la caridad universales, nos dejamos llevar por las pasiones de facción y, finalmente, traicionamos a Cristo. Sí, sin contemplación, sin la íntima, silenciosa, secreta búsqueda de la verdad mediante el amor, nuestra acción se pierde en el mundo y se hace peligrosa. Más aún, si nuestra contemplación es fanática y falsa, nuestra acción será tanto más peligrosa. No, debemos perdernos con el fin de ganar el mundo, debemos sumirnos en las profundidades de nuestra humildad con el fin de hallar a Cristo en todas partes y amarle en todas las criaturas: de lo contrario, le traicionaremos, al no verle en aquellos a quienes dañamos inconscientemente mientras le rezamos en nuestra "inocencia."

La esencia de mi Regla monástica se contiene en estas pocas palabras: "No preferir absolutamente nada al amor de Cristo" . . . y en este amor de Cristo, de Cristo en sí mismo y de Cristo en nuestro prójimo, es como se construyen Nuevos Mundos sobre bases duraderas. No se construirá un Nuevo Mundo entre nosotros mediante la deformación rusa de la dialéctica marxista. No se construirá un Nuevo Mundo mediante las pasiones destructoras del militarismo fascista. No se construirá ningún Nuevo Mundo mediante la magia engañosa de la tecnología imperialista. En cuanto a la diplomacia del dólar, hay poca esperanza de que origine algo más que decepciones y confusión para todos. El hemisferio occidental es enormemente rico, más rico quizás que todo el resto del mundo, y sus riquezas pertenecen a los que viven en él; pero la mera explotación de estas riquezas y su justa distribución no resolverán nuestro problema. Por encima de todo está el problema de la comprensión y del amor, el problema de la unidad, el problema del hombre. Esto es lo más importante de todo, pues el hombre es la imagen de Dios, y cuando está plenamente unido, dentro de sí mismo con sus hermanos, y con su Dios, entonces el Reino de

Dios ha venido y se manifiesta en la tierra para que todos lo vean. Pero esto no puede lograrse jamás, excepto en Cristo, y mediante el poder de Su Cruz, y la victoria de Su Resurrección.

Esto, entonces, es lo que me parece a mí tan importante con respecto a América . . . y la gran función de mi vocación en ella: conocer América *en su totalidad*, ser un americano completo, un hombre de todo el Hemisferio, de todo el Nuevo Mundo; y desde este punto de partida, ser también un completo cristiano, un completo contemplativo, y de este modo, ayudar a traer a Cristo en la plenitud de la madurez, en todo el Cosmos, "hasta que arribemos todos a la unidad de una misma fe y de un mismo conocimiento del Hijo de Dios, al estado de un varón perfecto a la medida de la edad perfecta según la cual Cristo se ha de formar místicamente en nosotros; por manera que ya no seamos niños fluctuantes, ni nos dejemos llevar aquí y allá de todos los vientos y opiniones humanas, por la malignidad de los hombres que engañan con astucia para introducir el error; antes bien, siguiendo la verdad del Evangelio con caridad, en todo vayamos creciendo en Cristo que es nuestra cabeza." (I Efesios 4:13-15)

¡Ojalá los que lean este libro y yo que lo he escrito quedemos unidos en este ideal y en esta lucha! Trabajamos juntos como americanos y cristianos, como hermanos y como constructores. Yo con mis oraciones y con mis libros, vosotros con vuestro trabajo y vuestras oraciones. Separados, somos incompletos. Juntos somos fuertes con la fortaleza de Dios. ¡Oh, hermanos míos del Sur! Me alegro de que este libro nos haya reunido en Cristo; pero el libro no era necesario: ya somos uno en nuestro amor a la verdad, nuestra pasión por la libertad, y nuestra adoración del Dios Vivo.

THOMAS MERTON
Abadía de Gethsemaní
Pascua, 1958.